THE MEN IN MAMIE'S LIFE
and what she *really* thought of them

BURT REYNOLDS: "High on jive but low on substance."

ROCK HUDSON: "We slid on Mother's waxed linoleum as we struggled for traction, groping for handholds . . ."

JOE NAMATH: "In my bedroom, Joe proved his ability was just as great off the football field as on it."

JOHNNY CARSON: "The opportunity to make love with Johnny was tempting."

STEVE MCQUEEN: "Unabashedly wonderful in bed."

PLUS: WARREN BEATTY, HENRY KISSINGER, ELVIS PRESLEY, HOWARD HUGHES, JACK DEMPSEY, BO BELINKSY, FRANK SINATRA and MANY, MANY OTHERS!

Turn the page for rave reviews . . .

5 min, before 9 p.m.

THE CRITICS ARE WILD ABOUT MAMIE!

PLAYING

THE

FIELD

MY STORY

MAMIE VAN DOREN

WITH

ART · AVEILHE

B

BERKLEY BOOKS, NEW YORK

This Berkley book contains the complete
text of the original hardcover edition.
It has been completely reset in a typeface
designed for easy reading and was printed from new film.

PLAYING THE FIELD

A Berkley Book/published by arrangement with
G. P. Putnam's Sons

PRINTING HISTORY
G. P. Putnam's Sons edition/September 1987
Berkley edition/November 1988

ISBN: 0-425-11251-9

A BERKLEY BOOK® TM 757,375
Berkley Books are published by The Berkley Publishing Group,
200 Madison Avenue, New York, New York 10016.
The name ''BERKLEY'' and the ''B'' logo
are trademarks belonging to Berkley Publishing Corporation.

PRINTED IN THE UNITED STATES OF AMERICA

10 9 8 7 6 5 4 3 2 1

This book is dedicated to
my devoted husband, Thomas Dixon,
my faithful son, Perry Anthony,
and my always caring mother and father,
Lucille and Warner Olander.

Prologue

◈

For me, Hollywood is a haunted town, full of ghosts and memories. A lot of blonde bombshells and platinum goddesses didn't make it. They died long before the wrinkles and lines they lived in fear of had a chance to appear in their beautiful faces. A number of them committed suicide.

There was a time when I contemplated suicide too. My career was on the rocks, my life sad and lonely. The future seemed behind me. But I couldn't join all those blondes who had taken that route. My will to live transcended Mamie Van Doren, movie star. It was born of a steel forced in the soul of Joan Olander, my Christian name before I became Mamie.

From the beginning, my name has been linked with sex. I have been called a sex symbol, sex kitten, sexpot, and sex goddess. If that seems terribly glamorous, try having those words connected with your name when you're trying to have a parent-teacher conference about your child, or set up a mortgage with a bank's loan officer.

A favorite question of interviewers has always been, "Is there a Hollywood casting couch?" Did I ever find myself on it? The casting couch did exist and I did occasionally find myself on it. Many of us who made a career out of the movies did—many, many more than want to admit it.

What I felt when I was *on* the casting couch is a question I have never been asked, presumably out of delicacy, but it is every bit as important. The phrase "casting couch" implies that an actress has to have sex with someone as the *necessary* price for being cast in a film. Fortunately, it was not necessary for me. If you are young, healthy, energetic, and possessed of the normal set of biological urges, the casting couch can also be fun with the right person.

Fun, I believe, was where I excelled. I was not, however, manipulative. Marilyn Monroe once told me, not entirely in jest, that she believed I was smart enough to sleep with the "right" person. Without regret I can tell you honestly that I was not. All too often I bypassed the casting-couch activity that would have furthered my career, and followed the instincts and urges of my heart. By and large such romances did nothing to advance my career. Often, in fact, I became involved with a man despite stern warnings from the studio. I couldn't understand why women could not have the freedom to do that. I also turned down the advances of several powerful and important men in the industry because they simply didn't appeal to me.

Hollywood in the 1950s exhibited the double standard and the repressed sexual mores of the rest of the country—it was okay for men to play around, but nice girls could not. The difference in Hollywood was that if nice girls *did* sleep with the right guy, they could get ahead in "the business." That was the game you had to play.

When I left Hollywood, it was in the process of leaving me, and I decided to hell with a career. I was tired of playing an endless succession of dumb blondes. And I was tired of playing the endless Hollywood games. I walked away and didn't look back.

I always marched to the beat of a different drummer. I went my own way and made love to whomever I wanted, and learned to live with the career consequences. In light of today's sexually liberated and independent woman this attitude seems commonplace and accepted, but in the 1950s and early '60s it made people talk.

But to give you a real sense of what it was like for a blonde bombshell in the golden days of Hollywood, I must take you back to Hollywood. I must take you back to the glittering city where I lived and worked and played. The place where I discovered something much more fun than just playing the game—playing the field.

Chapter One

Midway through January 1953, the first month of my contract at Universal International, I was called in to speak to Al Horowitz, head of the U.I. publicity department.

"Mamie," Horowitz said, "we're beginning a big publicity campaign to get your name in front of the public and we'd like you to be seen with one of our top stars. I've already spoken to McHugh about this."

Jimmy McHugh was a popular songwriter whom I had recently hired as my manager.

I was discovering it took a little practice to get used to people calling me by my new name. When someone at the studio called me Mamie, it often took a moment to register. At home, my parents still called me Jo.

"Wonderful," I answered.

"We'd like you to attend the Photoplay Awards at the Beverly Hills Hotel on Saturday night. And we'd like you to go as Rock Hudson's date."

It was my first taste of a social event arranged by the studio. The evening would, after all, help to get my name launched. Rock was on the verge of the superstardom he would later enjoy.

"If Jimmy said it was all right, okay."

"He loved the idea. I've already called the wardrobe department and arranged for them to make up something appropriate for you to wear. Give them a call to set up a time for a fitting. Rock has his own car, or . . . well, maybe we could have a studio limo take you two. Yeah, I think the limo.''

''That sounds fine to me,'' I said.

''Good, good. You like Rock, right?''

''Oh, sure. We see each other all the time in class.''

''Good. Then you kids'll have a good time.''

Later that day in the commissary, I discussed my upcoming date with a friend.

''Of course, you know *why* they're sending you with Rock?'' she asked with the air of one who's in the know.

''I guess it's about the rumor that's going around.''

''Rumor? Honey, he *lives* with that well-muscled young man you've seen riding in the car with him.'' She looked around to make sure no one was near enough to hear. ''The studio executives are frantic that someone will get ahold of the story. If *Confidential* printed that—all hell would break loose!''

''So they're using me to make him look good?''

''Sure! Plenty of pictures with U.I.'s bosomy new starlet. A few stories about how you looked into his eyes or how he was ever-so-attentive to you at the awards—that'll do wonders for Mr. Hudson's sometimes shaky masculine image.''

''It's too bad—Rock's really handsome. And butchy. You could never tell he likes boys.''

''Well, he does, Mamie. It'll be like going out with one of the girls. You'll be as safe as if you were with your mother.''

Rock Hudson pulled up in front of my parents' new house in the San Fernando Valley in his convertible instead of the studio limo. When he came to the door to get me, a momentary flash of disbelief passed across his face. In the dress the studio had made for me, I looked like some kind of prom queen. It had a beaded, strapless bodice and a flared skirt with acres of crinolines. The studio's idea was to make me look as innocent and schoolgirlish as possible. I felt a little foolish.

Rock smiled bravely though, and escorted me to his car. It was a cool February evening and I shivered as we drove away. A blast of cold air blew in from a tear in the convertible top.

''Nice car,'' I said without much conviction.

"Thanks. I told the studio not to send a limo. Too stuffy."

I rubbed my goose-pimpled arms vigorously.

"Nothing stuffy about *this*."

"Oh, yeah," Rock said, laughing. "I forgot about the hole in the top. Here, I'll flip on the heater."

Warm air engulfed the front seat, but I continued to shiver. Rock gave me a look of understanding. "Nervous?"

"Yes," I admitted. "I don't know what to do at one of these functions."

"That's all right. Just follow me and smile. You look terrific."

"Thanks, Rock."

"Really, you're going to be a big hit."

The Beverly Hills Hotel, illuminated with spotlights, lit up the darkness of the surrounding neighborhood. As we got out of the car at the entrance, the flashes from photographers' cameras went off with blinding rapidity. The crowd of fans behind the barriers roared: "Rock! Rock Hudson!"

Rock gave them his easy, toothy grin and waved.

"Say hello to your fans, Mamie," he told me quietly.

I waved. Behind the roped-off walkway I could see them looking at me, trying to figure out who exactly I was. I was so new on the Hollywood scene that few of the fans knew my name. But when tonight was over, the papers would carry my picture along with those of the many other stars at this event. And tomorrow, in accordance with Universal's publicity department's strategy, Mamie Van Doren would begin to become a celebrity.

As Rock and I entered the hotel, I realized that my dream was unfolding.

Downstairs in the Crystal Room, the Photoplay Awards banquet was already under way. Rock and I made our entrance after speaking to a couple of reporters. We sat at our assigned table with Joan Crawford and her date.

In no time I realized that Crawford was on the way to becoming blind drunk. Every so often she'd knock back a slug of her drink and look around the room malevolently.

Marilyn Monroe was cavorting on the dais at the front of the room. She was the center of attention in a slinky gold lamé gown that clung to her like it was painted on. It was just the kind of dress I'd hoped the studio would make for me for this event.

Off to our left sat Gary Cooper, laughing at something Grace Kelly said across the table. Tex Ritter came onstage and sang the title song from their new film *High Noon* before accepting an award for it. John Wayne and Maureen O'Hara both accepted awards for *The Quiet Man*.

My head was swiveling around all over the room as I picked out all the stars in the audience. For a moment I was once again Joan Olander, star-watcher. Mamie Van Doren, starlet, was still someone new to me and it took conscious effort to play the part.

At one point in the evening, Marilyn wiggled her way up to the microphone to accept an award for Best Newcomer. Joan Crawford, looking at the dais, took a long pull at her drink.

"Shit," she muttered. "Bes' newcomer my ass." She said something unintelligible to her date, then turned and spoke to Rock.

"Whole goddamn placesh is fulla newcomers if ya ask me. Right, Rocko?"

"There are a lot of new faces, all right, Joan," he answered.

Crawford drunkenly tried to flirt with Rock but it only made her look like she had indigestion. Finally she turned her attention venomously on me.

"Lotsha pretty new faces with nothin' goin' on behind 'em. Pretty few fuckin' real stars here . . ." She giggled a moment and waved to the waiter for another drink. "*Fuckin'* stars are what they are . . . 'cause thatsh how they got here—fucking!"

I didn't reply. It was especially painful for me to be treated that way by Joan Crawford—my mother had named me Joan because she was such a big fan of Joan Crawford's. But Joan was hardly responsible for what she was saying, I told myself.

I remember her compelling performances in *Mildred Pierce* and dozens of other films and how I had worshiped her as a great talent of the screen. I had jumped at a chance to do a scene from *Mildred Pierce* in an audition at MGM. Before tonight she had seemed larger than life.

I didn't understand her meanness then. I couldn't know that her drunken rage was directed not at me, but at what I represented: the new wave of glamour girls—Marilyn, Grace Kelly, myself, and the many girls under contract to the various studios around town who were the changing guard. We were the ones who would feed the insatiable appetite of the movie industry for new, pretty faces.

And we were the ones in years to come who would or would not survive the next new wave.

"Excuse me," I said, getting up.

I made my way across the crowded banquet hall to the ladies' room. I locked myself and the bushel of crinoline I was wearing into a stall and sat on the toilet to check my makeup. While I made repairs in the reflection of my hand mirror, I heard a familiar voice among the others in the rest room as congratulations were offered.

"Thanks," the soft voice said. There was a formal sound about it. Rehearsed. "Thanks so much. It's a real honor."

I stayed fixing my lipstick for several minutes. The conversation had died down in the ladies' room and I could tell by the occasional scrape of a high heel that there was still one other person in there with me. When I came out of the stall, Marilyn Monroe was looking at herself in the mirror. Without turning from the mirror, she looked at me, a little tipsy, with a flash of recognition.

"I told you you'd make it somewhere."

"Yes, you did," I said to her reflection in the mirror. "You said that if I didn't make it at Twentieth Century-Fox I'd make it at some other studio. I thought for a while that you had managed to keep me from getting my contract there."

"Fat chance. So you're screwing Jimmy McHugh?" She said "screwing" in that innocent little-girl way that was already becoming a trademark.

"Not on your life. He's my manager. He's such an old bastard."

"I didn't think you were, Mamie. See? I even know your new name. You look like you're smart enough to screw the right one. But be careful of Louella Parsons, Jimmy's girlfriend. She's powerful." Louella Parsons was Jimmy McHugh's girlfriend, and she, along with Hedda Hopper, ranked as one of the two most influential and powerful columnists in Hollywood.

"I've already found that out. But I've always got Hedda."

We both laughed. Marilyn turned back to the mirror and gave her hair one final pat. "Well, back to the party. Welcome aboard, Mamie Van Doren."

"Thanks, Norma Jean."

"Yes, well, Norma Jean isn't here anymore. Joan won't be after a while either. You'll see." She blew a kiss to our reflections in the mirror. "This is what we are now."

I breathed a sigh of relief at the end of the evening as the valet closed the car door and Rock got in behind the wheel. We pulled out of the Beverly Hills Hotel and began winding up Coldwater Canyon Drive.

"Have a good time?" Rock asked.

"Well . . . sure, pretty much."

"Sorry about the scene with Joan Crawford."

"You couldn't help it, Rock. It was just kind of a shock to me." I explained to him that I had been named after Joan.

"Yeah. But just think, you could have done a lot worse. Look at me. My namesake's some goddamn boulder next to the highway between Palm Springs and Hemet."

"What?"

"My agent or some genius in the P.R. department got the idea for my name coming back from a weekend of golf."

As we laughed about some of the names chosen for different players around the lot, we drove past Rock's house off Coldwater Canyon and kept on toward the Valley where I lived. We stopped in front of my parents' house.

"This really has been fun, Rock," I said, meaning it. "I didn't know what to expect from something, you know, arranged by the studio."

"I've enjoyed it too, Mamie. And you handled it perfectly. Just like a veteran."

We got out and walked to my front door. I turned, expecting a goodnight peck on the cheek. Instead, Rock said, "Have you got any coffee in there?"

"Sure," I said, surprised. He acted pleased to be invited in.

My parents were asleep, so we tiptoed out to the kitchen

and closed the door. As I made coffee, we talked shop about the studio executives, various directors, producers, and of course other actors and actresses.

When I went to the cupboard to take out the coffee cups, I felt Rock's hands on my bare shoulders. He turned me toward him and kissed me. My first thought was that it would be a little smack on the mouth between friends. Instead, to my surprise, Rock gave me a deep, searching, passionate kiss and his body was pressed against mine. I could feel him hardening against me as the kiss grew more ardent. Soon we were breathing heavily and pawing each other.

As we necked, we slowly sank to the kitchen floor. I was laying half on top of Rock, helping him unzip his fly. When I got it open I realized that the boulder his agent had named him after must have been a big one: Rock was well-endowed.

He rolled me over to get on top, but suddenly found himself engulfed in a cloud of crinoline. "Jesus," he muttered, trying to push some of the petticoats aside.

Every time I moved my back against the cold linoleum, the beads on my dress popped off and rolled across the floor. That sound was punctuated by the plunk-plop of the coffee percolator and our muffled voices trying to give directions.

"Wait . . . oh . . ."

"I . . . just let me . . ."

"No . . . not there . . ."

I tried to guide him inside me but couldn't reach him through the forest of underskirts. We slid on Mother's waxed linoleum as we struggled for traction, groping for handholds.

"Mamie . . . I'm . . . ah-umph, ah-umphing . . ."

"What did you say?"

Rock let out a long sigh and his weight collapsed on top of me.

"I said, 'I'm coming,' " he groaned softly.

We got up and straightened ourselves out. I searched around in my crinolines and cleaned up the damage. I poured our cups of coffee, long since perked, and we sat at the kitchen table.

Rock asked, "Would you like to have lunch tomorrow at the commissary?"

"Sure. I'll meet you about noontime."

"Maybe after lunch you could come over to the set where I'm working."

"Why over at the set?"

"Oh, there'll be some photographers over there. It'll be good for you to get some exposure. We're getting a lot of attention with this picture."

The picture he was working on was another in a long line of Universal westerns called *Gun Fury*. It was the usual shoot-'em-up plot about good guys and bad guys in the Old West and was notable only for bolstering Rock's macho image.

"It'll be good for all of us," I said pointedly.

Rock gave me a sheepish look. "I hope I didn't ruin your dress."

"No, no. It's the studio's dress anyway. They're probably used to this sort of thing."

The next morning before I went to the studio, my mother let me have it.

"What went on in here last night anyway?"

I studied my glass of orange juice intently.

"Oh, nothing."

"Nothing! The throw rug was pushed into the corner and the coffeepot was on all night. It's a wonder it didn't burn up."

"Sorry."

"What's the studio going to say about your dress?"

"What about it?"

"The beads, Jo. It must not have a bead left on it. When I came out into the kitchen this morning to fix your father's breakfast, I nearly fell and broke my neck on all those little beads rolling around on the floor."

The commissary that day was jammed with extras, production people, studio executives, directors, writers, actors, P.R. people, and gossip columnists. The U.I. commissary was, like the commissaries of other studios, the traditional meeting place and wellspring of movie-business gossip. A colorful, multicostumed, chattering group convened there to eat and catch up on the business every working day.

Rock came in fresh from the set of *Gun Fury*, dressed in western costume. We sat at a small table. Back-to-back with him, at a table behind us, sat his current lover, who was in the same picture and was also dressed in cowboy garb.

"How's the shooting going over on your set?" I asked.

"Huh? Oh, fine." He leaned his chair back on two legs and said over his shoulder, "How was I in the scene we just finished?"

I couldn't hear the answer over the din in the commissary. Rock laughed and nodded and said something I couldn't hear. He let his chair down on the floor and took a bite of his lunch.

"Yes," he said to me, "it's going pretty well. You coming over to the set this afternoon?"

"Sure, if you want."

Rock smiled and waved at someone a few tables over where the publicity people normally sat with columnists setting up interviews. I turned and saw Harrison Carroll of the Los Angeles *Herald Express* and his assistant, Army Archerd, both wave back. Sitting not far from him was James Bacon of Associated Press, who grinned at us.

Rock leaned back again and said over his shoulder, "There's Bacon over there too."

Rock and his friend carried on a conversation for several minutes while I tried to participate. But it was a losing battle. Finally I turned my full attention to my lunch and let Rock play his little game.

I was obviously just there to boost Rock's image with the media. The situation made me uncomfortable until I remembered the night before. Then the whole charade seemed very comical. I wondered what Rock's lover would say if he knew about the impromptu wrestling match Rock and I had had on my mother's slippery kitchen floor. Or the sticky spot on my petticoats that I hoped the wardrobe department would ignore.

I started to giggle. Rock stopped talking and looked at me.

"What's so funny?"

"Crinolines."

Chapter Two

I was born in the little town of Rowena, South Dakota, nine miles outside of Sioux Falls, on February 6, 1933, the daughter of Warner and Lucille Olander. My dad worked in a rock quarry to take care of us. He was paid thirty-five cents a load and on a good day he brought home seven dollars.

The township of Rowena consisted of a church, a school, a railroad station, a grain elevator, a hardware store, and a combination grocery-store/filling-station/post-office/dance-hall, owned by my Great-Uncle Ben.

My dad's parents were well-to-do farmers; they attended the Swedish Lutheran church they helped to build. My mother and father met there one Sunday, but they were listening to their own inner voices more than the sermon. Consequently, I arrived a bit early. They were married in August and I came quickly afterward in February. That would make little difference today. In 1933, however, it made a great deal of difference. The town gossips counted the months on their fingers and had something to talk about.

But the love which began in church that Sunday, and that hastened me into the world, has lasted to this day. Now my parents have been together for more than fifty years, and their love is still in bloom.

My maternal grandmother was born in Göteborg, Sweden,

and emigrated around 1880. My father's people were Black Swedes, adventuresome dark-featured descendants of the Mongolian hordes that settled in Scandinavia. Many of the people of Rowena were immigrants, or from immigrant stock: Germans, Swedes, Norwegians, and Irish.

When I was four years old my father got a better job as a mechanic in Sioux City, Iowa. He and Mother moved to Sioux City and I went to live with my maternal grandparents, the Bennetts, on their 160-acre farm in Rowena so I could be assured of a warm bed and three meals a day. It was the Depression, and times were that hard.

I grew up around plain, stoic, hardworking people, many of whom had their ideas of the world formed in the preceding century. I was a sensitive, serious child, and often lonely, looking to my family for more love than they were capable of expressing outwardly.

My special name for Grandma Bennett was "Dah," pronounced like the A in "half." She was the dominant figure in the household. She ran the house, if not with an iron hand, with at least a firm one. The house had to be cleaned just so, her little collection of exotic plants watered ever so gently, and everyone had better damn well mind their manners. She was meticulous about her clothes and never went into town without a hat. She kept her ramrod-straight, proud posture until the day she died.

My Grandpa Bennett, known to me as "Pa," was a small wiry man, with great reserves of strength, and a fun-loving twinkle in his Irish blue eyes. He parted his snowy white hair in the middle and slicked it down before driving us into town on Saturday. He could play the fiddle and dance a jig. He loved to have a drink and argue with the men in the pool hall about how Franklin Roosevelt was sending the country to hell in a handbasket.

Uncle Cliff, my mother's brother, was a teaser. During the daily milking, he would take aim with the cow's tit and squirt warm milk in my eyes. I could milk a cow myself when I was very young.

Barnstormers occasionally flew over the countryside, buzzed our little community, then landed in a farmer's field to give airplane rides.

One time Pa's sense of adventure got the better of him,

and he took me out to see it. The handsome young pilot with his leather helmet smiled at us and asked if we wanted to go for a ride, just fifty cents each.

There was seldom a spare half dollar around in those days, but when I looked at Pa, the mischief was popping in his eyes.

"What do you think, Joanie?" he asked.

"I don't know, Pa. Should we? Isn't it dangerous?"

He smiled and put a hand on my shoulder.

"Young feller," Pa said to the pilot as he dug into the pocket of his faded big overalls, "what do you say to takin' me and my granddaughter here up for a half dollar? She'll sit on my lap and she's no bigger than a minute."

The pilot looked around the field. No one else was around yet anyway. "Well," he drawled, "since you're the first ones here . . . why not?"

We climbed in, and as the engine coughed to life, I sat on his lap in the front seat of the old biplane. We flew over the patchwork quilt of fields and farms, my eyes watering, thrilling to the wind in my face, and the roar and smell of the airplane's motor. It was over too quickly. When the plane rolled to a stop, my heart was still pounding from the view I'd had of the countryside.

But the giant Atwater-Kent radio with its ornate woodwork and big black tuning knobs was our main link with the outside world. It brought us music, the Joe Louis prizefights, the early ravings of Adolf Hitler, and the fireside chats of FDR (whom Pa would cuss roundly).

We had no indoor toilets. We had to go to an outhouse in the cold, and in those howling South Dakota winters it got to ten and twenty degrees below zero. We had no electricity. And no gas or running water. We trudged out to a cistern to pump water, summer or winter.

Growing up on the farm gave me a fine opportunity to see what work was like. Everybody pitched in. My grandfather had four or five sturdy plowhorses and I remember him holding a plow handle all day long, from sunup to sundown, with the plowhorses pulling the plow through the rich black soil. Pa used to come home black from plowing, with the dirt caked on him from head to toe. My job was to carry thermos bottles of water out to the fields for Pa and the hired men so they wouldn't drop from the heat, and dinner at midday so they could eat in the fields. And they had to eat and drink a lot.

For all that Grandma Dah loved me, I think she was tired of raising children. She had raised four girls and a boy already. Dah really talked to me and was relieved when my mother and father drove the ninety miles from Sioux City to visit and take me off her hands. I was usually so thrilled about my parents' visits that I wouldn't sleep the night before.

Dah was an austere woman who found it hard at her age to identify with a little girl's problems. Though endowed with large breasts herself (all of her daughters were too), she seemed at a loss when mine started to grow at an early age.

"Stop scratching there, Joanie," she snapped.

"Dah, it itches bad," I said. "I can't help it."

My tiny nipples were swollen and red. She shot a glance at Pa.

"She's starting early," he said.

"Just like her mother, Lucille," Dah replied.

I was sick a lot as a youngster. There was no refrigeration on the farm and we didn't pasteurize the milk. Living in the country, we didn't have the convenience of a nearby doctor. And back then, we didn't have all the drugs that are available today—penicillin and other antibiotics. You saw the hearse going by three or four times a month because of polio, scarlet fever, chickenpox, or tuberculosis.

One year, I had undulant fever and my temperature shot up to 106. They put me in the hospital in Sioux Falls—something unheard-of. But several times my Grandma Dah sent me to school when I was sick because she didn't want anybody in the house during the day. I remember walking the mile and a half to school in the snow running a temperature.

I attended a classic two-room country school that included kindergarten through grade six. One room contained grades one through three, one aisle for each grade, and the other room with grades four through six.

The best time of year were the Christmas holidays and the high, hot Midwestern summer. Christmas especially was full of excitement and festivities as the family gathered to feast on traditional Swedish ludefisk (a kind of boiled whitefish) and other foods, washed down by the sovereign Swedish cure for cold winters, glüg. Glüg is a drink made with boiling cinnamon and other spices in equal parts of red wine and whiskey. When the glüg flows, the Swedes shed much of their cold reserve, and the little farmhouse on the hill would ring with laughter and song.

In 1939, when I was six years old, I moved to Sioux City, Iowa, to be with my mother and father. Living on the farm, I had had few children my own age to play with. But my father's sister also lived in Sioux City, and my younger cousin, Colleen Mennenga, became my favorite playmate. Sioux City, unlike Rowena, had bright lights—hotels, restaurants, department stores, and dime stores with lunch counters. There were places where my mother and dad went dancing, and even a half-block red-light district. Pre-World War II Sioux City might not have been a grandiose place, but to a little girl fresh from the farm, it might as well have been Prohibition-era Chicago. It was there that I first went to the movies. For me, it was like a dream come true.

Both my parents worked that first summer, and they couldn't afford a baby-sitter. So when I wasn't in school, they left me at one of the three movie theaters in Sioux City. Often I was there all day. In the evening, when Mother came to pick me up, I'd be sleeping in a front-row seat, dreaming of my favorites: Clark Gable and Carole Lombard, Spencer Tracy and Katharine Hepburn, Fred Astaire and Ginger Rogers.

I'd try to dance like Ginger Rogers. I announced to my mother that I wanted platinum hair just like Carole Lombard's. Whenever there was a church social or a school talent show, I'd always be in the middle of it. I won a declamatory contest, as they were called in those days, with a dramatic reading called "Mama." I also had a flair for posing for cameras, one foot in front of the other, wearing a cute little smile. I tried to fashion myself after my favorite heroines in the movies. I was fascinated by the beautiful clothes they wore, the independence they seemed to have. They were dressed to the nines, talked elegantly and with sophistication, wore beautiful jewelry, and drove expensive cars.

I was enormously attracted to the secure, glamorous lives

they seemed to live. The movies were the perfect tonic in those dark days of the Depression.

The other thing the movies seemed to promise was love. In every one of those celluloid fairy tales, the heroine lived happily ever after in the company of the man she loved. How I yearned for that.

It was then that I set my heart on becoming a Hollywood star.

Chapter Three

In May 1942, when I was nine, my family moved to Los Angeles, only a few miles from Hollywood. We were lucky to find an apartment quickly. People were flocking to the West Coast as the country geared up for the war effort and jobs by the thousands opened up in defense plants.

After a short stay in a boardinghouse, we managed to find a little courtyard apartment on Raymond Avenue. Unfortunately, they didn't allow children. The landlord finally relented, but my parents had to hide me so the other tenants wouldn't object. While Mother and Daddy came and went by the front door of the apartment, I had to sneak in and out by the back door.

We hadn't been there more than a few days when my mother spotted an article in the newspaper telling of a gala Hollywood party to be held at one of Hollywood's most glamorous nightclubs: the Mocambo. I was excited, and begged to go watch. As soon as we finished dinner that night, we took off to see our first Hollywood stars in the flesh.

In front of the Mocambo, we found ourselves standing in a crowd of noisy, restless people craning their necks to see the arriving limousines bringing the stars to the party.

Clutching my brand-new autograph book tightly, I sidestepped and squeezed my way to the front of the closely packed group behind the police barricades. My eyes popped as the bejeweled, tuxedoed, fur-wrapped, and sequined stars climbed smiling and waving out of their cars and walked through the bright lights and the shouting, waving, dazzled gauntlet formed by the fans.

They looked so small in person. What looked like a little girl hurried out of a limo and into the Mocambo. It was Bette Davis. Only a few of the more experienced fans recognized her.

By now my mother and father had worked their way near the front where I stood. A collective sigh escaped the crowd as a giant black Packard limousine pulled up to the curb, disgorging the most glittering creature I'd ever seen. It was Mae West.

Clad in twinkling silver sequins, her pale blonde hair encircling her head like a halo, she was escorted by an entourage of half a dozen tanned and beautiful well-built men. If a genie had suddenly appeared, I would have gladly traded anything I had to be just like her.

I wanted desperately to ask for her autograph. "Go on, Joanie, ask her," my mother encouraged me, knowing how much it meant to me.

"But what if she says no?" I said with a quavering voice.

A strange woman spoke up. "Go on, honey. She won't say no to someone as cute as you are."

"Yeah, kid," someone else put in. "Go on."

I looked from the woman's eyes to my mother's. Mother nodded encouragement.

My knees shook as I slipped under the barricade and solemnly held out my autograph book and pen.

"May I have your autograph, Miss West?"

She stopped and looked down at me. Her eyes pierced me with their blue crystalline depths. Her smile was like a bank of bright lights.

"Sure, baby. What's your name?"

"Joanie . . ." I managed to croak through a dry throat.

She made a flourish and I heard the pen scratching on the paper.

"There you go, Joanie," she said with that unmistakable throaty Mae West voice.

She handed back my autograph book and swept past, her entourage trailing in her wake. "Best of luck to Joanie, a very pretty girl,'' she had written. I stood in the walkway looking after her until my mother pulled me back behind the barrier.

The doors of the Mocambo opened and closed repeatedly that night, swallowing up celebrities and stars. More than anything in the world I wanted to be behind those doors. I, too, wanted to be the toast of Hollywood, adored, envied, catered to.

It was late when my father picked me up in his arms and carried me to the car. I had fallen asleep on the edge of a planter next to the building. I shivered with the cool night air and snuggled into the warmth of my mother's lap as we drove back to our apartment. That night I crawled sleepily into bed, clutching my autograph book tightly as I drifted off to sleep, dreaming of Hollywood, of the future.

Chapter Four

The breeze coming in the window of the bus tugged at my hair. Outside, on the sidewalks lining Sunset Boulevard, people hurried to and fro in the pale sunshine of early summer. Post-World War II Los Angeles was bustling with crowds of uniformed servicemen and civilians. There was an air of prosperity in the city as the strangers who had come west during the war settled in to make a life in California.

I smiled inwardly, remembering the conversation with my mother as I left the house only a short while before.

"You're too young to be running around Hollywood alone, Jo."

"I'm thirteen and I'm not alone, Mother. Hollywood's full of people. Besides, you never say anything when I go to work at the Pantages."

Just after my thirteenth birthday, I convinced the manager of the Pantages Theater on Hollywood Boulevard near Vine Street to give me a job as an usherette. At last I was able to see all the big movies that played there for free—*Notorious*, starring Cary Grant and Ingrid Bergman, *The Spiral Staircase*, starring Dorothy McGuire and George Brent, and *Heartbeat*, with Ginger Rogers and Jean-Pierre Aumont. (Little did I know that years later I would star with Jean-Pierre in a film in Buenos Aires.) I wore an usherette's uniform with a little pillbox hat, and carried a flashlight. It was the perfect job for someone as infatuated with the movies as I was.

My daytime hangout on the weekends and after school was a drugstore on the corner of Hollywood and Vine. Everyone knew the story about Lana Turner's discovery in Schwab's drugstore, it was part of Hollywood mythology. And even though it never happened, it made Schwab's the most famous drugstore in the world. It became a mecca for aspiring actors and actresses sitting around drinking coffee and Cokes, waiting to be discovered. But Schwab's was too crowded for a loner like me.

Already I had dyed my hair platinum in the hopes of attracting the attention of the talent scouts. And although I was only thirteen, my figure had filled out nicely.

One day, while I was sipping a soda and thumbing through a movie magazine, a man's voice caused me to look up.

"My card," he said formally.

He was a tall, distinguished gentleman with graying hair and broad shoulders. His face, though not handsome, had a certain masculine strength to it. He was dressed in a conservative business suit.

His card said: Niles Thorn Granlund.

"You're a Swede too, Mr. Granlund?"

"Yes. What's your name?"

"Joan Olander."

He nodded.

"You know, Joan, you look very much like Jean Harlow." Jean Harlow was my favorite glamour girl. "Thank you."

"I have a television show, Joan. I'd like you to be on it."

My dad had brought home a television not long after we moved out of our little court on Raymond Avenue and into a large flat on Harvard Boulevard. Television was then in its infancy. It was okay, but it wasn't the movies.

"What would I do?" I asked.

"I'm hosting a new show here in Hollywood. It'll be broadcast live from the Florentine Gardens nightclub. We need lots of pretty faces like yours to decorate it."

"Well, I don't know . . ."

"Of course, if you're already in a movie . . ." His voice trailed off and he looked at me with a knowing smile.

"No, no. I'm free right now. Let me think about it, okay, Mr. Granlund?"

He put a hand gently on my arm.

"Call me NTG. Ask your mother about the show and give me a call."

That night I discussed NTG's offer with my parents. They didn't think much of it.

"Jo," my dad said, lighting a cigarette, "your mother and I don't want to see you get disappointed."

"Honey," my mother said, "we don't want to see you get into trouble with some of these people, either. Remember the Black Dahlia?"

The Black Dahlia murder case in the 1940s had been one of the most shocking and sensational crimes in L.A. history. The dismembered body of Elizabeth Short, a girl in her twenties trying to break into the movies, had been found in a vacant lot. The crime had never been solved.

"Oh, Mother! I can take care of myself." I turned to my father. "And as far as being disappointed is concerned, I've got just as good a chance as anybody to make it in movies."

"Well," Daddy said, shaking his head, "there's an awful lot of competition out there."

My mother glanced at my father and he shrugged. "Okay," she said. "I'll go to the television show with you."

The Florentine Gardens the next day was a madhouse, with banks of oven-hot lights, cables snaking over the floor, and dozens of beautiful girls milling about waiting for the show to begin.

NTG waved and came over.

"This must be your mother," he said to me. He shook Mother's hand and said: "Thank you for coming, Mrs. Olander. And thank you for allowing Joan to be on the show."

"What do I have to do?" I asked anxiously.

"We have a number of businesses here in town that want you and the rest of the girls to model their clothes or jewelry, or say something about their services on television."

"But I . . . I don't know what to say."

"It'll be all written out for you. Just memorize it."

"*Memorize!*"

My mother nudged me. "Don't worry, Mr. Granlund, Joan can do it. She won a declamatory contest when she was just six. She's very good in front of people."

"Call me NTG, Mrs. Olander. Now, Joan, don't you

worry, you'll do just fine. You're going to have a very special place on the show, Joan. You're going to be the flower girl.''

They coated all the girls appearing on the show with thick white Pancake makeup and brown lipstick. We looked like creatures in a horror movie.

The show was a landmark—a kind of prototype of the modern talk show. It was one of the first shows originating from Hollywood. Once a week, NTG would interview a movie star, talk with the audience, and do jokes about the girls onstage who were modeling clothes or selling products. Occasionally NTG would call on me to distribute flowers to members of the audience or do some little chore onstage.

After that first broadcast, I was on the show often. I was known as Little Joanie, the Flower Girl. Mother and I became friends with NTG and the owner of the Florentine Gardens, Mark Hansen, another Swede. Because Mother trusted the two Swedes, I was allowed to do NTG's Hollywood show for nearly a year.

All the girls worked for free, our only compensation a pair of Willy's of Hollywood stockings with the seam up the back, and the chance to be discovered.

For a while after I started doing the NTG show, I began to think my father was right about all the competition. Nothing seemed to be happening to advance my ambitions. I was still in school, and although my blossoming fourteen-year-old figure and blonde hair got me noticed by plenty of boys, as well as earning me disapproving looks from my teachers, no Hollywood agents came knocking on my door.

The next summer, at the age of fifteen, while Mother and I were staying at the Montecito Motel in Palm Springs, the owner of the motel suggested I enter the Miss Palm Springs beauty contest, sponsored by the Montecito. Mother agreed to allow me to enter, and I won.

During my reign as Miss Palm Springs, while making an appearance at a meeting of the Los Angeles Press Club, I was asked to be the press club's beauty queen for the coming year—Miss Eight Ball. Last year's representative had been a lovely young girl named Marilyn Monroe.

Between the two beauty titles, my picture was soon all over the Los Angeles and Palm Springs papers, and one day, in answer to my prayers, the phone rang in our Harvard Boulevard flat.

"This is Bill White, director of casting at RKO Studios. I'm calling for Joan Olander, please."

"This is Joan."

"Joan, I was wondering if you could come over to my office on Gower and Melrose sometime this week. I'd like to discuss a contract with you."

"With me?"

"Yes, we're considering offering you a contract with the studio. This *is* Joan Olander, Miss Palm Springs and Miss Eight Ball, correct?"

"Yes."

"And you would, I imagine, like to be in the movies, wouldn't you?"

"Yes, yes, I would."

"Then come to my office and we'll see what we can work out. Why don't you drop by about ten o'clock on Thursday?"

"That . . . that's great."

"We'll meet for a little while and then I'll introduce you to Walter Kane, Howard Hughes's right-hand man."

"Howard Hughes?"

"The studio's owner," he said, laughing good-naturedly at my confusion.

Later I described the call to my mother. "What do you think I should do, Mother?"

She thought a moment and said: "Well, it's Howard Hughes. You should probably go."

I arrived at RKO on the appointed day and was given a brief interview by Bill White. Afterward he showed me to an outer office where I waited for Walter Kane, RKO's executive vice-president.

After cooling my heels for several hours, I went back to Bill White. "Is Mr. Kane coming or not?"

Mr. White smiled in a way that implied he'd been through this before.

"Apparently he got tied up in a meeting. Why don't you come back at ten o'clock tomorrow? I think Howard Hughes will want to meet you then too."

"Are you sure he'll be here?" I asked skeptically.

"Be here at ten."

The next day I met Walter Kane, a stocky mid-fortyish Irishman with an egg-shaped head and red face, who seemed to fancy himself a fashionable dresser. One of the duties of his executive position was the pleasant task of screening the young girls that his wealthy boss wanted to meet. We talked for a while about my acting ambitions, the pictures RKO was doing, and various roles I might play. He left a vague sort of impression that I might get some work at RKO. In a friendly way, he also made many double entendres that went over my head, though there was no mistaking his tone and the twinkle in his eye. Nonetheless, I found myself liking him.

When Kane asked in a casual tone, "Do you have any black stockings?" I was surprised. "The kind with the seam up the back?" he went on, his voice becoming just perceptibly thicker.

"I don't wear them, Mr. Kane."

"Walter. Well, we need to get you some stockings." He got up from the chair and opened the door to his office. "Come on." I realized it was the only way I was going to see Howard Hughes. Reluctantly I got up.

He drove me to Saks Fifth Avenue, where he bought me a new pair of silk stockings with the seam up the back, exactly as he had described. Back in his car he said, "Now, let's go to my house and you can model them for me."

I looked at him, thinking: Damn, he looks old enough to be my grandfather!

"Don't worry, Joan," he said, reading the expression on my face. "I just want to see the stockings." He smiled warmly. "Really. We won't even be alone. My maid's there."

We went to his apartment on Sunset at La Cienega, a well-appointed place in the same building as Paul Hessy's photo studio, which would serve as a favorite meeting place for the security-conscious Howard Hughes. I went into Kane's bedroom alone and put on the stockings.

As I modeled the stockings for him out in the living room, Walter watched me intently with watery blue eyes. I did a few cheesecake poses for him on the arms of chairs. He wet his lips carefully several times. Then we drove back to RKO.

I asked him if I was going to meet Howard Hughes today. He said he thought not, but assured me that Mr. Hughes wanted to meet me very much.

"Why?" I asked.

"He's seen your picture in the papers as Miss Palm Springs."

"And Miss Eight Ball," I added.

"Right. Howard Hughes likes beautiful girls very much."

"Then why doesn't he come out and meet me?"

"My dear," Walter Kane said sagely, "you have a great deal to learn about Howard Hughes."

A few days after my meeting with Walter Kane, I got a call from Bill White saying that RKO wanted to use me in a movie called *Variety Footlights*. It was a bit part with no lines. I agreed, nonetheless, enthusiastically. My scene was the final one of the movie, as the camera panned across an empty theater to find a boy and girl still necking in front of a black screen. I played the girl; the boy was a good-looking young actor named Jack Paar. Paar was very sweet, a little shy. Even then he was wearing a toupee.

While I carried out my Miss Eight Ball and Miss Palm Springs duties, I met any number of people in the movie business. Among them was an actor named Conrad Janis, who was shooting a film on location near our flat. I wanted so much to get into movies that I took every opportunity to make a good contact.

Conrad came from a wealthy eastern family and was just beginning to establish his acting career. One evening he invited me to the Mocambo for a glamorous night of dinner and dancing.

The floor show that evening was the Nat King Cole Trio. I tingled with excitement at being behind the frosted-glass doors that had beckoned me so tantalizingly years before while autograph-hunting. We danced until the wee hours when, dizzy with champagne, Conrad deposited me giggling on my doorstep and kissed me good night.

The next morning I was still sleeping when the phone rang.

"Hullo?" I answered sleepily.

"This Joan Olander?" a husky male voice snapped.

"Yes . . . who's this?"

"Johnny Meyers here. I saw you at the Mocambo last night."

"That's nice."

"A friend of mine thought it was very nice."

"Well, it's very thoughtful of you to call and tell me so, Mr. Mayor."

"Meyers. Johnny Meyers."

I looked at the clock on our mantel and saw that it was not quite nine o'clock. My head was throbbing from last night's champagne, and my stomach was churning.

"Mr. Meyers, I'm not feeling well this morning, so if you'll excuse me . . ."

"Wait! Joan, my friend is Howard Hughes and he wants you to have lunch with him."

"Oh, God," I groaned. "Here we go again. Why doesn't Howard Hughes call me himself?"

"Howard Hughes never calls anybody. I work for him. He'd like you to meet him today at—"

"Today? You must be kidding."

"Howard Hughes never kids about these things. Do you realize that aspiring young actresses all over town would give . . . anything for an opportunity like this."

"How about tomorrow?" I said, half-pleading.

"Today. It must be today, Joan."

I tried to stop my head from spinning so I could look at my reflection in the mirror across the room. Could I hide the ravages of last night's champagne?

"Okay."

"Good," Meyers said positively. It was like he'd just closed a sale. "Before you have lunch you'll come to Paul Hessy's photo studio to meet Mr. Hughes."

"Isn't that where Walter Kane lives?"

"Be there at eleven-thirty."

"Are you *sure* Howard Hughes is going to be there?"

"You can count on it, Joan. He's looking forward to meeting you."

"Okay, Mr. Meyers. Eleven-thirty."

"Oh, Joan, one more thing. Make sure you wear a white sweater . . . with no bra."

I showed up at Paul Hessy's studio dressed as requested. Johnny Meyers greeted me and took me into another room, where I saw Walter Kane and a tall, disheveled man who looked as though he hadn't shaved in several days: Howard Hughes.

Hughes had an amused look on his face and a mischievous glint in his eyes as he greeted me. He wore one of those houndstooth jackets with sleeves made of a different material that were so popular in the forties, baggy brown slacks, a nondescript shirt, and no tie. His shoes were a pair of scuffed tennis sneakers. Except for the shoes, his clothes were clean but rumpled, as if he had slept in them.

We shook hands and Johnny Meyers announced for my benefit that we were eating at a restaurant close by on Sunset Boulevard, called The Players.

Walter Kane stayed behind while Johnny Meyers, Hughes, and I climbed into one of his fleet of Chevy sedans, all of them as nondescript as his shirt, and drove the several blocks to the restaurant.

We parked behind The Players and entered through the back door. We were met in the kitchen by the maître d' and led to a quiet booth in a back room roped off from the rest of the restaurant. Meyers sat on the far side of the booth and Hughes sat to my left. Meyers had made small talk with me up to now, but he abruptly fell quiet.

"Well, Joan," Hughes said, "I'm glad you could come to lunch."

"Thank you, Mr. Hughes," I said. "I'm glad we finally get to meet."

He smiled from behind his scraggly growth of beard. He looked at Johnny Meyers and then back to me. Meyers got up and left the table. When he was gone, Hughes asked me, "Are you a virgin, Joan?"

My jaw dropped in surprise. "Am I . . . a . . . a . . . what?"

"You know. A virgin?"

"You mean have I ever . . . ever been to bed with anyone?"

"Yes."

"That's something you'll never know, Howard," I said, brashly using his first name.

He blinked at me dumbly for a moment. A wave of annoyance passed across his face, soon to be replaced by a look of genuine amusement. He grinned broadly at me.

"Only time will tell."

A waiter brought menus to the table and we ordered. He took the menus away before Hughes spoke again.

"Do you live at home?" he asked pleasantly.

"Yes. With my mother and father."

"That's good. Were you born here?"

I filled him in on my South Dakota history, explaining that we had come to California almost seven years before. In return, he told me a little bit about growing up in Texas and how much he liked California. Before long we were talking like old friends, each laughing at the other's remarks.

Then suddenly he adopted a businesslike tone of voice. "The boy you were with last night, was that a serious date?"

"Conrad? Oh, no! We've only gone out a few times."

"A pretty girl like you isn't going steady with someone?"

"No, Howard." I shook my head and smiled across the table at him. "No one."

He seemed pleased by that.

At last the conversation drifted to the movie business.

"I'm making a picture up near Las Vegas called *Jet Pilot,*" he said. "There's probably a part in it for you, if you're interested."

"Oh, yes. Very interested."

"Good, good. You'll be hearing from, uh, someone at the studio in a few days. In the meanwhile, I'm going up to Palm Springs this weekend to stay at the Racquet Club. Would you like to go along?"

"Uh, well, I'm going to Palm Springs myself with my mother. I've got to attend a Chamber of Commerce function as Miss Palm Springs. We'll be staying at the Montecito Motel."

"I see. The Montecito. Would your mother mind if I sent a car for the two of you? You can ride up and we can see each other when you get there."

"No, I don't think she'd mind. It sounds like fun."

Early the next Saturday morning, Mother and I sat in the back of one of Hughes's Chevys, rolling through the San Gabriel Valley. The driver was discreetly quiet after picking us up at the Harvard Boulevard flat.

"Well, Jo," Mother said sotto voce, "I've certainly never seen a limousine like *this* before. Are you sure this is *the* Howard Hughes?"

"I think Howard is a little eccentric, like all the stories in the papers about him."

"Yes, I believe he is," she sniffed disdainfully. "He let you call him Howard?"

"He did *not* let me. If he can ask me if I'm a virgin, I can call him Howard."

"I just don't know about all this."

"He really is nice, Mother. You'll like him. And he wants to put me in his new movie. I hope we can see him right after the Chamber of Commerce luncheon."

The driver dropped us at the Montecito in midmorning and Mother and I settled into our room. It was still early enough for us to get some sun before the luncheon. As I was putting on my swimsuit, the phone rang. Mother picked it up.

"It's for you, Jo," she said, covering the mouthpiece. "Howard Hughes."

"Hello, Howard?"

"Hi, Joan," Hughes said with his Texas twang. "Did you have a nice drive up?"

"Oh, yes. Thank you for the lift."

"My pleasure. Was that your mother who answered the phone?"

"Yes."

"She has a lovely voice. Sounds as young as you do."

"People mistake us for sisters all the time. She's very beautiful." I gave Mother a wink.

"I'm sure," Hughes said. "Now, what I'd like to do is have you come over here for lunch right now. After lunch we could . . . we could spend some time together. Get better acquainted."

"Well, Howard, I have to go to this Chamber of Commerce luncheon first. That's why I'm up here in the first place. But I could come—"

"I'll send the driver right away."

"I can't do that, Howard. These people are expecting me."

He persisted in trying to get me to come to the Racquet Club immediately, his voice taking on a hard edge.

"Let me call you back," I finally said.

"When you call back, ask for Mr. Murphy. That's my code name. No one knows I'm staying here."

I hung up the phone and turned to my mother. "What am I going to do, Mother? He wants me to come over now."

"Jo, you have an obligation to the people at the Chamber of Commerce."

"I know, but—"

"No buts about it. You have to go!"

After arguing for a few minutes more, I dialed the Racquet Club and asked for Mr. Murphy. Johnny Meyers answered; he handed the phone to Howard.

"Yes?"

"It's Joan," I said. "I can't come over, Howard, until I get through with luncheon. But as soon as it's over I'll—"

Johnny Meyers' gruff salesman's voice interrupted me.

"Joan, Howard's very angry with you right now. He came up here especially to get better acquainted with you. I suggest you forget this other thing and get over here right now. If you don't, you're going to screw everything up."

I gave one last appealing glance to my mother. She folded her arms and shook her head.

"Well . . . I can't come, so that's that."

Throughout the Chamber of Commerce luncheon I was in a daze of disappointment. My one chance at getting to know Howard Hughes, gone because of a roomful of smiling businessmen!

After the luncheon, Mother and I discovered that our chauffeur was no longer available. We had no way back to Los Angeles from Palm Springs. We ended up taking a Greyhound bus. I was furious at Howard Hughes for leaving us high and dry. And I was just as furious with my mother for ruining what I thought was my big chance to get in the movies.

Much to my surprise, a few days later Bill White from RKO called. He told me to ask my mother if I could leave for Las Vegas in two days.

"Why?" I asked skeptically.

"You're going to be working in *Jet Pilot,* starring John Wayne and Janet Leigh."

I let out a scream. "You're kidding!"

"A ticket on TWA will be waiting for you at Burbank airport. Plan on being up there two days."

"Wonderful."

"Everybody I talk to should be so excited over a bit role. Report to the wardrobe mistress when you get there, so you can be fitted."

"I will, Bill. Thank you."

"The plane leaves at ten o'clock. Don't miss it."

"I won't, believe me. Thanks, Bill."

"Don't thank me. You must have made an impression on the boss."

I worked two days on *Jet Pilot* without ever laying eyes on John Wayne. Janet Leigh was cool to me, but nice enough to share her limo and give me a ride to the Air Force base where we were filming. When I flew back to L.A. after my two days' work, I felt like I had at least made some kind of start in the movie business. Hopefully, it would just be a matter of time until the larger roles came along.

I appeared in two other pictures at RKO in the months ahead: *His Kind of Woman*, starring Jane Russell and Robert Mitchum; and *Two Tickets to Broadway*, starring Tony Martin and Janet Leigh. *His Kind of Woman* was a romantic adventure set in an exotic tropical locale, the exteriors of which were built on the backlot of the old David O. Selznick studio in Culver City where *Gone with the Wind* had been filmed. Bob Mitchum played a soldier of fortune with laconic humor, the kind of role he would later develop into a screen persona uniquely his own. Jane Russell was a consummate professional who did her job without noticing much of what went on around her. Mitchum, on the other hand, was fresh out of jail on a marijuana-possession charge and glad to talk to anyone and everyone on the set—from Jane Russell down to the lowliest grip and bit player.

The second movie, *Two Tickets to Broadway*, was a garden-variety rags-to-riches story with every pretty unknown in Hollywood playing a bit role. If there had been a beauty contest on that set, I would have come in last. Janet Leigh pretended not to remember me from our limo ride on *Jet Pilot*.

Around this time an agent I had met at the studio suggested that I take up acting lessons to improve my skills. I enrolled with Natasha Lytess, a well-thought-of acting teacher in Hollywood, taking several lessons a week in her gloomy house off Highland, up in the Hollywood Hills. In fact, the house had no electric lights at all. Natasha spent most of our lessons talking, however, and there was very little time left, after her long-winded speeches on the art of acting, to actually perform for her.

Another student of Natasha's was a chubby-faced blonde I had seen at modeling layouts around town, and the girl who had preceded me as Miss Eight Ball. She was about seven years older than me, and her name had been Norma Jean Baker, though she had taken lately to calling herself Marilyn Monroe. We met one day on the walk through the trees that surrounded Natasha's little house. She wore faded jeans and an old sweatshirt. Her hair was groomed as a sort of after-thought, dark roots in need of a touch-up. We said ''Hi'' to each other as I went in for my lesson.

I asked Natasha about her.

''Oh, she is talented,'' Natasha said in heavily accented English. ''When she finds herself, someday she will be recognized.''

I stopped taking lessons from Natasha after a short time. I felt I wasn't learning anything—Natasha couldn't or wouldn't stop talking long enough to teach.

One day on the set of *His Kind of Woman* the same agent who had spoken to me before told me I should go over to Twentieth Century-Fox. I was the Twentieth Century-Fox type, he said, and they were looking for Betty Grable-type girls who could sing and dance. He made an appointment for me to be interviewed by their casting department.

At Fox, first you interviewed with casting; if they liked you they gave you a script to study and you came back the next day to test. My interview went well and my test was the next day.

I gave it my best shot although I was nervous and sweating under hot lights and the glare of a bored crew. The most notable thing about the screen test was the blonde standing in the shadows watching. Her face was familiar. As I was leaving the studio after my test, I saw her walking toward me across the parking lot. The clogs she wore went clippity-cloppity, clippity-cloppity on the pavement. She had on a tight pair of green pants and a sweater, both of which seemed to have missed their last washing. Her platinum hair was disheveled and sticking out at wild angles. Thirty years later the hair would have been punk.

We approached each other warily, like a couple of gun-fighters on a deserted street. But when we were a few feet apart, she smiled.

"Hi again!" said Marilyn.

"Hi."

"I saw your test this afternoon." The voice was soft, a little thin, friendly. "You did real well."

"Thanks," I said, making a little wave of my hand. "Are you still taking lessons with Natasha?"

"Sure. I haven't seen you there in a while."

"No. Without any lights on inside that dark house, she gave me the creeps. And all she did was talk. I never got to *do* anything."

"I learned a lot from her." She smiled at me a moment and went on. "But she does talk a lot. Your name's Joan, right? You were Miss Eight Ball after me, huh?"

"Yes. I remember seeing you model at a Blue Book Model Agency session by the Ambassador Hotel pool. You were Norma Jean then, weren't you?"

"Oh, sure. Have you done some modeling too?"

"Sure. And I've done some pictures at RKO."

"Good parts?"

I weighed the idea of a lie for a moment.

"Bits! I got to say 'Look!' as John Wayne flew by in *Jet Pilot*. I came here hoping to get something."

She smiled wistfully again and nodded her head knowingly. "Sure. You probably will. If not here, then somewhere else."

When the agent called me back about the screen test, he told me not to be discouraged.

"They liked you very much, Joan," he said.

"Just not enough to give me a contract."

"But they *liked* you. The only problem is that they have another girl under contract who looks too similar to you. Her name's Marilyn Monroe."

Chapter Five

By the time I finished *Two Tickets to Broadway*, I could see that there was no future for me at RKO outside of playing bit parts.

It was a frustrating realization for me as I approached my seventeenth birthday. It seemed that the world was moving too fast around me and my progress was too slow. And my parents were part of the anchor holding me back. Suddenly I felt smothered at home. I did well in school, but longed to get out into the *real* world where I felt my future beckoned. I began looking around for a way to get out. I found it at the boxing matches.

My father took me to the Hollywood Legion boxing matches every Friday night, where we had season seats close to ringside. Sitting next to us every week there was a ruggedly handsome man named Jack Newman who looked me over appreciatively and soon struck up a conversation with my father.

I found the boxing matches exciting and adventurous. The blood lust in the spectators' eyes, the smells of sweat, rosin, and canvas in the smoky room, the sounds of cheering and booing and punches landing, and two men intent on combat was a thrilling combination.

Jack Newman made friends with my father while we watched the fights week after week. Both men were gamblers and loved to bet on the fights. Before long Jack asked me out and though he was more than ten years older, my parents allowed me to go. It gave me a taste of the good life, as Jack was rich.

Jack was a very successful manufacturer of men's sportswear. He was a bachelor with a luxurious apartment in Beverly Hills, a new Cadillac, and a desire to spend money on me. I was the perfect foil for such a man: a poor and oversexed nymphet. After much dating of boys my own age and older, I was an avid practitioner of all variations of heavy necking, petting, and making out. Miraculously, I was still a virgin.

When Jack asked me to marry him, I swiftly agreed. He was my ticket out of my parents' house and into womanhood. We eloped to Santa Barbara, where I lied about my age to the judge who married us.

During our honeymoon in San Francisco, I began my initiation into the joys of married life. Our athletic sex lived up to my expectations, but I soon discovered that afterward we had to live with each other. And some things were not what they were cracked up to be—like trying to sleep with someone snoring in bed beside me. By the time we returned to L.A., I was beginning to feel that I might have made a mistake.

Jack had told me before we were married that he had been wounded in the war. A slight head wound, he had said. But I found out during our first month of marriage that the wound was considerably more severe: a steel plate had been installed in his skull. Whether or not the steel plate affected his behavior, I can't say. But I became aware that his moods were erratic.

Jack seemed pleased when I looked nice. He encouraged me to charge plenty of lovely, expensive clothes at I. Magnin's, always with matching hats, which he thought made me look older. However, when we went out, Jack became furious when men took notice of me. Though he managed to stay controlled in public, he would fly into a jealous tantrum when we got home. Several times he even hit me. These angry scenes became more frequent and I sensed that a crisis was approaching.

Jack came home very drunk one night and began raging around the apartment threatening to kill me. He broke all the wedding gifts given to us by my relatives. Then, as I watched tearfully, he cut my beautiful clothes and hats to shreds.

When I could stand it no more, I picked up a heavy ashtray and threw it at him.

"Jack! Stop it!" I shrieked. "Please stop it!"

The ashtray bounced harmlessly off the wall next to him and he turned on me. "Why, you goddamn little bitch," he growled.

He attempted to throw me off the second-story balcony of our apartment. I managed to struggle free and my screams brought the neighbors to break up the fight.

I called my parents, who took me home to my cozy little room in the flat on Harvard Boulevard. They were understanding and began legal proceedings to extricate me from the marriage. Jack called a few times and tried to get me back. When we were in court he even offered me a new Cadillac. But I was too afraid of him.

What should have felt like a dream come true had rapidly become a bad dream. My visions of being the wife of a rich man with an elegant apartment, a maid to take care of it, my own car, and charge accounts at I. Magnin's and Saks were shattered. The reality was: I became a battered wife and nearly a homicide victim from an alcoholic blaze of temper.

When the dust had finally settled from my marriage, summer vacation was near and it was too late in the year for me to go back to school. Mother and Daddy took me with them to Las Vegas. We had been up there many times over the years, making the long drive across the desert and leaving our cares behind us with each mile. Now the therapeutic desert scenery and the glitter of the Strip helped me forget the disappointments and insecurities brought on by my failed marriage.

My father had taught me to shoot craps when I was so small that I had to stand on a stool to throw the dice. Now, as a young woman, I attracted a lot of attention at the crap tables. Men wanted me to bet with their money; they wanted me to come to their rooms when their luck turned with the dice. Although I didn't go to their rooms, I found the first two facts of Las Vegas life very exciting and profitable.

The owner of the El Rancho Hotel and Casino noticed me one afternoon at the crap tables. As my father and I walked away, he stopped us and offered me a job as a showgirl. A showgirl in Las Vegas in early 1950 dressed up in costume for two shows a night, and before and after the shows circulated around the casino, shilled at the tables a little, and looked pretty. There were nice rooms for the showgirls to live in at the back of the hotel, and the pay was excellent.

Since it was summer vacation, my parents agreed to let me work there.

Vegas was a middle-class fantasy land in high gear twenty-four hours a day. The Strip consisted of only a few hotels then and they did their level best to separate the out-of-towners from their money. For a time Vegas' bright lights dimmed my movie-star ambitions, but all the longing, all the memories of those magic stories on the screen still burned just below the surface.

During the day, while the customers jostled for positions at the tables, there was little for those of us who worked there to do. Most days I was poolside working on deepening my tan.

While I was cooling off one day swimming laps in the El Rancho's pool, I bumped into someone swimming in the other direction.

"Sorry!" I said, sputtering while I hung on to the side of the pool.

"My fault," a tall, long-necked girl with icy blue eyes answered. She removed her swimming cap and shook out a shock of long blonde hair. "Should have been watching where I was going."

She introduced herself as Danielle Cory and we discovered to our mutual delight that we had both worked at RKO studios.

"Did you have to let old what's-her-name, the director, shoot photographs of you in nightgowns over in his trailer?" I asked.

"Oh, sure," Danni said. "He does that with all the girls on the lot. Occasionally he even finds one that will give him a blow-job."

"He hinted around about it, but it just didn't seem worth the trouble. He didn't insist."

"He never does," Danni said knowledgeably. "He only insists on the pictures."

When I told Danni that my one burning ambition was to get a studio contract, she explained that she wanted to be a model and was trying to save enough to get to Paris, where the field was wide open.

Danni and I hung around together for the time she was in Vegas. She introduced me to pot and we made the rounds of the casinos and lounges, laughing and giggling. And we naturally attracted the attention of lots of men.

To my surprise, I found that Danni was a lesbian. She made a pass at me one night outside the door to my bungalow. I was caught off guard when she leaned toward me, her lips brushing against mine. She tried to hold me, but I pushed her gently away.

"Danni, I can't, really."

"You might like it if you tried it, Joan," she husked.

"It's not me. You'll have to accept that if we're going to be friends."

She appraised me a long moment. "Okay. I do want to be your friend."

Danni soon went back to L.A., but visited several times during the summer, and our friendship ripened. Our lives would cross and recross over the years.

In Vegas I quickly became the darling of the mobsters. I often dated Nick the Greek Dondolis, who never bet against the house; I was frequently seen in the company of Russian Louie.

One day while I was lounging by the pool at the Flamingo Hotel, I noticed a man watching me. Instead of the usual once-over, this short, compact little man in a bathing suit kept peeking around a corner. After a few minutes he went into a bookie room the hotel maintained near the pool so their patrons could bet on horse races around the country. Before long he came out again smoking a cigar.

When he at last came over to where I was sitting, I noticed he walked with a limp. He had a mane of white hair and a well-conditioned body for a man in his fifties. He introduced himself as Charles Fisher from Detroit, and we talked for a few minutes.

"How would you like to go to the fights tonight?" he asked finally.

"I'd like that," I said. "I'll meet you there."

"No, no. Come up to my penthouse here at the Flamingo."

Later that night we went to the fights and ended the evening in the wee hours at the hotel's coffee shop. Charles ordered prunes.

"Eat prunes every night and you'll never have any problems," he said.

"So you're Fisher as in Fisher Body in Detroit?"

"Ummm," he grunted noncommittally. "Yeah, I've done a lot of body work in Detroit."

I really liked him. Unlike ninety-nine percent of the men I met, he didn't seem to expect the quid pro quo most did for an evening out. In fact, he took me back to my bungalow at the El Rancho and gave me a chaste kiss on the forehead.

The next day I ran into the public-relations man for the Flamingo and asked him to tell me about the penthouse tenant that built cars in Detroit.

He laughed loud enough to make heads turn by the pool. "Cars? He doesn't build cars." He lowered his voice. "Joan, that's Charlie Fischetti, as in the Fischetti brothers. They're Al Capone's cousins."

My jaw dropped. "Al Capone?"

"Don't worry," the P.R. man went on, "he's well-protected here."

"Protected? You mean my life could be in danger?"

He shrugged. "Only if they throw the bomb close to you."

I still continued to see Charlie, though. He was a good companion who took the time when we went out to make sure things were the way I liked them. We made a striking couple around town. Charlie wore the most gorgeous suits I'd ever seen on a man. And he was generous to me without being the least bit demanding.

After a week, during which we were together every spare minute, Charlie announced he had to return to Chicago. And his wife.

It was not exactly a surprise to me. Once I found out who he was, it was easy to come up with plenty of information about Charlie Fischetti. In addition to a wife in Chicago, he also had a heavy date in Washington, D.C., with the Kefauver Congressional Committee investigating organized crime.

"Listen, Joan," he said to me the evening before he left. "You told me you want to be an actress, right?"

"Yes, Charlie. More than anything."

"And what does it take for you to do that?"

"Schooling. Dramatic lessons. Dance lessons. Voice training. I've had some acting lessons, but I need more." I hung my head. "I'm tired of being just the pretty background for someone else. I want to headline here in Vegas someday. And I want my name on movie marquees. But the lessons take money. That's why I'm up here—saving money."

Charlie rubbed his hands over his deeply tanned face and grinned. "Kid, you're the only person in the world who ever came to Vegas to *save* money."

After Charlie went back to Chicago, he kept in touch by phone and sent envelopes filled with crisp hundred-dollar bills wrapped in a plain piece of white paper, unsigned.

When I finished my long summer in Vegas and came back to Los Angeles, I used some of the money I'd saved to buy a shiny MG TC roadster that had belonged to Humphrey Bogart. Danni and I would cruise the Sunset Strip, smoke a joint, and go listen to Billie Holiday or Charlie "Bird" Parker at Tiffany's on Eighth Street, or Shorty Rogers at the Lighthouse in Hermosa Beach. Occasionally we'd drive up to Palm Springs and spend the weekend.

I refused to go back to high school. After my marriage, I felt too mature and experienced to return to school.

I heard from Charlie Fischetti regularly. We'd talk on the phone occasionally and the plain envelopes full of cash continued arriving.

Then in late September Charlie called and asked if I could come see him in Chicago. My mother agreed for me to go as long as I stayed with my Aunt Norma in Evanston. Charlie sent the money for the plane ticket and in a high state of excitement I left.

The afternoon I arrived, Charlie picked me up at my aunt's apartment wearing a handsome cocoa-brown suit and driving a new Cadillac convertible. We went for a drive in the bracing autumn air and I snuggled close to Charlie, happy to see him.

We drove around the lakeshore and he pointed out the sights. We had a quiet dinner, and since his wife was out of town, went back to his town house overlooking the lake. It was an ostentatiously furnished place with gold flocking on the wallpaper and mammoth rococo Italian Renaissance furnishings. It was just the kind of place a Mafia chieftain or a seventeen-year-old girl would find classy.

Charlie Fischetti was a very sexy man. He had piercing dark eyes, a symmetrical face with a clean jaw, and strong white teeth. He cultivated his tan by spending most of the year in Las Vegas or on his boat the *Blonde Witch* in the Caribbean. Even his limp somehow added to his charm.

During our time in Las Vegas, he had been physically undemanding. Now, with only the slightest urging I responded to him with all my soul. Charlie had the gift of being a great lover. Any other man would've seemed far too old to me, but Charlie's lean, well-muscled body excited me. We melted into each other's arms and made love in his big antique bed by the moonlight reflected off the waters of Lake Michigan. He played my young body like a musical instrument, leading me carefully through the act of love until we breathlessly climaxed in a harmony of passion. In the languorous times afterward, Charlie told me what was on his mind.

"I want you to come live here, kid. I'll set you up in a nice apartment not far away. We'll have great times, Joan. We'll see a lot of each other."

"You mean when your wife's in Europe buying clothes?"

"She doesn't have to go anywhere for us to see each other."

"But she's always there."

He sighed heavily.

"She's a fact of life. Like winter."

I raised myself on one elbow and looked at him.

"Charlie, I want to be an actress."

"So, you can't act in Chicago?"

"Not very much, honey. Chicago's the wrong place. I need to be in Los Angeles. Or New York. Those are the places actresses make it and that's where I need to be."

He was quiet for a long time.

"I understand."

"Do you? Really?"

"Look, Joan. We'll have a good time while you're here. We'll go to the best places. Do everything you've ever wanted to do. When you leave, I'll make sure you have plenty to keep you going every month, more than I've been sending you. You'll go to the best goddamn acting teacher you can find, okay?''

I hugged him and our bodies pressed closer together. I felt his arousal again.

"Okay," I whispered.

"You'll be the best damned little actress in Hollywood. We'll get you everything you need."

I fell more than a little in love with Charlie Fischetti that week in Chicago. The day I left, the sky was turning that steely gray I hadn't seen since leaving South Dakota. Snow was coming.

Sitting in his car outside the airport, he gave me a pair of ruby-and-diamond earrings as a remembrance of our visit. They were beautiful. But I didn't need them to remind me of Charlie.

Back in Los Angeles one morning, Danni called me to ask if I'd seen the latest issue of *Variety*.

"I found something you might be interested in. Albert Vargas is auditioning girls for his new series of drawings in *Esquire* magazine."

Though I was aware that I had a good figure, it had never occurred to me that I was pinup material. As it turned out, I was—I was part of a small group chosen by Vargas for one of his calendars.

Danni called again with a lead from *Variety* that looked potentially more rewarding.

"There's a revival of the twenties musical *Billion Dollar Baby* in New York, starring Carol Bruce and some comic named Jackie Gleason," she said. "They're after blondes. You'll be perfect. The agent's name is Harry Gold. He's interviewing at the Beverly Hills Hotel."

I knocked on the door at Harry Gold's suite the next day and he told me to come in. He looked me over with that peculiar meat-market quality that agents have.

"Okay," he said.

"Okay?" I asked. "Is that all?" I had been to some brief interviews but this one was the prizewinner.

"Yep. When can you leave?"

"Leave?"

"Leave for New York. That's where they're doing this musical."

"You mean I got the part? Just like that?"

"Just like that. What's your name again?"

The next day I was packed and at the airport to fly back with Harry Gold and the other Golden Girl, Marie Allison. I brought my mother along but by now I was old enough that she didn't have to sign a release. I felt like I was on my way: I had just turned eighteen and I was on my way to New York to do a Broadway show.

Billion Dollar Baby had lots of pretty girls, songs, and jokes. It was a rags-to-riches story set in Atlantic City. It was due to open at the Monte Proser Café Theater at Forty-ninth and Broadway, near Jack Dempsey's restaurant and saloon. Dempsey was a frequent member of the audience.

During the rehearsals of *Billion Dollar Baby,* I stayed at the estate of a wealthy friend of my mother's in Douglaston, Long Island. After the show opened, however, the long commute forced me to move into Manhattan. I registered at the Barbizon Hotel for Women.

As lead showgirl in *Baby,* I wore a scanty (for its day) butterfly costume with a pair of green wings. The show's lead dancers were a husband-and-wife team—Bob Fosse and his wife at the time.

Not long after the show opened Jack Dempsey put on a big party in his restaurant for the members of the cast. The next day one of the other girls in the show stopped me.

"Joan, how come you missed the party at Jack Dempsey's last night?"

"I had a date with Eddie Fisher," I answered.

Eddie Fisher at the time was a protégé of Eddie Cantor's. He was singing at the Café Theater.

Eddie had had a hit song called "Thinking of You," and was already very popular. He had been hired by the Monte Proser Theater to save *Billion Dollar Baby* from disaster. The show was not doing well and the management thought it might help to have a rising young star like Fisher sing before each show. I'm afraid, however, that whatever good Eddie accomplished in drawing people to the show only prolonged the inevitable closing of the play.

Eddie was short and small-boned with an easy smile. He was (and is to this day) a nice guy. There was a gentle, sexy quality about him which attracted me. When *Billion Dollar Baby* was over and I returned to L.A., he stopped on the West Coast, clad in USO uniform, on his way to entertain the troops in Korea, and we dated again.

The girl before me gave a jealous sneer. "Well, Dempsey was fit to be tied because you didn't show up. I think he gave the party just so he could meet you."

One night Jack Dempsey met me outside the stage door. His craggy features showed his Cherokee Indian blood; his black eyes were as intense as a hawk's. He towered over me, his big hands flexing and fidgeting with a life of their own.

"Joan," he said gruffly, "I'm Jack Dempsey. I'd like to have dinner with you." His words were slurred in the punch-drunk fashion of so many longtime fighters, and he leaned forward on the balls of his feet as if he was about to take a step forward.

While we ate he told me of the poverty he endured growing up. My own childhood sounded like a fairy tale in comparison. For Dempsey in his day, as for many boxers today, the professional ring was a way out of the depths of poverty.

I began seeing Jack regularly. He took me to places I had only dreamed about: the Stork Club, 21, El Morocco, and the Copacabana. We danced, drank champagne, and ate fancy dinners every night after the show.

On our first date at the legendary Stork Club (which has since been torn down to make way for a public park), we were met at the door by the club's owner, Sherman Billingsly, who seated us at table number one. When the press arrived, alerted by Billingsly, I was busy inhaling hors d'oeuvres, and my lipstick was smeared when the photographers began snapping pictures. We were seated at a table with Ethel Merman and William (Hopalong Cassidy) Boyd. Merman got up and sang "Anything You Can Do, I Can Do Better" and Ginger Rogers was persuaded to dance. When I went to the ladies' room during the course of the evening, I found actress Marie (The Body) McDonald fixing her makeup next to me in the big mirror. It was a memorable evening.

Wherever Dempsey took me, he was recognized and given the celebrity treatment. The Copacabana, 21, the Stork Club, all the places around town where the beautiful people gathered, Jack Dempsey was known and treated with respect.

Jack took delight in getting me tipsy with sweet liqueurs, then taking me to bed. He was older than my father (as my mother would soon remind me) and it gave me a strange feeling to be in bed with him. He was a big man, still retaining some of the muscular bulk of his prizefighting days, despite the assaults of rich food and strong drink to which he was accustomed.

Our first time in bed was frightening. He was just the opposite of Charlie Fischetti. Where Charlie had been skilled and concerned for me during our lovemaking, Dempsey was clumsy and preoccupied with his own pleasure. This would prove to be the norm throughout our relationship. Only occasionally, when I engineered the feat, would Dempsey rise above himself as a lover. Unfortunately, to put it generously, *that* was never spectacular.

I had thought the nightlife in Los Angeles was fast, but the pace of New York was staggering. It was all I could do to fall into bed back at the Barbizon as the sun was coming up and get a few hours of sleep before it was time to go to the theater.

Jack loved to station himself at a front table of his restaurant, at the window looking out onto Broadway. We often had our dinners sitting like two fish in a fishbowl. People would walk by and point and wave. Tourists came in asking for his autograph, and with an air of noblesse oblige, he signed them.

Before long, Jack and I became an item around town. Our romance was taken note of in the "Cholly Knickerbocker" column, then written by Igor Cassini, brother of fashion designer Oleg. I even received a call from an up-and-coming young columnist for the New York *Post*, Earl Wilson, trying to find out the scoop on the Champ's new romance.

Dempsey had told me that if people inquired about our relationship to say we were engaged. That's what I told Earl Wilson. The next day the engagement of the former Champion of the World to Joan Olander, complete with pictures, ran in the *Post*, then in the "Cholly Knickerbocker" column syndicated in the Los Angeles *Herald Examiner*. My mother called the next day.

"Jo, how can they print that about you and Jack Dempsey?"

"Because that's what I told them, Mother."

"Oh, Jo," she sighed. "I think you're making a mistake—again. Jack Dempsey is older than your father. I hope you'll reconsider this."

I swore up and down that I would not and that Jack and I would soon marry. But there were, when I admitted it to myself, some serious misgivings in my heart about the whole thing.

Dempsey could be less than gracious, especially to his many acquaintances who were down on their luck. Like many men who have become successful after poor beginnings, Jack Dempsey became known as a soft touch. But he was unable to just give a man money when asked if he could spare a few bucks. He would empty his pockets and scatter the money around the sidewalk. It seemed to give him a perverse joy to see grown men scrambling around on their hands and knees picking up his loose change.

At the same time, my financial situation was becoming more and more precarious. There were several times that I thought I wouldn't be able to make the rent on my tiny room at the Barbizon. Taking acting lessons in New York as I had once hoped to do was out of the question. Between my $150 weekly salary from *Billion Dollar Baby* and the money Charlie Fischetti sent less and less frequently, I was barely squeaking by.

Dempsey allowed me to sign for meals in his restaurant, but stubbornly refused to give me any financial help. Whenever I asked him for money his stock answer was: "Keep your butt off the canvas, kid. Keep your butt off the canvas."

Since the Champ was willing to have *my* butt on his canvas, or have me hanging on his arm around town, I thought I deserved better. Especially since he was willing to have nationally syndicated columns print that we were engaged.

It began to look like I might have to force his hand. If he wouldn't marry me, I wanted to go back to L.A. when *Billion Dollar Baby* closed its run. Tightfisted as Dempsey was, I knew he would never give me the money to get home. And

I was too embarrassed to admit defeat and ask my parents for it.

When *Billion Dollar Baby* closed, I managed somehow to hang on, living from hand to mouth. I now had more time and energy, if less money, to devote to New York City's nightlife. Many times Dempsey would drop me at the Barbizon after dinner, where I could change and go out alone.

My first musical love was jazz. I'd perch in the bleacher seats with the rest of the aficionados at Birdland to hear Miles Davis, Dizzy Gillespie, or J. J. Johnson. It was a wild and exciting time in New York. I longed to stay. But I sensed that my future did not lie there.

Just as I was wondering what to do about staying in New York, I received a telegram from Charlie Fischetti. He asked me to join him in Bimini, where he was cruising on his yacht. It was the perfect solution to my unemployment problem and the situation with Jack Dempsey.

I gathered up my clothes from the closet in the tiny room and threw them in my suitcase. While I packed, I turned the radio on. I half-listened while an announcer read the news. Suddenly my attention was riveted by a news bulletin.

"Mobster Charlie Fischetti, one of the Fischetti brothers of Chicago, died today of a heart attack . . ." the announcer began.

I didn't hear the rest. I stared dumbly at the little brown radio while the voice droned on. How could it be true? Charlie dead? It wasn't possible! He just sent me a telegram. He couldn't be dead!

By the time I had cried myself out, the sun was well up over the Manhattan skyline. I saw myself as just another one of those people scrambling around after Jack Dempsey's tossed-aside pocket money. Or Charlie Fischetti's. It was time I started making my own career. Time I started depending on myself for money instead of a man. But first I had to get back to L.A.

I phoned Jack Dempsey at his apartment in the Mayflower Hotel.

"Jack, I need to see you tonight."

"What's wrong, Joan?"

"I can't tell you on the phone. Can you meet at your restaurant for dinner? Eight o'clock?"

"Sure, kid, sure. Eight it is."

When I arrived under the giant neon sign that said "Jack Dempsey's," the sidewalk was still ankle-deep with confetti from General Douglas MacArthur's 1951 ticker-tape parade. He had addressed Congress the day before and today made a triumphant entrance into New York. The streets were still crowded with people.

Jack was having a drink when I sat down at the usual table by the window. We ordered dinner and I got right to the point.

"Jack," I said quietly, "I'm pregnant."

He strangled on his Scotch. "What?"

"You heard me."

He wiped his face with a napkin and looked around the room. When he looked back at me, he raised his bushy eyebrows.

"Are you sure?"

"You can't fool a woman about these things, Jack. I missed my period three weeks ago. I went to the doctor last week and got the test results this morning. Positive."

Dempsey took a long pull at his Scotch and rubbed a big hand across his face. There was the faintest hint of a smile on his lips.

"Well, I'll be goddamned."

"Jack, are you going to marry me?"

"Marry you?"

"Yes. Is that such a difficult question?"

"Well, no, Joan. It's just that this needs to be thought about a little bit. Are you . . . ? Are you sure that it's . . . it's . . . ?"

"It's yours, all right, Jack. There hasn't been anyone else."

"Yes, yes, of course. I didn't mean . . ."

"I *know* what you meant, Jack."

"I just don't see how we can . . . can get married, Joan."

"Tell me why."

He proceeded to give me every reason in the book except the phase of the moon or the postwar economy. Finally he concluded with: "I think it would be best if we found a doctor who can, uh, fix the situation."

"I already have."

"You have?"

"I had a feeling that you'd react this way, so I spoke to a girlfriend of mine. She knows a doctor out on Long Island who'll take care of it. For a price, of course."

"Of course, yes. Well, naturally, I'll take care of that. How much?"

I screwed my courage to the sticking place and took a deep breath. Remember, I told myself, this is to get you back to L.A., and this man has taken up a lot of your time.

"One thousand dollars."

"*Jesus!*" Dempsey bellowed. He quickly lowered his voice. "I've heard of people getting it done right here in town for a couple hundred."

"Do you expect me to hand myself over to some butcher— some veterinarian—to have this done?" I demanded.

"No, no, of course not. I just meant there might be some, er, uh, more economical way . . ."

"I've checked and my girlfriend says there's no one else as good. She had to have one done herself not long ago."

"Okay." He swallowed hard. "A thousand it is, a thousand you'll get. When are you going to have it done? I want . . . I want to go with you."

"No," I said quickly. "There's no need for that. I'll stay with my girlfriend out on Long Island. She can take care of me there and help me afterward. Don't worry."

"Well, I *do* worry. After all, it . . . it's our . . . uh . . . you know."

"I want to go tomorrow. The sooner the better."

"That's pretty soon, isn't it?"

"The sooner the better. Don't you have the money?"

"Just sit tight."

He got up from the table and disappeared through a door in the rear of the restaurant. In a few minutes he came out and motioned me over to the telephone near the ladies' room. He counted out ten one-hundred-dollar bills into my hand. I put them in my purse and we walked back to the table to finish our dinner. Dempsey smiled and whistled a jaunty tune.

When I got back to the Barbizon that night, I changed and went to Birdland. Miles Davis was cooking onstage. At ringside I saw the suntanned and silver-bearded face of Papa Hemingway, sitting with Marlene Dietrich. They smiled at one another, toes and hands tapping in time to the beat.

I stayed out late. I remembered to tell the switchboard operator to tell Mr. Dempsey I was out all the next day.

It was three days before I took any calls from Jack. When I finally returned his call, I kept my voice weak.

"Oh, Jack," I moaned.

"Joan! Did you do it? Are you all right?"

"I'm okay. Don't worry."

"Is there anything you need? Anything I can send over?"

"No," I whispered. "I just need a few more days' rest."

After a decent interval of time, I told Jack I was returning to Los Angeles. He ranted and raved that he wanted me to stay, but I knew there was no future in continuing to see him. For Jack Dempsey, I was what I suppose I had been for all the "older" men I had gone out with: a decoration—a boost to the male ego.

In Dempsey's case, I provided a little youthful spice to his life. He was able to feel that he could still not only get it up but also sire a child by a voluptuous eighteen-year-old. He never knew there was no baby or that his money compensated me for all his tightfistedness during the time I went out with him.

As I sat in the airplane seat droning westward toward home, I remembered his satisfied grin in the restaurant the night I told him. He looked out onto Broadway where MacArthur had ridden by just a few hours before and said dreamily: "Old soldiers never die . . . they just fade away."

Chapter Six

GOSSIP columnists work in cruel and devious ways. Absolutely corrupted by their almost infinite power, they could be the most jealous and vengeful false gods in the Hollywood firmament.

Louella Parsons was still powerful in 1952, the Queen Bitch of all Hollywood gossip columnists. She enjoyed a long, merciless reign of terror over Tinsel Town throughout the 1930's, 1940's, and 1950's, backed from on high by the patronage of William Randolph Hearst himself. Her throne was secure in his vast newspaper empire. She was, unlike Lucrezia Borgia, able to syndicate her poison and sell it nationwide for nearly three decades.

Louella, make no mistake, was a bitch. And she tried to ruin my career. In fact, to be more accurate, she tried her damnedest to prevent me from ever having a career.

Louella declared war on me after I met Jimmy McHugh. Jimmy was in his late sixties or early seventies when I introduced myself to him at the urging of a mutual friend in New York, songwriter Sammy Fain. Jimmy, overweight, bald on top, with hair on the sides of his head, had a charming Irish twinkle in his eyes. He lived in a lovely house with a swimming pool on Alpine Drive in Beverly Hills, and boasted a fine collection of paintings.

He could well afford his handsome life-style. Jimmy, with

lyricist Dorothy Fields, had written such hit songs of the thirties and forties as "I Can't Give You Anything but Love, Baby," "Don't Blame Me," and "I'm in the Mood for Love."

Jimmy took an interest in my career and signed me to a management contract. He had other starlets and female singers under contract as well. I was nineteen years old, and I thought I had really made a breakthrough by signing with a professional manager. Especially since Jimmy seemed to enjoy playing my "Henry Higgins."

"I think you should study acting," he advised me one day at his home. "You're a fine singer, but you need to develop your acting ability," he said. "I'm going to put you through drama school myself," Jimmy announced.

I was genuinely surprised. It was a generous offer and a real vote of confidence. I thanked Jimmy and told him I would pay him back when I started working.

Jimmy arranged for me to attend Ben Bard's Theater. Ben Bard was an older actor who had started an acting school and theater located between the mid-Wilshire district and downtown Los Angeles. Aaron Spelling was directing the plays staged at Ben Bard's, and Carolyn Jones, his girlfriend—they were living together at the time—was involved in the workshop and classes and helping Aaron.

When I walked through the door, Aaron seemed impressed. Right away he put me in a lead in *Once in a Lifetime.* Then he put me in *At War with the Army,* and right after that I played Dixie in the theater's production of Clifford Odets' *The Big Knife.*

The plays were well-attended by talent scouts, casting agents, producers, and directors. I went to several parties with Jimmy McHugh, where I sang his songs and met some of the movers and shakers in the film industry, including Darryl F. Zanuck and Buddy Adler from Twentieth Century-Fox, and Louis B. Mayer. Before long, Jimmy phoned me with exciting news.

"Paramount wants to give you a screen test," he said.

I don't remember what I answered—I was on cloud nine; already I could see my name in lights. Paramount. A major studio. A screen test. I wanted to pinch myself.

Then all hell broke loose.

After Louella Parsons' husband, "Dockie" Martin, died—a casualty of too many years of hitting the sauce—Jimmy McHugh became her lover. How much Jimmy actually loved Louella, I never knew. How much he enjoyed the fringe benefits that went with being Louella's lover was eminently clear to everyone in Hollywood. Louella was on everybody's A-list, so Jimmy escorted her to all the important premieres, the best parties, the biggest charity balls. Through Louella, he got to spend half of his life in a tuxedo sipping Dom Perignon and nibbling beluga caviar. And he shared the frame when flashbulbs popped, as the paparazzi that always stalk Hollywood celebrities recorded Louella's image for newspapers across the country and a multitude of fan magazines. Jimmy McHugh loved it. After the anonymity that he had known as a composer, he was thrilled to bask in the limelight, even if that light only reflected from Louella. Jimmy was even given small roles and bits in pictures by producers who hoped to get their films plugged in Louella's column.

Now, Louella was furious with Jimmy. She had been with him at several of the parties he had invited me to attend to sing his songs. She had barely acknowledged my presence, sitting across the room alternately pretending I wasn't there and glaring daggers at me. Somehow she had found out that Jimmy was sending me to Ben Bard's at his expense. She accused him of paying far too much attention to me and threatened to stop seeing him if he didn't dump me. Jimmy feared losing all those invitations to star-studded premieres, parties, banquets, balls, and other social gatherings.

To prove she meant business, Louella swung her hatchet. Jimmy summoned me to his home, explaining that he had something important to discuss with me that he did not want to go into on the phone. When I arrived, I discovered Jimmy lounging beside his swimming pool, working on his tan.

"What's so important that you couldn't tell me on the phone?" I asked.

The Irish twinkle was missing from his eyes. From the pained expression on his face I could see someone was twisting his balls.

"I'm taking you out of Ben Bard's school," he continued.

"Why?" I was completely stunned. "I'm doing really well there."

"There's a problem."

"A problem?"

"You can't go back there. It would spell trouble. Ben doesn't want trouble."

"Trouble?" I said uncomprehendingly. "What are you talking about, Jimmy? How can I cause Ben Bard . . . ?" Suddenly it hit me. "Louella! Louella's behind this, isn't she?"

"Leave her out of this."

Jimmy never wanted to say anything negative about Louella, especially when he knew it was true.

"Why should I? She's trying to ruin my career." Jimmy knew Louella had talked to Ben Bard, and I later confirmed that she had, with an unimpeachable source at Ben's theater. Ben had to obey or Louella would dissuade aspiring and working actors from taking classes at his school or appearing in plays at his theater. She had the power to put him out of business.

"Listen," Jimmy said, "we've got to be careful. Louella's jealous and we don't want to stir her up any more than she already is. She thinks we're sleeping together."

I barely stifled a laugh. "Sleeping with you?" Jimmy was friend and manager but hardly a lover. "There is nothing going on between us. Doesn't she allow you to have friends?"

He spoke impatiently. "Look at it from Louella's point of view. You're a beautiful young girl and you're . . . you're . . . very well, uh, endowed. I've told Louella there's nothing happening between us. I've told her it's strictly business, but it didn't register. She's mad as hell." A note of fearful concern crept into his voice. "I don't want to get on the wrong side of her. I could find myself *persona non grata* from the Polo Lounge to Chasen's. Hell, with Louella against me, I probably couldn't get a spot to park at Dolores's Drive-in."

"You make it sound as though my career isn't as important as a hamburger."

He gave me a defeated look. "You can't fight city hall."

The truth of that was a bitter pill, but I had to swallow it. "It isn't fair."

Jimmy shrugged. "Whoever said it was?" He thought for a moment. "In a few days, when Louella cools off, suppose

I speak to Harry Hayden and arrange for you to join his theater?''

Harry Hayden and Leila Bliss ran the Bliss-Hayden Theater in Beverly Hills. Marilyn Monroe, Debbie Reynolds, Veronica Lake, and many other actresses had been showcased early in their careers in Bliss-Hayden's excellent productions.

''Would you, Jimmy?'' I smiled for the first time that day.

Jimmy nodded. ''I'll talk to Harry in a couple of days. In the meantime, you continue preparing for that test at Paramount.''

I said good-bye and left Jimmy soaking up the afternoon sun.

In the days that followed, I concentrated on preparing for my screen test. Carolyn Jones had helped me with a couple of roles at Ben Bard's and she continued to help me, rehearsing with me, critiquing my line readings, and being generally supportive.

While I was at Ben Bard's, Aaron Spelling had coached me privately for a fee, which was against the school's rules. Nevertheless, I felt I needed the coaching and Aaron certainly needed the money I paid him under the table. He and Carolyn were living in a tiny studio apartment in Hollywood, struggling to make *one* end meet. Though he would go on to produce television hits like *Dynasty, Charlie's Angels,* and *Fantasy Island,* in 1952 the gaunt young Aaron was fighting for a foothold like the rest of us.

Carolyn, Aaron, and I became friends. And I felt Aaron coached me to the best of his ability and mine.

For my screen test I decided to do the scene in *The Big Knife* in which the lead female role, Dixie, has been drinking heavily. It's a poignant scene that comes just before the play's climax, when she is hit by a car and killed. It was an emotional scene and I knew I could let out all the stops to give Paramount a good example of my ability.

A couple of days before my screen test, I went to the studio to be fitted. Edith Head, the famous Academy Award-winning costume designer, looked me over. She was an imposing figure in her tailored suit. She was also warm and friendly.

Gazing at my bust, she said, ''You've got a lot. Like Liz.'' She thought for a moment. ''I know the perfect gown for you.''

She arranged for me to wear the same strapless gown that Elizabeth Taylor had worn in *A Place in the Sun*.

On the day of the screen test I went to the studio early. I felt excited, confident, and full of energy. I was determined to do well. I had worked hard and I was ready.

I went first to makeup and then to wardrobe, where Edith Head had the gown ready for me. There were four or five other girls being tested that day. When my turn came to go before the camera, I felt fully into the character of the beautiful, tipsy blonde. I played the scene with as much intensity as I had ever played a role, feeling the character's pain and anguish so acutely that it became my own. I knew when I finished the scene that I had not missed a beat. I had brought the character and the situation to life. I had turned myself into Dixie.

The director thanked me and I left the set. I changed back into my clothes, returned the dress and fur I had worn to wardrobe, and drove away from the studio. As I raced along the Hollywood Freeway I felt better than I had at any time since I had had to withdraw from Ben Bard's Theater.

The suspense over the next couple of days was excruciating. Each time the phone rang my pulse quickened. Finally Jimmy McHugh called.

"I just heard from Paramount," he said.

I held my breath and braced myself.

"They loved the way you tested," he went on. "They're going to offer you a contract."

I felt a wave of excitement surge through my body. I was so happy I wanted to laugh and cry at the same time. My childhood dream was coming true. I felt so emotionally charged that it took me hours to calm down.

Eagerly I shared the news with my mother and father. Though pleased, my father received the news with typical Swedish reserve. Mother clapped her hands and hugged me in excitement.

"I always knew you could do it, Jo," she said, beaming.

It wasn't long, though, before the bubble burst.

Negotiations with Paramount seemed to be taking an inordinate amount of time. I phoned Jimmy McHugh and questioned him about the delay.

"We've hit a snag," he admitted.

"Why? What kind of a snag?" I pressed him.

"Everyone loves your test. But a couple of executives think your look is too close to Marilyn's."

It was a familiar story. I was constantly told by producers, directors, or actors, and even people on the street, that I looked like Marilyn Monroe.

"The verdict's not in," Jimmy said. "Maybe they'll still decide to sign you."

"And if they don't . . . ?"

"We'll *burn* that bridge when we get to it. I spoke to Harry Hayden. You're starting there on Friday." Jimmy hung up.

I was desolate. I had already been turned down for the same reason by Twentieth Century-Fox, MGM, and Columbia. It seemed that I was destined to be haunted by the image of Marilyn Monroe.

A day or two later Paramount made its decision. They weren't going to sign Joan Olander. It might be too hard to market her in competition with Twentieth Century-Fox's blonde bombshell, Marilyn.

The bottom had fallen out of my whole world. My spirits, which had been soaring with hope, skidded all the way to the bottom. I moped around the house, solemn and withdrawn.

You can't give up, a voice within me argued, you can't quit.

I pulled myself together, rose out of the depths of my despair, and vowed never to give up.

By Friday, when I was due to start working at the Bliss-Hayden Theater, I convinced myself that no matter how unlikely it seemed, somehow, someday, I was going to be a star. When I reported to the Bliss-Hayden Theater, Harry Hayden and Leila Bliss immediately offered me the ingenue role in William Inge's play *Come Back, Little Sheba*—the role of Marie that Terry Moore played in the film version. The play was opening in three days.

While I was rehearsing the play, I discovered that Paramount had *not* turned me down because Marilyn and I were similar types. They had been pressured into not signing me by Louella Parsons! She made it clear to the studio that if they signed me to a contract she would never again give Paramount, its pictures, or its stars a line of publicity in her widely syndicated column. Losing their access to Louella's millions of readers just to sign a starlet named Joan Olander was too high a price for Paramount to pay. The Queen Bitch had once again proved that Hollywood was her realm; keeping me in exile was simply a matter of making a phone call.

I was furious. I wanted to squeeze Louella by the throat. Instead I stole half an hour from rehearsal to confront Jimmy McHugh.

"Sure, I knew," he admitted, sitting at the piano in his elegant living room. "But what was the use of burdening you with all that? I figured it'd just put you further down in the dumps." He looked at me as though he expected me to thank him. We both knew he didn't give a damn about my feelings. He simply didn't want to deal with the fact that he was my manager and his girlfriend was sabotaging my career.

I knew that complaining to Jimmy was a waste of time and energy. I was stuck in a bad situation and had to figure a way out of it.

As angry as I was, I managed to get my emotions under control and concentrate on the play. I simply was not going to let anything that Louella Parsons had done to me interfere with my performance. Whether it led to anything or not, I was going to give the part my best shot.

Opening night, we had a good audience that really seemed to enjoy the play. Marie, the character I portrayed, was something of an exhibitionist who flaunted her shapely body in tight shorts and blouses. At the curtain call, when I stepped forward, along with the applause there were approving whistles.

Phil Benjamin, a casting director at Universal International, was among those in the audience and he phoned Jimmy McHugh the next day. Universal was shooting a picture called *Forbidden* starring Tony Curtis and Joanne Dru. Phil Benjamin thought I might be right for the role of a nightclub singer.

I drove to the studio and met Phil Benjamin and the producer, Ted Richmond—a veteran producer whose recent successes included *Bengal Rifles* with Tyrone Power.

"You'll have to meet the director," Ted Richmond said, after we talked briefly about my acting background. He introduced me to the director, Rudy Maté.

"Can you sing?" Maté promptly asked.

I responded by singing "I Can't Give You Anything but Love, Baby."

He smiled approvingly.

"You're going to have to start right away because we've got to shoot this scene," Maté said.

"Oh, my God!" I said. I hadn't expected to be working right away and suddenly I felt nervous.

Phil Benjamin said, "They'll give you the song and the movements. Go home and work on them. You'll get fitted for the costume tomorrow."

The song I was to sing was called "You Belong to Me." I went home and worked on it and the movements and gestures Rudy Maté wanted.

I was so nervous I bit my fingernails down to the quick that evening. They took one look at my nails the next morning and sent for a manicurist. After all, when you're a nightclub singer, you should have pretty nails. After the hairstylist did my hair, the makeup artist worked on my face. The most difficult part was the eyelashes. I had never worn false eyelashes before, and I had a difficult time trying not to blink while the makeup man glued them in place.

The nightclub scene had been beautifully designed. The gown I wore had been rented from MGM especially for the scene, a white satin evening gown that had been created for Jean Harlow. I was to be photographed in the white evening gown against a white background. It was something that hadn't been done before—photographing white on white—and James Wong Howe, one of the finest cinematographers in the industry, was called upon to do it. Since this scene would also serve as my screen test, I was extremely fortunate to have him behind the camera.

I was led to the elegant nightclub set, and when Tony Curtis, Joanne Dru, and the other actors were in place, Rudy Maté cried, "Action!"

The song went well. The only tense moment was when I had to pick up a cigarette with those ridiculously long nails, but I managed it without a hitch.

As I was singing, I noticed a large group of men on a ledge near the rear of the soundstage. Later I learned that the group included Milton Rachmil—the head of Decca Records, parent company of Universal—members of his executive staff, all of whom had just flown in from New York for their once-a-month meeting, and the studio's top local management. All the right people were there; it was just timing and luck. Of course, I knew none of that at the time, which was probably just as well. I didn't need any additional pressure. I only knew that I had a larger audience than I had expected. I simply put my heart and soul into singing "You Belong to Me."

When Rudy Maté called: "Cut!" Ted Richmond came over and said, "Joan, you did an excellent job. Everybody thinks you're just dynamite. We've been talking about a contract for you here at the studio. They really like you. The rushes will be in late this afternoon. I'll call you after I see them."

Then he told me who the cadre of executives were who had watched my scene.

I went home hoping my luck was at last beginning to change. Fortunately, Louella Parsons had departed a few days earlier for Europe, ostensibly on vacation. Actually she had gone there, I learned from McHugh, to undergo cosmetic surgery. Louella was having a face-lift, her eyelids tucked—even her elbows. She was also having fat removed from her arms and other parts of her body. Ironically, she wanted the major overhaul to be done far from Hollywood to avoid, as much as possible, being the subject of malicious gossip. Upon her return to Hollywood, she wanted to be able to attribute any improvement in her appearance to a long, restful European vacation.

Later that afternoon, true to his word, Ted Richmond called.

"You got it," he said. "We're going to negotiate with your manager. A seven-year contract with two-year options. I don't know what kind of money they're going to offer you, but you'll be attending the talent school here and they're willing to give you a big buildup, the whole bit. It's a real opportunity, Joan."

I still couldn't believe it. My recent experience had taught me not to believe in anything as far as Hollywood was concerned until I saw the dotted line in front of my own eyes. I still feared Louella would get wind in Europe of Universal's intentions and phone in another thunderbolt.

But this time the deal went through. McHugh did indeed

negotiate a seven-year deal for me with two-year options. The studio agreed to pay for singing lessons off the lot as well as for my wardrobe. I was to receive two hundred sixty dollars a week—in those days a good starting salary.

When I signed, the studio decided I needed to change my name. Through some logic that still escapes me, I was told, "You don't look Swedish, you look more Dutch." I didn't question their reasoning. Why rock my ship now that it was coming in? Besides, I thought, what's in a name?

They decided my last name should be Van Doren. And because I signed my contract on January 20, 1953, the day Dwight D. Eisenhower was inaugurated for his first term as President of the United States, I was given the name Mamie.

Mamie Van Doren. I liked the sound. It had a certain quality about it, a ring to it. Nor did I mind discarding the name Joan Olander. It just didn't sound like a movie star's name. But Mamie Van Doren—now, that was something else.

When I went to bed that January night I was probably the happiest girl in Southern California. My childhood dream had turned into reality. I seemed to have outflanked my number-one enemy. I was riding the crest of a marvelous wave, thrilled by all that was happening to me. It would be a while before I learned the awesome price of being a movie star and a sex symbol.

Chapter Seven

✦

In January 1953, after I had received my contract at Universal and my new name, I began to pay the price. I suddenly had to work a lot harder than I played.

The first order of business was to get a movie. But that was a process over which I had minimal control. Jimmy McHugh, my manager, and the powers at Universal would have as much to say about that as I would. Scripts were constantly being selected to be put into production in Universal's giant movie factory, and I was being considered along with the other starlets on the lot for roles in each of them.

While that was going on, I began studying at Universal's famed talent school. It was said that the actors who went through it received a million-dollar education in the art of movie acting. I realized that with my lack of experience the school would be a great boon, and I dived into it with all my energy. I doubled up on diction lessons, scene study, ballet lessons, riding lessons, all of the curriculum offered. I received my high-school education there and took college courses from UCLA professors as well.

A typical morning would find a group of us on horseback taking riding lessons, straggled out across the hills of what is now Universal City in the San Fernando Valley north of Los Angeles. Among those in the class were Dennis Weaver, David Janssen, Jack Kelly, Barbara Rush, Kathleen Hughes,

Hugh O'Brian, Anita Ekberg, Piper Laurie, Clint Eastwood, Russ Johnson, Tony Curtis, and Rock Hudson. There was occasional grumbling about the early hour, agents, directors, and the other actors.

Rock Hudson would grouse: ". . . so I told the son of a bitch: 'You're my agent! You're supposed to get me *more* money!'"

Or Anita Ekberg would snap: ". . . well, the role was so *small* and actually they needed someone with dark hair."

At one time I overheard David Janssen mumbling: ". . . she told me that she's already missed one period." It was the perfect place to air grievances and gossip.

The talent school was available to all contract players on the Universal lot. All of the new contract players were expected to take advantage of it, and many of the established stars sat in on classes between pictures.

Among the classes were fencing lessons—mostly for the men who would play swordsmen in swashbuckling costume dramas, though women were expected to fence as well, to build poise and confidence—ballet, jazz, tap, and ballroom dance classes. Dennis Weaver looked a little out of place in dance tights rather than Levi's and cowboy boots, but all the male actors, as well as the women, were required to take a certain amount of dance for grace and agility. And who knew when you might need those dancing skills for a part.

There was a gym where we could work out with exercise equipment. The little man who ran the gym was famous for his rubdowns with a vibrator. Some of the girls even learned to box.

Every day during my first month I came to work and threw myself into the classes. My dream, so far, had come true—now if I could just get a movie. So far, except for the date with Rock Hudson that the studio had arranged, there had been little word from the front office.

Over the next few weeks I became more and more nervous as no suitable script came along. Jimmy McHugh's warning rang in my ears: "You've got your contract, now you've got to get a movie. If you don't—if they don't find anything they like you in—they'll drop you."

One day Jimmy called to say there was a script Universal wanted to discuss with me. At last! I was ecstatic. The film was a college-football movie called *The All American*, which the studio wanted ready for a fall release. It would star Tony Curtis, with whom I had played a bit role in *Forbidden*. Now I was to be his costar.

I met with the director, Jesse Hibbs, a forty-plus-year-old man who had himself been an all-American football player, to rehearse for my screen test. Hibbs subtly made it understood that if I was nice to him, he'd be nice to me—the age-old show-business equation. When we rehearsed my scenes in his office, he encouraged me to fondle him, taking my hand and putting it on his crotch.

I was frightened. Universal International was very strict about fraternization between the contract players and other studio employees, from the top on down. Hypocritically, such fraternization was tolerated and occasionally expected. It was a precarious moment for me. I needed the movie *The All American* and it appeared I would have to take the peccadilloes of its aging all-American director with it. Hibbs would direct my screen test and could make me look good or bad.

When I asked Jimmy McHugh that evening what I should do about it, he hit the ceiling.

"He what?" he bellowed. "He put your hand where?"

"I didn't know what to do, Jimmy. If I don't get this role, God knows what will happen. The studio will probably drop me. He can make me or break me with the screen test."

"Yeah," McHugh growled, "but for crying out loud, you shouldn't have to do that stuff. Can't you just *talk* nicely to him?"

"What do you think I've been trying to do? I don't get a thrill out of groping a guy with more wrinkles than a box of raisins."

McHugh winced. He was very sensitive about his own age and wrinkles.

"Well, just tell him *no!*"

"And what about the screen test?"

"You've got your screen test with the star himself, Tony Curtis. How bad can he make you look?"

"He could shoot over my shoulder. He could light me so I look like a lump of dough. Jimmy, you know as well as I do that he can make me look pretty bad."

"Mamie, now look, you know what to do. Do the right thing. Just go do it!"

Some advice.

I was young and naive enough to think that I had to put up with it. I allowed Hibbs to put my hand on his crotch the next time we met in his office to go over the script. But I batted my eyes and smiled coquettishly and pretended that, well, "I just *couldn't* do anything else." To my relief, he bought it and soon tired of the game. It was difficult to imagine Jesse Hibbs doing anything else. When my hand was resting on his crotch, there was very little there to feel. Happily, when they started principal photography, Hibbs, a rookie director, was too busy to bother with me.

After I got the role, Tony Curtis and I had to work together a lot. He was helpful in many ways. He is very knowledgeable about his craft, and works hard to achieve what he's after. We worked on scenes day after day during the rehearsal weeks to perfect our roles. Often his wife, Janet Leigh, would check on us. It was just before she began filming *Walking My Baby Back Home*. She was no longer as nice to me as she had been when we shared her limo on *Jet Pilot* at RKO. She was watching carefully to make sure I didn't make any headway with her man.

Tony Curtis and Janet Leigh were at that time Hollywood's dream couple. They were the cutesy love affair of the year, but it was no great surprise to me when they broke up. There was something essentially unsound about their marriage. Why else would Janet feel she had to check up on Tony?

Tony was at that time an extremely insecure actor. He was incredibly vain about what side he was photographed from and who was in the shot with him. It was particularly tough during *The All American*. The location shooting was done at the Rose Bowl, and the place was teeming with honest-to-God all-Americans. Tony constantly feared being upstaged by the real athletes. He was doing his own quarterbacking in the film and worked hard to master the game.

For all of the insecurity, though, Tony tried to be friendly. He even went so far as to encourage me to sign with his agent at MCA. I couldn't sign, however, as I was under exclusive contract to Jimmy McHugh.

We completed filming *The All American* in six weeks in

the summer of 1953, and the studio executives and McHugh began discussions on my second picture. Even as postproduction work on *The All American* progressed, I was given the role of Lilith opposite Jeff Chandler in the Universal film version of the best-selling novel *Yankee Pasha*.

While *Yankee Pasha* was still shooting, I was asked to a meeting one Sunday afternoon at Jimmy McHugh's house. Jimmy had taken time out from a luncheon he was having with a group from the Catholic church he attended. He took me outside by the pool, sat me down, and looked at me solemnly.

"Mamie," he began, "U.I. just previewed *The All American* for the studio executives. I just got the results."

My heart sank as I looked at the expression on his face. Oh God, I thought, I must have bombed.

"And they didn't like it?" I asked weakly.

"Almost unanimously the preview cards the execs filled out showed they . . . *loved you!*"

A huge smile split his round face.

"What?!"

"They loved you and they thought the picture was a smash. Most of all, the audience wanted to see *more* of Mamie Van Doren!"

I jumped up and threw my arms around him.

"Oh, Jimmy!"

He grabbed my wrists anxiously.

"Shush, Mamie, for Pete's sake!" he said, pointing inside. "Do you want the whole Catholic Church to see?"

Universal management was delighted with the work I'd done in *The All American*. In fact, they decided to send me on tour to promote the picture around the country in September, 1953.

The first stop on the tour was Detroit. I was scheduled to appear at the premiere of the film with Tony Curtis, who had Janet Leigh in tow, and Richard Long.

As I stood outside the theater in Detroit I could see my breath in the cool fall evening. People were lined up waiting to get into the theater. I gazed up at the brightly lit marquee. There, in bold neon letters, were the words "Starring Mamie Van Doren." Publicity pictures had been appearing in magazines and newspapers for some weeks now and I'd done several interviews back in L.A. But tonight, for the first time, people were seeing me on the screen in a starring role.

I wondered if there was a little girl in the audience who would sit in the dark dreaming of stardom as I had. Would she dream of me the way I had dreamt of Lombard and Bette Davis? Would she beg her mother to see the feature just one more time? Would she vow to be up there on that silver screen herself someday? Would she be as lucky as I had been?

Chapter Eight

Yankee Pasha was a movie based on Edison Marshall's best-selling novel, set in the 1800's. The story concerned a man who sails across the ocean to rescue his true love, a young woman who has been captured by pirates and sold into white slavery. Jeff Chandler, my costar, and I hit it off right away. Though he was one of U.I.'s sexiest, most masculine stars, Jeff and I never became more than friends. Though incredibly sweet and well-liked at the studio, he was very self-centered. There was a fussy, little-old-lady quality about him that killed any sexual attraction I might have felt for him.

The director of Yankee Pasha, Joe Pevney, on the other hand, although in his forties, was both sexy and friendly, and I was very much attracted to him. Before long Joe and I were necking shamelessly in his office. Oddly enough, we never got around to having sex. Either we didn't have enough nerve or there were too many outside distractions for both of us.

Because we were on a hectic eight-week shooting schedule, I was required to work six days a week. (Shortly after Pasha was wrapped, there was a union dispute that resulted in a five-day work week for actors in films.) Most of the film's location shooting was done on the Universal back lot. Often we would shoot from early morning until late at night, and then shoot all night the next evening. The constant juggling of the shooting schedule kept me feeling tired all the time, and before long I could see the difference in my figure.

A few weeks into the picture, I called Jimmy McHugh in a panic.

"Jimmy, I don't know what to do."

"About what, Mamie?"

"I'm losing weight and I don't know what to do."

"Are you sick?"

"I don't think so. I think it's because of the long hours I'm working."

"Then what's the problem? Eat more."

"The problem, Jimmy, is that my breasts are getting smaller."

"That's no big deal, Mamie."

"That's what I'm afraid of."

"What I mean is, get yourself some falsies. Go up to the wardrobe department and tell them you want some . . . padding up there."

"Padding?"

"Sure. Who's going to know the difference?"

"No one, I suppose."

"Good. Do it tomorrow."

The next day I followed Jimmy's advice, and took my problem to the wardrobe department.

A major stumbling block to the creativity and freedom of the movie industry during that period was the censors. The film industry had to police itself with regard to the wholesomeness of its product. In the thirties and forties there was the Hays office; later it was the dreaded Johnson office. The self-styled moralists that peopled these quasi-official bodies had the authority to dictate to moviemakers matters of such dire importance to the nation's morals as the length, in seconds, of a kiss, the fitness of dialogue, and the amount of an actor's or actress's body that could be exposed. Two of their greatest horrors were shots of cleavage and belly buttons.

These were issues that affected all the studios' so-called glamour girls. (The term "sex symbol" was still not in wide use. Merely the mention of the word "sex" was a touchy matter.) The amount of cleavage allowed was strictly limited. And God forbid that a child should be corrupted by the sight of a female belly button. Men routinely appeared with chests bared and navels showing, as Chandler did in *Yankee Pasha*. My harem costume in the same picture, however, had pants that discreetly covered my own belly button lest some man become inflamed and violate the nearest woman.

This curious form of sexual discrimination had some funny consequences.

Since the censors forbade exposing more than a few centimeters of cleavage, the studios, in their efforts to outdo each other, encouraged their glamour girls to use padded bras, and went for sheer size. Eventually, the padded bras built us out to such mammoth dimensions that we felt a little self-conscious. The bullet-shaped cones under out tight sweaters were just short of becoming hazards to navigation.

One of the bullet-bras in the U.I. wardrobe department was far and away the most comfortable and the most well-proportioned. That was the one we all vied to get for a day's shooting. More often than not, I got there early and strapped myself in before the others arrived.

"Good God, Mamie!" Jeff Chandler said to me the first day I wore the bullet-bra during the shooting of *Yankee Pasha*. "Is that all you?"

I leaned forward and shook them at him mock-lasciviously.

"Very impressive," Jeff replied.

"I lost so much weight recently, the wardrobe department made me pad them out. With all these well-stacked Miss Universe contestants around here, I don't want to be out-gunned."

Miss Universe candidates from at least fifteen different countries had been cast in *Yankee Pasha* to fill out the harem scenes. And were they filled out! It made all the ingenues under contract feel more than a little insecure knowing a bevy of beauties was waiting in the wings. Fortunately, most of the Miss Universe girls couldn't speak English.

Jeff had just lost a lot of weight himself. William Goetz, the head of U.I., told him to knock off twenty pounds for the start of *Yankee Pasha*. Goetz took an active hand in shaping the careers of the Universal stars.

Jeff turned his profile to me and smoothed the skin on his face. "You don't think it makes my cheekbones stand out too much?"

"No, Jeff. You look fine. You've got the greatest cheek-bones in Hollywood. Why not show them?"

There was a good deal of pressure on Jeff during the film-ing of *Yankee Pasha*. It was U.I.'s first CinemaScope movie. The studio had picked on one of its most bankable stars to debut the expensive new wide-screen color process. For Jeff it was a big step forward. His career had consisted of a lot of Indian roles up to that time, most notably a couple of Cochise movies. Jeff made no bones about being glad he was free of them at last.

"Now, if I can just get a shot at a musical . . . Mamie, you and I would be great together in a musical."

"Musical?"

"Sure. I want to be a singer. My biggest ambition is to play a Las Vegas showroom."

I told Jeff I took singing lessons outside the studio, and we discussed the merits of voice teachers.

"One of the songwriters here at the studio is helping me put together some songs for a nightclub act. He's Lou Gersh-enson's assistant. Guy name of Mancini. Have you met him? He's scoring *Yankee Pasha*."

Jeff pointed across the set to a brown-haired young man with large chocolate-brown eyes. "That's him over there. He's been watching us shoot this morning. Hank! C'mere, Hank. Mamie Van Doren, meet Hank Mancini. Hank, this is Mamie."

We shook hands and Hank gave me a big grin.

"Mamie, I just saw the rushes of your first entrance in the movie. Great stuff."

"Thanks, Hank," I said.

"Wait'll you hear the music I wrote for the entrance. Waa-waa wa-wa-wa, waa-waaaa wa-wa-wa. You'll love it!"

I had no way of knowing then that the unassuming Hank Mancini would soon become the hottest composer in Holly-wood.

Jeff's other costar in the picture was Rhonda Fleming. Though recognized as a star, she was not under contract to any studio at the time. Rhonda was always coolly correct with her fellow workers. Her aloof attitude occasionally made us feel that she felt she was a cut above the rest of us.

One scene in the film called for Rhonda and me to fight

over Jeff. Movie fights are elaborately choreographed so that no one will get hurt. Pevney, the director, blocked out the fight for us, and the stunt coordinator carefully rehearsed our movements. During the fight, Rhonda was to hit me, sending me sprawling across the bed. When the cameras rolled and the fight started, everything worked as it was supposed to— until the end. Rhonda's punch was supposed to miss me by a comfortable margin. The camera angle would make it look like her fist had landed squarely on my jaw. When the moment came, though, she landed a solid right cross that dislocated my jaw and made me see more stars than a Hollywood premiere.

Late one afternoon as I was walking across the lot to my car I saw a man up ahead walking toward me in full Indian costume: giant feather headdress, beaded breastplate, fringed buckskin breechclout, and moccasins. He shuffled along tiredly; I thought he looked familiar from the way he walked. As I approached, I recognized the actor under the dark bronze makeup and colorful warpaint as none other than Rock Hudson.

Rock stopped and gave me a rueful grin.

"Hi, Mamie."

"Rock you look . . . great!"

"Like hell I do. I've got bronze makeup in my ears and practically up my ass! It'll take me two hours to shower this stuff off. Goddamn, I'm sick of it."

I thought he made a handsome Indian, but he was in no mood to be told that.

"When did you start playing Indians?"

"About the time your costar, Jeff Chandler, stopped. He made a deal with Bill Goetz not to play any more Indians, and now I'm stuck with them."

"Well, it's better than being out on the street, Rock," I said to try to cheer him up. "And it could be worse. You could be making Ma and Pa Kettle movies. Besides, it won't last forever. You career's on the way up. Before you know it, you'll make a deal with Goetz too. Then somebody else'll inherit Cochise."

The picture that would make Rock a superstar, the remake of *Magnificent Obsession,* was still in the future. And following *Magnificent Obsession* would come a starring role in *Giant* with James Dean and Liz Taylor. By then he would wear no more war paint. But for now it was a humiliating experience.

"God, I hope so," Rock went on. "In the picture I'm Son of Cochise. I've gotta get out of these roles before some wise guy in the front office comes up with the idea for *Grandson of Cochise Meets Ma and Pa Kettle*."

Chapter Nine

Bob Palmer, head of U.I.'s casting department, got word to me on the set of *Yankee Pasha* that he wanted to see me. After a few pleasantries, Palmer got down to business.

"Mamie, the reason I called you is MGM has requested that you audition for a new picture they're doing."

"Great," I said enthusiastically. MGM had been the first studio I approached for a contract, when I first signed with Jimmy McHugh. I had walked through the MGM gates full of hope, with warm memories of all the hit MGM musicals. But MGM had passed on signing me. Now they were *asking* for me. "What am I auditioning for?"

"*Oklahoma!* Oscar Hammerstein and Richard Rodgers have approval on all the major roles. They want you to audition for Ado Annie."

I knew of *Oklahoma!* from my stint in New York, although I had never seen the show. It was *the* great American musical. And I knew that Ado Annie was the perfect role for me: a cute, perky, corn-fed Midwestern farmgirl. With my background, the role was a natural.

My eyes must have gotten as big as saucers. Palmer grinned at me. "It's a great opportunity for you, Mamie. Buy the Broadway cast album and learn Annie's main number. They want to see you day after tomorrow. If they like your audition, they'll give you a screen test. I tried to call Jimmy

McHugh to tell him, but his secretary told me he was in the hospital.''

"He went in last week," she said. McHugh's health had been steadily deteriorating over the past year. He complained about every little ache and pain. At first I thought he was a hypochondriac. But as time went on, I could see it was something serious. "The doctor said it was some kind of heart problem. He's known about it for a while. They put him in the hospital to control his diet and make him rest."

"Well, give Jimmy my best when you see him."

On my way back to my parents' house, I bought a copy of the *Oklahoma!* album. For the next two days I listened to it every spare minute I had, memorizing Ado Annie's big number, "I'm Just a Girl Who Can't Say No." I rehearsed in front of a mirror to get the facial expressions just right. By the time of the audition, I was ready.

When I met the famous team of Rodgers and Hammerstein, they looked like an unlikely combination. The two men could not have been more different in looks.

Oscar Hammerstein had a large head perched atop a tall, bulky body. His round face was cratered like a moonscape, from which two blue eyes sparkled. His shirt collar was pulled open around a big neck. His rumpled mien had the same homey appeal as a pile of your mother's laundry.

Richard Rodgers was the exact opposite of his collaborator. A compact man, Rodgers was dressed like a bit of a dandy, with a sharp suit and tie and a brilliant shoeshine. He sat at the piano to play for my audition.

When I launched into the first lines of the song, Hammerstein's eyes widened. Rodgers turned and looked at me intently while he played. I hadn't even finished the last note when Hammerstein started talking excitedly.

"Yes!" he exclaimed. "I definitely want to test you. As soon as possible. What do you think, Dick?"

"Excellent," Rodgers agreed. "Mamie, take this scene home and learn it. We'll make all the arrangements with your studio. Who's your agent? We'll contact him when we make the arrangements for the screen test."

"Jimmy McHugh's my manager, but he's in the hospital right now. Just let the studio know and they'll tell me."

As I drove home from MGM, I patted the script in the seat

next to me. It was a big chance for me, the movie version of the biggest musical on Broadway. Sitting at a light, I turned the rearview mirror to myself.

"Ado Annie," I said softly to my reflection.

I couldn't wait to take the script to my acting teacher, Jean Grahame, mother of Academy Award-winning actress Gloria Grahame, to study for my screen test. Mrs. Grahame was an austere woman. I always called her Mrs. Grahame because she was so intimidating. But she was a good teacher.

Word came from MGM through U.I.'s front office that my screen test was set for the next week. I studied hard with Mrs. Grahame during that week. We went through the scene line by line, building the character, working on motivation, preparing my line readings. When I had the scene down pat, Mrs. Grahame asked if she could have the script to keep for a few days.

"I'd like to have some of my other students work on that scene."

"Sure," I said, handing her the script.

During that week I also rehearsed steps to go with the song with choreographer Agnes DeMille. And there were costume fittings at MGM's wardrobe department. By the time the big day came, I was beginning to feel like a regular on the lot.

The day of the test I arrived at the soundstage costumed and made up as Ado Annie. Inside the cavernous stage was a large outdoor set. A huge curved scrim made the blue sky and prairie appear to stretch away into the distance.

I was introduced to a stocky man in his early forties who had a cocky smile and aggressive manner. His dark hair was slicked to one side and he was in his shirtsleeves.

"Mamie Van Doren, I presume?"

"Yes . . . ?" I turned to him.

He took my hand and shook it.

"Mike Todd, Mamie. I'm very pleased to meet you."

Though I had never seen him before, I recognized the name. Mike Todd was a producer on the MGM lot who was making a name for himself. He had developed a color process called Todd-AO that would rival CinemaScope and which MGM was using for *Oklahoma!* He had yet to begin the colorful Elizabeth Taylor phase of his life.

I was introduced to Fred Zinnemann, the director. I could tell that he was not crazy about the idea of testing me for the role. It was only because of the enthusiasm of Rodgers and Hammerstein that he was forced into directing the test. I would read my lines with Zinnemann, then do my song. I would be accompanied by a piano player off-camera.

We ran through the scene a couple of times before Zinnemann said he was ready to shoot.

"Okay. Places, everyone."

I found my marks for the opening shot and Zinnemann barked, "Action!"

The scene was one in which Ado Annie confides her love life to Laurie (the character that Shirley Jones would ultimately play) while they sit on a bench in the middle of the sprawling prairie. The scene culminates with Ado Annie singing "I'm Just a Girl Who Can't Say No."

The scene went off without a hitch. While I sweated out the next week, waiting for word from MGM, I went over every moment of the test in my mind. I replayed and analyzed every word of dialogue, every note I sang, every step I danced. I felt that in spite of Fred Zinnemann's lack of enthusiasm for me, I had done a very good test.

I tried to reach Jimmy McHugh several times, but his long-time secretary was taking his calls. I confided in her about the screen test and told her I needed to talk to Jimmy.

"I'm sorry, Mamie. I can only give him the message. He's under strict orders by the doctor to stay clear of any excitement. Jimmy's very ill."

"I understand, Lucille. But this could mean a lot of commission to Jimmy, not to mention what it could mean to me."

"I'll give him the message, Mamie. Sorry."

When I found myself in Bob Palmer's office again, looking across his desk, I was sweating bullets.

"Mamie, although Richard Rodgers and Oscar Hammerstein both liked you, MGM's decided to go with someone else for the part."

I was devastated.

"Was it because Fred Zinnemann didn't like me?"

"No, he seemed to think you fit the part pretty well."

I could feel my eyes burning and I gripped the arm of the chair.

"Then what was it? Why didn't I get the part?"

"I think the studio brass felt that they had to go with some-one who had a little more recognition at the box office."

"And who is that?"

"It looks like they're going to use Gloria Grahame." My mouth fell open. "They must figure that winning the Acad-emy Award for best supporting actress last year in *That Bad and the Beautiful* makes her a bigger draw."

"Yes," I said weakly, "that's what they must think."

"It's too bad McHugh couldn't get involved in this one. He might have been able to help."

"Yeah."

"You take acting lessons from Gloria's mother, don't you, Mamie?"

I thought for a moment about Mrs. Grahame borrowing the script. It took a moment to get my voice under control.

"I used to."

I cried over that one. Luckily, I was able to go home to Mother and pour out my grief. When I was finally cried out, Mother said, "It's all right, Jo. There'll be other parts."

"Not like this one, Mother," I moaned. "It's not fair. I know Gloria's mother gave her that script."

"She shouldn't have done that," Mother agreed. "But it wasn't meant for you to play that part, and that's all there is to it."

When Bob Palmer called me back to his office a couple of weeks later, I thought perhaps MGM had changed their minds. Or Gloria Grahame had come down with some dire disease that would prevent her from playing Ado Annie.

I had immediately changed acting teachers after giving Mrs. Grahame a clear piece of my mind on the subject of her ethics as a teacher. I began taking acting lessons from Batami Schneider, a Russian immigrant who had studied with Stani-slavski himself. She lived in the San Fernando Valley with her husband, Benno, who was head acting coach at Columbia Studios.

"Mamie," Palmer said, "Columbia has asked us to loan you out for a picture called *Pushover*, starring Fred Mac-Murray." He held up his hand and silenced me before I could speak. "You might as well know that it's fallen through and they've decided to cast someone else."

"Then why did you bring me in?" I asked in disappointment. "A phone call would've done just as well."

"I wanted you to understand something, Mamie. I called your manager to tell him about this loan-out. I hoped he could get on it right away because they were anxious to test you. I left a message with his secretary and he never returned my call. He also never called Columbia."

"Jimmy's been sick—"

"I know that. But I also know that because you had no one to represent you at Columbia, they passed on you and decided to develop their own sex goddess. Some girl named Novak. Her first name's Marilyn, but they've decided to change it to Kim. The fact is, Mamie, you've got to have an agent or manager who's on the ball to represent you. We can't represent you to another studio. But we'd like for you to be loaned out. It makes big money for us *and* it builds your career."

"I understand. I'll have a talk with Jimmy."

That night I phoned Jimmy McHugh in his hospital room. He answered and we exchanged amenities for a few minutes before I got around to the point. I reminded him that I'd lost out on Ado Annie, then I mentioned the role at Columbia. Jimmy exploded.

"How dare you call me in the hospital about a part? I'm lying here at death's door and you have the gall, the ingratitude, to call me because you missed out on some role in a movie!"

"I'm sorry, Jimmy. I didn't mean to upset you. But because you're so ill, perhaps you should let me sign with an agent to help with my career—"

"I'm taking care of your career, Mamie. But I want you to know that I'm not ever answering the phone here in the hospital again. My doctor tells me that the telephone is one of the most upsetting things in the world. Now, don't call me again with any of this whining about not getting roles. If it wasn't for me, you wouldn't be where you are now!"

He slammed down the phone and left me staring at my receiver.

What he said hurt. I knew that he had helped me get my

start in Hollywood, and had engineered my contract at Universal International. And I was damned grateful. But what good was getting a start if you didn't follow through? I was getting publicity now, and now was the time to capitalize on it. Why not turn me over to someone else until he was feeling better?

The dust still hadn't settled when I received a message through the studio that Burt Lancaster wanted to see me about a role in his next movie.

Burt Lancaster had set up one of the finest independent production companies in Hollywood. What has now become common practice in the film industry was then a daring venture that smart money around town thought was doomed to failure.

As I had so many times, I took my mother along with me when I went on the interview. She waited in the car while I went into Lancaster's office on Santa Monica Boulevard.

Burt's first words were: "Jesus, you look so young."

I was shocked that he said so. Though I felt very mature and sophisticated at twenty years old, my publicity stills of the period show I still had a nice layer of baby fat.

We talked for a few minutes more about the movie—it was called *Vera Cruz*—before Burt said, "Mamie, I want you to read for the part of the contessa that seduces Gary Cooper. But let's go somewhere that's more quiet where we can concentrate. Okay?"

I agreed. I didn't want to tell him my mother was waiting for me in the car, so without saying a word to her, we went out the back door of the office and got into Burt's car. We drove a short distance to a small apartment in the back of a well-manicured apartment house.

Inside, Burt kept up a steady and rather charming stream of chatter about the film, as well as the next picture he was planning, *Trapeze*.

He picked up two scripts and handed one to me.

"Read the part of the contessa. She's an experienced, wealthy woman of the world."

He told me what page the scene was on and flopped on a chaise longue in a corner of the room. I sat on a chair and studied the scene for a moment.

"Come over here, Mamie," he said. He patted the edge of the chaise longue. "Sit down here and read. This is a love scene."

We read the scene together. When I finished, Burt pulled me down on top of him and kissed me on the mouth.

A scene from a movie I had seen when I was in junior high school flashed through my mind. It must have been the first movie Burt Lancaster appeared in—*The Killers,* a gangster movie with Ava Gardner. I remembered how tough and sexy he was. He was even sexier in person. He spoke my name softly.

I pulled away and sat up.

"Burt, don't," I said. "I'm sure this scene works with a lot of the girls around town. But I came here to audition for a part. Not to go to bed."

A surprised look came over his face.

"Look," I went on, "if we end up working together, whatever happens between us just . . . happens. But I'm not going to get the part this way. Okay?"

His eyes blazed with intensity. A smile crept up the corners of his mouth until that famous row of white teeth was showing.

"I respect that, Mamie," he said. He patted me on the leg with gentle camaraderie. "And I think you're absolutely right."

"Then how about if I read for the role?"

"Why don't you take your time and look over the script?"

"Burt, listen, I have a confession to make. My mother came with me to your office and is still sitting in the car outside—if she hasn't gone to call the police."

"Holy Christ! Why didn't you say so?"

On the way back to his office Burt said, "Mamie, take the script with you and work through the scene. Do you have an acting coach?"

"Batami Schneider."

"Good choice. Go over the scene with her and come read for me. I'm going to check into the hospital for a rest before we start shooting *Vera Cruz.* Call me and you can come there to audition."

I went back and auditioned for Burt, but was not surprised that someone else was cast in the role. But I felt that I matured in the process of auditioning. I had held my own and called Burt Lancaster's bluff.

Yankee Pasha had finished shooting some four months ago and I was hoping for another script soon. I was starting to feel a little discouraged. I'd had three turndowns and Jimmy McHugh was barely talking to me.

But then, as if to give the rain on my parade a silver lining, U.I. asked me to attend the premiere of *The Glenn Miller Story.* Being seen at this type of event was another facet of the million-dollar publicity buildup that U.I. gave its stars-to-be. Part of my daily routine often consisted of interviews with movie magazines, newspaper writers, photo sessions. I was photographed in every conceivable position by the studio's veteran publicity photographer, Ray Jones, who had photographed such greats as Marlene Dietrich. Those shots appeared in movie magazines all over the world. And it was expected that I would appear at premieres and other media events to promote my name and the studio's. As Universal's "answer" to Marilyn Monroe, I was pulled along by all the enthusiasm of the 1950's for sexy, busty blondes. An impressive quantity of fan mail was already arriving for me at Universal's post office—and I had starred in only two films.

Attending a premiere of that size would be an exhilarating experience. Just the thought of it lifted my spirits. But I didn't have a date. I had to come up with an escort.

There is one thing that is a truism about being a so-called glamour girl: the phone suddenly stops ringing with guys asking for dates. Other girls in the same position say the same thing. Men believe that you are inundated with calls from guys wanting to take you out. So the phone stays silent.

I ticked off the possibilities at the studio, one by one. None of the contract players was an especially thrilling prospect, although they would have certainly acted as my escort for the evening. Most would have been glad for the exposure. The studio was adamant that I go to the premiere, so I had to make a decision of some kind soon.

Then I got an idea.

I called Al Horowitz, head of the U.I. publicity office, on the phone.

"I'd like you to do me a favor, Al."

"If you'll do me one: go to *The Glenn Miller Story* premiere."

"That's what I'm calling about. I just thought of the most eligible bachelor in town to take me to the premiere. Nicky Hilton."

"He just divorced Liz Taylor, didn't he?"

"Yes. And I'll bet he's very much available."

"Women must be beating down his door, Mamie," Horowitz said doubtfully.

"Just give him a call for me, Al. I can't do it myself. Tell him I'd like him to take me to the premiere."

Within the hour Horowitz was back on the phone to me.

"Okay, Mamie," he said. "You're on with Nicky."

I'd given a lot of thought to what I might wear. The studio was reluctant to make another gown for me as they had for my Rock Hudson date. And I was just as reluctant to be done up like a prom queen again.

I finally found a Ceil Chapman gown on Rodeo Drive that I could afford. Strapless and white beaded and *very* slinky—it was gorgeous. It was my first Hollywood premiere, and I was bent on knocking everybody for a loop.

When Nicky Hilton picked me up, he smiled appreciatively and I knew the gown had the desired effect. Nicky was boyishly good-looking, handsomely turned out in black tie. He kept up a steady stream of banter that put me at ease as we drove to the Pantages Theater.

As we approached the theater, I looked at the streets where I had hung out in the forties, reading movie magazines and walking to my job as usherette at the Pantages. The giant klieg lights lit up the night sky and there were throngs of movie fans clogging the sidewalks on both sides of Hollywood Boulevard, straining behind the police barricades.

We pulled up in front and I felt the chill of the night as I got out of the car. As Nicky took my arm and we started to walk up the red carpet into the theater, I heard the fans.

"May-mee! May-mee! May-mee!" they chanted.

I waved to them on both sides of the entrance.

"May-mee! May-mee!"

Suddenly I didn't feel the cold of the night. I felt only the warmth of the crowd's response from the other side of the barriers.

"May-mee! May-mee!"

Entering the theater's ornate lobby, I had a curious déjà vu feeling. The grand, brightly lit lobby was familiar and strange at the same time. The Pantages hadn't changed since I stood next to the big doors leading into the theater as a teenager, sneaking looks at the screen while I showed people to their seats. I could still remember the smell of the theater when I first came to work before the popcorn started popping, and the feel of the deep red plush velvet of the loges.

"Nicky, will you excuse me, please?" I said.

"Sure, Mamie. Everything all right?" he asked solicitously. I felt lucky to have Nicky as my escort tonight. He had been very poised in front of the chanting crowd outside. His smile had been genuine as he waved back to the throng. He was just modest enough to let the fans' attentions focus on me without shrinking into invisibility. The ideal escort. Strong but not overpowering.

"Fine. I just want to powder my nose."

The ladies' lounge was deserted. Inside was the giant mirror, lit with rows of lights, showing a warm, rosy reflection.

I sat on the bench in front of it and stared at myself. This was the mirror I had posed and primped in front of, pretending I was a movie star in my grand dressing room. I wasn't any different from the girl I had been a few years ago, shaking my blonde hair out from under the little pillbox usherette's hat that was part of our uniform. I still made the same silly faces at myself in the mirror when no one was around. And yet outside, there were people shouting my name. People who knew who I was and wanted somehow to bask in the glamour they supposed I had.

They couldn't know how scared I was. They couldn't know how worried I was that I wouldn't get another good part at the studio; they couldn't feel my terror over the fact that my option was coming up in a couple of weeks and I was afraid it might not get picked up. All they knew was that I got out of that big Cadillac with one of the richest, most eligible bachelors in town. As far as the fans were concerned, things were going just fine for Mamie.

The reflection in the mirror tried to smile. Underneath the more professional makeup job I'd learned to apply, trying to look more mature, there was the same young girl's face.

Back again in the glittering lobby, I found Nicky waiting patiently for me.

"You look wonderful," he said, smiling as he guided me toward the door into the theater.

We were ushered to our seats. And they were terrible.

"What are we doing way down here?" Nicky asked, craning his head around to look back up the aisle. We were just half a dozen rows from the front, looking almost straight up at the giant screen.

"I don't know," I said. I looked back up at the balcony loges and saw the stars and the U.I. studio executives. It was obvious that I had been given these seats deliberately. "Looks like maybe you said yes to the wrong starlet, Nicky." I was suddenly dejected.

Nicky took my hand and squeezed it. "I'll be damned if that's so. We're going to enjoy ourselves in spite of them."

He put his arm around me and said: "Hell, Mamie! You're with a Hilton!"

The next morning I could hardly move. Nicky had brought me home, kissed me good night, and asked if I would have dinner with him soon. I agreed enthusiastically. But even then I had not felt well. By morning I had a sore throat and was running a high fever. I was in no shape to go to work and I called Bob Palmer to tell him so.

"Don't worry, Mamie," he said when I explained how sick I was. "Just stay in bed and get well. Pictures of you with Nicky Hilton are plastered all over the papers this morning. You looked stunning."

"I looked so stunning, I think I caught pneumonia."

"The dress *was* pretty bare on top."

"I was freezing. And I got a crick in my neck from staring straight up at the screen. Whoever assigned me those seats was a real practical joker."

"What do you mean?"

"Bob, did you ever sit in the sixth row of the Pantages Theater?"

"No. Why?"

"Try it sometime. I'm going back to bed."

"Oh, Mamie, there's one more thing."

I blew my nose again, hard. "Yes?"

"I got a call this morning from RKO. Howard Hughes wants to see you."

"He can buy a *ticket* and see me."

"He wants to meet with you. Soon as it can be arranged."

"Howard actually called you?"

"Oh no, no. Howard Hughes never calls anyone. He had some flunky at his studio make the call. He wants to meet with you alone, Mamie. No agent or manager. Just you and him."

"That's easy enough to arrange. I don't have an agent, and my manager, McHugh, is still too sick to leave his house. How does U.I. feel about it?"

"You have our blessing. His representative said he wants to discuss a loan-out for RKO for a movie called *Susan Slept Here*. That's if he likes you for the part. You and Debbie Reynolds are two corners of a love triangle. It's being produced by Harriet Parsons, Louella's daughter."

"You know what Louella thinks of me. Why bother?"

"Hughes wants to meet with you anyway."

"It sounds like a wild-goose chase, but I'll meet with him. As soon as I'm well, okay?"

"Let me know when you feel well enough. Go back to bed."

Chapter Ten

The Jaguar I had bought a few months before eased to a stop in front of Paul Hessy's photo studio on Sunset. My mother sat in the passenger seat with her arms folded and an exasperated look on her face.

Mother was still my boon companion on jaunts like this. And she was my most trusted confidante. Though I drove a fancy sports car, I was still living at home with my parents for purely practical reasons. In 1954 I had little desire for an apartment of my own and the time-consuming responsibilities that went with it. I paid a token rent at home and took full advantage of the washing, ironing, and answering service, and especially the four-A.M. breakfasts Mother fixed for me when I had an early makeup call at the studio. Practically every other starlet at Universal was living with one or both of her parents. Universal management encouraged situations like that—it gave their girls respectability. I liked it both because of the benefits—clean clothes that someone else washed and ironed, meals, free time to pursue my career—and because I loved my parents very much.

My mother was not amused with our situation on this particular afternoon.

"I don't care what you say, Jo—I don't like Howard Hughes. He's . . . weird."

"Mother, please. I'm just going to talk with him about doing a movie."

"Phooey! Jo, he doesn't want you for a movie. Believe me, he wants you, just like he did five years ago when you were Miss Palm Springs, because he collects young, beautiful girls."

"Well," I said, opening the Jaguar's door and feeling the chill of the February late afternoon, "I won't be long. Just wait here for me, okay?"

"I wouldn't be surprised if he tried to rape you."

"He won't try to rape me, Mother. Don't worry about me."

Inside Hessy's studio, a young man dressed in a suit and tie led me to the rear of the building. He wordlessly let me into a darkened room lined with mirrors, closed the door, and silently went away. The only light in the room came from a window with the shade drawn. Two chairs were set up in the middle of the room, facing each other. I sat down in the one facing the door.

The muffled sound of traffic on Sunset Boulevard mingled with the sound of music from somewhere in the building. I wondered if it was coming from Walter Kane's apartment.

I got up and paced the room, looking at myself in the mirrors. I posed and adjusted my bra. It was the bullet-bra from U.I. and made my breasts look invitingly large under the smooth brown bodice of the dress I wore.

I danced a few steps, watching myself in the mirror. I did a pirouette, then a few Fred Astaire/Ginger Rogers steps, and posed again on one of the chairs.

Thirty minutes must have passed while I waited in the gloomy room. I began to think of my mother sitting in the car.

At last the door opened. Silhouetted in the opening was the tall frame of Howard Hughes. He was thinner than I remembered, and bareheaded, wearing the same kind of rumpled, nondescript clothes he had worn years before. For all I knew, they *were* the same clothes.

"Hello, Mamie," Hughes drawled. Texas was plain in his accent. "I can call you Mamie, can't I?"

"Oh sure, Howard."

"Used to be Joan, now it's Mamie."

He came inside and closed the door. He stood across the room looking at me and I noticed he had a Kleenex in his hand. He crumpled it and let it drop to the floor. Then I saw he was carrying a box of Kleenex in his other hand. He pulled one from the box and held it over his nose and mouth. He leaned toward me and cupped his ear with his free hand.

"How've you been, Mamie?" Hughes asked, muffled through the tissue.

"Fine, Howard. Just fine. Have you got a cold?"

"I see your publicity all the time," he went on, ignoring my question. "You're in the papers and movie magazines a lot." He grinned at me. "Beautiful as ever."

"Thank you," I replied.

An article about Hughes had appeared just a couple of weeks before in the February 9, 1954, issue of *Look* magazine—the same issue in which an article about me had appeared.

"We've both had write-ups in *Look*," I said.

He paced away to the far side of the room.

"I tried to stop that article from appearing. Even called Gardner Cowles, who owns the damn magazine. Said he'd print it come hell or high water."

"I thought it was a good article about you, Howard."

"Damn invasion of my privacy," he snorted. Another Kleenex fell to the floor and he pulled a fresh one from the box. I noticed he was not blowing his nose on them, but holding them in front of his face. "Had no business printing a bunch a lies about me like that. I told Cowles that if he insisted on printing that scurrilous piece, I'd order *Look* magazine taken out of every airplane in TWA's fleet."

I didn't know what to say to that one. I had been glad to get a nice write-up in a national publication like *Look*. Evidently it was not something relished by eccentric multimillionaires.

"I'm glad you could come today, Mamie." He dropped the subject of the *Look* article abruptly. "You look even more beautiful in person than you do in the pictures. You've grown up a lot since your Miss Palm Springs days."

"I guess I have."

"You were certainly the darnedest fifteen-year-old I've ever seen back then. How is your mother, Mamie?"

"Oh, just fine." I didn't want to admit she was waiting for me in the car. But Howard probably had his spies watching to see if I came with anyone.

"I want you to know how much I appreciate those parts you gave me at RKO back then."

"It's nothing." Hughes shrugged.

"But I had to leave when I saw that I would never get anything but bit parts."

He acted like he didn't want to hear that.

"You depend on your mother's judgment a lot, don't you? Her feelings about what you should do with your career?"

"Yes. Mother and I talk about everything."

"Good. That's a good thing to see."

He went to one of the chairs finally and sat down. We'd been doing a sort of stiff dance around the room—Howard pacing and me following. He gestured to the other chair and then did a strange thing—he pushed it a little farther away with his foot. I sat down and he stared into space for a few seconds.

"I'm very interested in having you do a part in a movie I'm making over at RKO. It's called *Susan Slept Here*."

"Bob Palmer at U.I. told me."

"Good. You might be very good for one of the roles. I've got a first-rate cast—Dick Powell and Debbie Reynolds are already cast. Harriet Parsons is producing."

"Well, frankly, I have my doubts about doing it—because of Harriet Parsons. Her mother detests me."

"So?"

"Howard, I don't believe for one moment that Harriet will like me any better than Louella does."

He laughed out loud. He took the tissue away from his face for a few moments and smiled at me. For all his peculiarities, Hughes had a charming smile.

"Mamie, if I want you to do this movie, Harriet Parsons will do as she's told." He said it without rancor or arrogance. It was just a fact of life: if Howard Hughes wanted something, he would get it. "But there's one thing that bothers me," he went on. "Why in the world would Dick Powell go back to Debbie Reynolds in the movie, after he's been with you?"

We talked for a while about the movie business, and Howard mentioned that he was seldom in Los Angeles anymore, that he did most of his business from Las Vegas.

He took another Kleenex from the box and covered his nose and mouth again. By now there were several dozen crumpled tissues scattered around the floor.

Howard stood and I sensed the interview was drawing to a close. I stood up and he took a step toward me. He looked down at my breasts with widened eyes. I could hear his breathing. After a moment more, he appeared to remember something and took several steps away from me.

"What do you want to do with your life, Mamie?" Hughes asked in a fatherly tone.

I shrugged. "Be the best actress I can be. I suppose more than anything that's what I want. That's what I've always dreamed about—a career in the movies, having all the things I want, being independent."

"There are a lot of ways to have the things you want."

I looked him directly in the eye. He smiled at me and I smiled back. "Yes. I've tried some of the easy ways. Most of them turned out to be harder work than I thought. If I'm going to get what I want, I'm the only person I can depend on to do it."

After a pause, Hughes repeated several times, "I think you'd be good in *Susan Slept Here*." He turned and walked to the door. He opened it and turned to me. "Good to see you again, Mamie. No, I don't have a cold. You can never be too careful."

A couple of weeks before I went to see Howard Hughes, I had been in U.I.'s film *Francis Joins the WACS*. There were two film series that were bread-and-butter for Universal International: the Ma and Pa Kettle movies, starring Percy Kilbride and Marjorie Main; and the Francis the Talking Mule movies, starring that sleek and well-fed devil, Francis, and the voice of Chill Wills.

These movies were responsible for keeping the lights on and the commissary stocked. They paid the salaries of most of us on the U.I. lot. They were cheap to make, received the widest possible distribution, and, thank God, the American public loved them.

But to all of us contract players they were anathema. A

new script for a Francis or a Ma and Pa Kettle movie was sure to scatter the actors and actresses to whatever hiding places we could find on the lot.

But while you could run, you couldn't hide. Almost everyone suffered through a turn in one or another of the films. Somehow I managed to skid by for a while, but when my one-year option was picked up at the beginning of 1954, my number came up.

One day, just before *Francis Joins the WACs* began shooting, I saw a familiar broad-shouldered figure walking down the hall. He had blue eyes, set off by a straight nose and a crooked grin.

"Hi, Clint," I said. Like me, Clint Eastwood was a U.I. contract player.

"Hi, Mamie. How's the new movie?"

"We start shooting in a week or so."

"No kidding?" He leaned toward me and said quietly: "Have you got any pull with the director? Do you think you could help me get in *Francis Joins the WACs?*"

"Gosh, I wish I could, Clint," I said, meaning it. I liked this tall drink of water, but Clint Eastwood couldn't seem to find a place for himself at Universal. "They practically had to break my arm to get me to do this one, so I don't think they'd listen to me."

Clint shrugged and grinned again. "Well, just thought I'd ask. You're lookin' pretty as ever, Mamie."

"Thanks, Clint."

He turned away and sauntered down the hall.

"That Eastwood," the publicity man I was with said, shaking his head. "Never gives up."

I looked at Clint as he walked out of the publicity office. "He'll get what he's after, eventually."

"Are you kidding? He's got no sex appeal."

"I wouldn't say that."

"He's got a monotone voice and a deadpan face. He'd better find himself a nice, steady job."

Clint Eastwood never did get a part in *Francis Joins the WACs*, but he made it into *Francis Joins the Navy*.

My costar in *Francis Joins the WACs* was Donald O'Connor. Like me, he was less than thrilled over the prospect of playing opposite a talking mule. There is no record of how Francis felt about costarring with us.

The fact was, there was only one star of the Francis movies—and he ate his oats from a feedbag and would heehaw your ear off.

Francis was actually played by several mules. Some were trained to do special tricks. Others were docile enough to be given the job of working long hours on the set under hot lights. A particularly distasteful fact about the Francis films was that the animal's mouth movements, which were later matched up to Chill Wills's voice, were induced by electric shock. It was a mild shock, to be sure. But after a long day of shooting his dialogue scenes, the poor animal's eyes were rolling around looking for relief.

Donald O'Connor and I dated occasionally while we worked on the picture. But my real romance at the time was with Nicky Hilton.

Nicky and I began seeing each other regularly soon after our first date at the premiere. We went to the most exciting places in Hollywood. We often had dinner at Romanoff's, invariably greeted at the door by ''Prince'' Mike Romanoff himself and shown to the best table. We'd often see Humphrey Bogart in a booth, hunkered down over a drink, surveying the room with those world-weary eyes and smiling crookedly at Nicky and me.

One memorable night at Chasen's, the venerable eating establishment where the cognoscenti of the movie colony gathered, we were steered to Nicky's favorite booth through a veritable sea of stars. We waved toward Gary Cooper and stopped by his table to exchange a friendly hello, paused to acknowledge Betty Grable's bubbly greeting, returned Spencer Tracy's self-effacing salute, and spoke briefly with Marilyn Monroe and her friend Sydney Skolsky, the Hollywood columnist. At a center table, I caught the eye of then president of the Screen Actors Guild, Ronald Reagan. His glance followed me across the room before his attention was diverted by a sharp nudge from Nancy.

Nicky was a fun companion, although I quickly discovered that he drank too much. Once seated at one of these star-studded watering holes, he would order a drink and begin his metamorphosis. He was actually a shy man who drank to excess to overcome it. After he'd had a few he became happy and sociable—a marked contrast to his bashful, almost diffident attitude when he was sober.

At the beginning, Nicky and I didn't make love. Prior to the pill in the 1960's, having sex indiscriminately with a man was risky business. Not all men were willing to wear a condom and girls were constantly riding the edge of the danger zone.

I saw Nicky was an almost acceptable risk, but I didn't want to give in to his advances too quickly. Nicky seemed to respect that and treated me with deference during the early part of our relationship. I think he was intrigued that I was one girl that didn't instantly fall prey to the charms of the famed playboy Hilton.

After Nicky and I had been dating for just over three months, he began acting more serious about me. It had been two years since he divorced Elizabeth Taylor, and though he never spoke about her or their marriage, it was obvious he was seriously contemplating taking the plunge again.

It was at that point that he took me home to meet Conrad.

Nicky's father, Conrad Hilton, was a legend. The head and heart of the Hilton Hotel chain, he was America's most successful innkeeper. The stamp of his personality was branded on each of his hotels around the world.

Nicky decided to bring me to his father's Bel Air mansion for dinner in an attempt to win his father's approval. On the appointed evening we drove through the estate's giant iron gates and up the long, winding driveway to the ornate front of the house. It was impressive. Divorced from Nicky's mother, Conrad lived alone there in unsurpassed elegance.

Although in his seventies, Conrad was an imposing figure of a man. Tall and broad-shouldered, he made Nicky, his favorite son—there was a younger brother, Barron—look small and weak. As Conrad showed us around the mansion, pointing out the remodeling he'd had done on the poolhouse where Nicky had lived for a time, I could see how thoroughly Nicky was dominated by his father.

Conrad made a point of ignoring me. It became obvious that I was not number one on Conrad Hilton's list of prospective mates for Nicky. In fact, I wasn't even in the running.

Barron was already married to an ideal mate for the Hilton dynasty—a good Catholic girl named Marilyn, who had already produced some heirs for Conrad. We had met and done the hula next to a swimming pool full of gardenias at a party at their home in Malibu. There was a kind of role reversal between Nicky and Barron. Although Barron was the younger brother, Nicky looked up to him as the successful one, the brother who could cope with the complexities of the Hilton empire. Nicky had taken me to meet them in a sort of little-brother gesture for approval, as though I was about to become part of the family.

But Conrad was another story. The three of us ate dinner in the formal dining room. The sumptuous meal was served on gold plates by a team of quiet servants. Conrad and Nicky sat at opposite ends of the twenty-five-foot table; I sat in the middle, halfway between them. The conversation was one-sided: Conrad talked to Nicky, Nicky talked to Conrad, and Nicky talked to me. When I spoke to Conrad, he answered me through Nicky. It was as though we spoke different languages and Nicky was our interpreter.

As the multicourse meal progressed, I fell silent while Conrad and Nicky discussed family matters, the hotel business, in which Nicky was only mildly interested, and what Nicky was doing these days with his life.

I noticed that every so often a noise would erupt from Conrad's end of the table.

"So, Nicky," Conrad would say, "perhaps in a year or so, you'll get all this out of your system—"

He would suddenly stop talking and a concentrated look would come over his face.

"Burrp!" He let out a loud belch and continued talking and eating as if nothing had happened. I did a double-take when I first heard it.

"Barron, you see, has done the right thing with Marilyn—Burrrrp!—and they have the beginnings of a fine family."

"Yes, Dad."

"It's what you need . . . a family—Burrrp!"

The conversation went on like that for most of the meal. Then, as the servants cleared the table and brought glasses of port, Conrad tilted slightly in his chair. From the depths of the upholstery of Conrad's elegant chair, a deep rumbling fart issued. I'm sure my mouth dropped open, but neither Hilton paid any attention. A relaxed, satisfied look came over Conrad's face. Nicky nonchalantly lit an expensive Havana cigar.

After the dinner with Conrad, it was obvious to me that there was little future in the relationship with Nicky—not, however, only because Nicky's father didn't approve of me. My own attitude toward Nicky was ambivalent, more for his attitude toward life than anything I saw about him in the presence of his father. Nicky did not really have a job. His entire life consisted of going out every night and drinking; going to Las Vegas, gambling, and drinking; going to Europe, screwing whatever girls he could find, gambling, and drinking. I had grown up around too many hardworking people. My father was still getting up early and coming home late five and six days a week from his job as a heavy-equipment mechanic. I was doing everything I could to make something of myself in the movie business. Meanwhile, Nicky slept until noon, put in token appearances at the Hilton corporate office, and bought a new Cadillac at least once a year. If there was ever a case of being from two different worlds, it was true of Nicky and me. But I continued to see him because it was, after all, fun.

The night Nicky and I double-dated with a girlfriend of mine named Jill and an oilman friend of his named Tex, Nicky gave vent to his frustrations.

Nicky and Tex took the two of us to a party. Both of them drank heavily throughout the evening. When we left the party, Nicky suggested we all go to another party.

We went to an apartment where this "party" was supposed to take place. Nicky and Tex started acting like maniacs. Tex hustled Jill off to the bedroom. Nicky started wrestling with me on the couch. By now he was sloppily drunk and clumsily began trying to force me to have sex with him. He tore my dress before I managed to knee him right where it did the most good.

Angry and in tears, I stormed out of the apartment and headed down the street. It was only a few blocks to Sunset Boulevard, where I knew I could catch a cab home. Nicky came running after me.

"Mamie, come on back! Hey, c'mon . . ."

He grabbed my arm and I turned and aimed another kick at his balls. He dodged drunkenly.

"Hey! Watch it, Mamie!"

"Watch it yourself!" I screamed. "You and your friend are just *too* cute."

"Shhhh! Don't make so much noise. Hell, we just wanted to have a little fun."

It was after two A.M. and lights started coming on in the darkened neighborhood. Nicky began to sober up quickly. I stalked off toward Sunset again. He ran after me, carefully staying out of kicking range.

"I'm sorry, Mamie. Really. That was a dumb thing for me to do."

"You're damn right it was!"

"Please don't shout. Don't go like this, okay? Let me take you home."

I stopped and turned to him.

"Nicky, you're a very spoiled man. You're so selfish you don't just ignore how other people feel, you're unconscious of it." I pulled at the top of my torn dress. "All this tough-guy act and fake-party stuff doesn't make it with me. Understand?"

He nodded contritely.

"I'll buy you a new dress."

As we walked back to his car, Jill began screaming from inside the apartment. She was nearly in hysterics and refused to be driven home in the same car with Tex. After we quieted Jill down, Tex ended up staying at the apartment while Nicky drove Jill and me home.

The next day Nicky sent flowers and called me on the phone.

"I was blind drunk, Mamie. Could we please try again?"

"Look, Nicky, you and I both know that last night's little performance was brought on by our dinner with your father."

"Now, listen—"

"*You* listen. Your father said something to you like: 'Son, you don't have to marry her to go to bed with her.' And I'll tell you something, Nicky, he's right. Only not for the reasons he thinks. I just don't see any reason why a woman shouldn't have the same rights as a man when it comes to playing the field.

"I like you or I wouldn't have continued seeing you after the premiere. We've had a lot of fun. We could have a lot more and let the marriage part of it take care of itself. But I'm not going to be strong-armed into bed or marriage or anything else by force or the Hilton fortune."

I was out of breath. I hadn't planned to do a lecture on my philosophy of life. In fact, I hadn't even thought it through before I said it.

"I understand, Mamie," Nicky said quietly.

"Then call me back when you decide what *you* want to do."

I'd no sooner hung up and walked away from the phone than it rang again.

"I've decided," Nicky said. "In a few days I'm moving into a new apartment. I just had it redecorated. When I get settled, why don't you come see it and we'll start over. Okay?"

"Okay."

While I was shooting *Francis Joins the WACs,* it was difficult for me to find time for dating Nicky. The shooting schedule was like any other motion picture—grueling. When I finally did visit Nicky's new apartment, it was a shocker. The decorator must have put everything in it he couldn't sell anywhere else. It had so many 1950's gauche furnishings that you could hardly find a place to sit down. Nicky's pride and joy was an enormous black-and-white television set (color was still a couple of years away) in his bedroom. Often we would spend hours lying in bed watching TV instead of going out.

It was on one of these nights that Nicky and I first made love. We sipped champagne and cuddled closer together. Finally Nicky turned off the bedside lamp and we made love in the flickering bluish light from the TV set.

Nicky was generously endowed as a lover. But there was a sadness about having sex with him. He tried to please, but there was an artificial energy about his lovemaking that came from his constant overindulgence in alcohol. From the first, I felt there was something missing. As we lay in his big bed afterward, Nicky seemed to withdraw into himself. He would hardly look at me.

After a few more nights of sex, it was plain that Nicky had the curse of so many alcoholics: he had virtually no interest in sex. What interest he had was effectively blocked by the effects of huge quantities of booze. And the nights he couldn't get it up because of drinking only made him drink more to drown the guilt.

We continued to see each other as often as my schedule allowed. Nicky was, in public at least, a genial and entertaining date. Often we attended some social event where we were photographed by the newspapers and fan magazines. At those times Nicky seemed at ease. He enjoyed being seen and photographed with me. Moreover, he seemed to thrive on the attentions of the acquaintances of his who would invariably stop by the table for a drink or two when we were out together. A party was what Nicky liked best, and the more people the merrier. There were times I was virtually falling asleep late at night while still another group of hangers-on drifted over to chat with the infamous Hilton playboy.

At home alone, however, lying alongside him in bed in front of that big TV, I felt that I was in the company of someone only half there.

In the end, I concluded that Nicky liked himself very little. However much money he was an heir to from his father's empire, the demands of that giant business concern were simply too great for Nicky. It might have been an advantageous marriage to make if I had been the kind of woman that married for money, and if I were willing to drop my career and become a professional wife. I'm sure I could have guided the situation to that end. But that has never been my style. And I wasn't willing to give up my career.

Chapter Eleven

While I was still dating Nicky Hilton, I began seeing a handsome young dance teacher named Dwayne Ratliff that U.I. hired to give private lessons to the actors and actresses. I wanted to develop my dancing skills, and having a dark, good-looking guy like Dwayne as a teacher made it that much more fun. He taught our lessons in a big, shadowy soundstage on the U.I. lot.

During that time I was very frustrated in my relationship with Nicky. What sex Nicky and I had was often somber and forced. Dwayne, on the other hand, was strong, virile, and happy-go-lucky. Unfortunately, he shared a little house in Hollywood with a live-in girlfriend. Consequently we could never go there to make love.

I always scheduled my lesson for late afternoon, doubling the usual one hour most of the others took. Afterward we'd find the darkest drive-in theater in the Valley and make love in the spacious comfort of his Cadillac. What a sight it must have been to the other moviegoers (if they looked up long enough from their own adventures) to see that big Caddy bouncing in the front row. But it provided an outlet for the unspent energies of my partially satisfied sex drive.

I'd finished *Francis Joins the WACs* and had been on hiatus for a couple of weeks when Jimmy McHugh phoned. He was out of the hospital and acting like he was interested in managing my career again.

"U.I. has a script they want you to star in, Mamie," McHugh said, sounding stronger than he had in a long time. "It's called *Third Girl from the Right*. It's being produced by a new guy on the lot, Sam Marx."

"What kind of movie is it?"

"Well, you won't have to work with a mule, that's for sure. According to Bob Palmer, this is U.I.'s answer to MGM's musicals. It's a story about a dancer who falls in love with a rich guy. Singing, dancing, big production numbers, lavish sets. They're going to test you and a few other girls in about a week. Are you still taking ballet from that guy . . . Radcliff?"

"Ratliff. Dwayne Ratliff. Yes," I answered, smiling inwardly.

"Stop by Marx's office and pick up a script, Mamie. You'll have to go to work on the scene they want you to test."

A few days later I was taking a lesson with Dwayne at the studio when he began to complain he wasn't feeling well.

"I think I'm coming down with the flu or something, Mamie," he said. "I ache all over and I feel sick. Feel my forehead. Have I got a fever?"

His skin felt warm to my touch and I suggested we cut the lesson short.

The pianist who played for the lessons had a house on the hill overlooking Universal just five minutes away and I took Dwayne there to let him rest for a while. When we arrived, his arms and legs began to cramp painfully. He cried out in agony as his muscles twitched and knotted. Like a flower withering in the heat, he began to curl up before my eyes, his hands and feet bent hideously out of shape.

I got him into a bathtub of warm water to relax the cramps. It gave him a little relief, but his overall condition worsened. His breathing became labored, each breath a deep, rattling struggle.

I half-carried Dwayne to my car and rushed him to Hollywood Hospital. By the time I got there, his fine strong body was twisted into a fetal position.

Dwayne was diagnosed as having polio. He was placed in an iron lung to assist his breathing. The doctor told me if

Dwayne had had an attack this violent when he was alone, he would've likely died. The doctor also said that I should be tested for the polio virus, since I had been in close contact with him.

I was panicked. This was 1954. Dr. Jonas Salk had only begun experimenting with his life-saving vaccine. Every year from summer to fall people lived in terror of the dreaded virus that left its victims crippled or dead. And the newspapers had been full of headlines this year about the worst polio epidemic in history.

I telephoned Jimmy McHugh right away. Jimmy had been head of the local polio foundation and was well-regarded by all the best experts in the field. He put me in touch with a specialist to give me the polio test. The test itself was painful and frightening. Using a spinal tap, they drew off a quantity of spinal fluid which could then be tested for presence of the virus.

The results of the test were negative. But for days afterward, as a side effect of the spinal tap, I was sick and had to stay in bed. I lost valuable rehearsal time for my upcoming screen test for *Third Girl from the Right*.

When the day came for the screen test, I was still weak from the experience with Dwayne. I had finally managed to squeeze in enough rehearsal for the test, but my energy level was down and it showed.

While I landed a part in *Third Girl from the Right*, the leading role of Sarah went to Piper Laurie. I won the part of Jackie, one of the supporting roles. It was a mystifying choice in some ways. Piper was (and still is) a fine dramatic actress, but she is not primarily a song-and-dance performer. My first role for Universal, in *Forbidden*, was as a singer, and my dancing was well-respected around the lot. Kenny Williams, U.I.'s dance director, had been instrumental in my getting a contract at Universal. Plus, at that moment, I was in the news constantly, much more than Piper. In fact, when the film was released, many posters for it did not show Piper at all, but instead featured me dancing in the front row as though I was the lead. I was deeply disappointed.

I blamed myself. I did not feel well enough when I did the screen test.

For the first time I seriously questioned the type of roles

Universal International management was arranging for me. All my roles so far, including Jackie in *Third Girl*, were dumb blondes. I wanted to play something else.

In the real world there must be as many dumb brunettes and dumb redheads as there are dumb blondes. But in the story lines of most movies, the perky little brunette is the smart one, and her blonde girlfriend is the boy-crazy scatter-brain.

Any actress worth her salt wants to play more than just one kind of role. Especially when the role is too often a stereotype. I wanted more for the characters I'd played. Susie Ward, the little waitress from the wrong side of the tracks I played in *The All American*, was a bit more than the stereotypical blonde. She was both wise and a hard worker. But she didn't get the guy in the final reel—Lori Nelson, the brunette, did. (My role had originally been written as a *bad* girl. When the producer, Aaron Rosenberg, and the director, old cop-a-feel Hibbs, saw the depth that I brought to the character, they had it rewritten to make her a good girl *almost* going bad. She ends up saving the day—the home team wins the big football game and the players carry Susie off on their shoulders.)

The character of Lilith the slave girl in *Yankee Pasha* was cute, chatty, blonde, and funny, but *not* an intellectual giant. My character, Corporal Bunky, in *Francis Joins the WACs* was of the same mold, as was Jackie in *Third Girl*. A pattern had been set, and though I was working steadily, I was not happy with the roles I was landing.

As we worked on *Third Girl from the Right* (which would be released as *Ain't Misbehavin'*), my romance with Nicky Hilton finally fizzled completely. My occasional dates with other men were severely limited by *Third Girl's* shooting schedule.

A friend of mine named Bob Francis, who was also a student of acting coaches Benno and Batami Schneider, and a contract player at Columbia, called me one morning to ask if I would like to go out with a friend of his. Bob and I had been buddies since we met one day at the Schneiders'; we used to meet for an occasional lunch or run into each other at parties. Neither of us had any idea his call would change my life forever.

"He's a very famous guy. They call him the 'Million Dollar Bandleader.' And he looks like a miniature Cary Grant. Let's have dinner together. Just the three of us.''

"Well . . .''

"I'm not asking you to marry him, Mamie. Just have dinner.''

"Okay, I'll go. What's his name?''

"Ray Anthony.''

Ray Anthony turned out to be a fascinating man. He was extremely funny and kept Bob and me in stitches. And we found we both shared a love of music and a common background—the Midwest. He told me that he was in town having a discussion with Twentieth Century-Fox about doing a role in an upcoming Fred Astaire movie, *Daddy Long Legs*. Sometime during the evening, I remember thinking: Now, this is a guy I could really go for.

The evening ended early. Ray had to go back on the road again and was leaving first thing in the morning and Bob had an early date to go flying.

"I love flying," Bob enthusiastically told us over the dessert. "Every time I land, I can't wait to get back up there.''

When I got to the studio the next day, I was met by the tragic news that Bob Francis had been killed that morning in a plane crash. His plane went down not far from our house in the San Fernando Valley. He died in the midst of a blossoming career, including a part in *The Caine Mutiny* with Humphrey Bogart. I was distraught over the loss of a good friend.

A day or two later Ray Anthony called and we commiserated over Bob's death. Ray and I both felt that we had found something special together during the course of our dinner. We made a date for the next time he was back in L.A., which, it turned out, would be soon, since he had gotten the role in *Daddy Long Legs*.

While Ray was on the road, I found myself suddenly without any desire to date anyone else. There was little time for dating anyway with the filming of *Third Girl* in full swing. But even the occasional contract player on the lot—and there *were* some good-looking ones—failed to ignite as much of a spark as Ray Anthony.

Nonetheless, the studio imported someone just for a day

who could have, under different circumstances, been a contender.

The publicity department called me one day when I wasn't scheduled to work.

"Get over here right away, Mamie! We've got a prince that's dying to meet you!"

When I got to the soundstage where *Third Girl* was being shot, one corner was crammed with studio execs, starlets, photographers, security men, and gawkers. Piper Laurie was there along with other members of the cast. In the center of it all was a tall, distinguished man who looked ill-at-ease in all the commotion.

His name, I discovered as I was introduced to him, was His Royal Highness, Prince Axel of Denmark. He smiled down at me from a great height. And I noticed his eyes were a deep, dreamy blue. He bent and kissed my hand. Flashbulbs popped everywhere.

"Miss Van Doren, so great is the pleasure to meet you," he said in broken English.

"The pleasure is mine, your highness," I replied.

"Please forgive my bad English."

"Your English is wonderful. Much better than my Danish."

He laughed and squeezed my hand.

"I speak a little Swedish," I went on. "My mother and father are Swedes." He listened as I demonstrated that I could count from one to ten in Swedish.

The prince laughed delightedly. He pointed to a short, dumpy man standing nearby.

"He will understand you. He is the Swedish ambassador." Some of the studio executives elbowed their way in and began babbling at the prince while his male secretary translated. The prince replied to them in Danish through his secretary.

The reception for the prince went on interminably. People jostled to get close to him, but he always managed to maneuver so that he remained by my side.

I was beginning to wonder how I could gracefully get away from all this, when I felt a persistent tug on my arm, and found myself gently pulled backward through the crowd and out a side door of the soundstage.

I looked up into the face of Prince Axel. His secretary was standing with us.

"His highness is hungry," the young man said simply.

"Mamie," Prince Axel said, "is there a place where we could get a good American corned-beef sandwich and a bottle of beer?"

"Of course," I answered. "The commissary."

His secretary stayed behind. I led the tall prince to U.I.'s commissary, where we sat on the back stools of the lunch counter. It was late for lunch and there was almost no one there.

While we waited for the food, he said, "These affairs are so dull, I find."

"Yes, I understand," I said. "Hungry work."

He took a moment to think about my idiomatic English, then nodded. "Yes, yes. Work that makes hungry."

The prince wolfed down his corned beef on rye, liberally slathered with mustard, and drank a bottle of beer.

"Ah," he sighed as he chewed the last bite of his sandwich. "Only in America can you find such corned-beef sandwiches. But in Denmark, we make much better beer."

Just then a chorus of voices came from the front of the commissary.

"There he is! We've found him!"

The prince smiled sweetly at me. "Mamie, this has been so pleasant, having lunch with you."

"I've enjoyed it too, your highness."

"Please call me Axel. Will you come to Denmark and visit me sometime?"

"Why . . . yes, of course."

"Good."

His secretary rushed to him with an apologetic look in his eyes. The prince said something in reassurance to him. He leaned down and kissed my hand and turned to join the crowd again.

It was not the last I heard of Prince Axel.

Several weeks later, I received an invitation through the studio to perform at a benefit for a crippled children's foundation in Denmark as the special guest of Prince Axel. I was to be his guest and stay at the palace.

It was a temptation. But I was in love with Ray Anthony.

The studio was willing to provide my wardrobe and give me the time off to go, even though by then I was shooting my next picture, *The Second Greatest Sex*. But I declined.

Before Christmas of that year, I received another invitation from Prince Axel to celebrate the Yuletide at the Danish royal palace. Once more I declined.

There was a third invitation sometime the following spring, but I was far too preoccupied by then to go. I never heard from Prince Axel again.

When Ray got back into town after a couple weeks touring in the Midwest, he began work on his first movie role as the bandleader in *Daddy Long Legs*. The plot revolves around a rich older man, played by Fred Astaire, who falls in love with Leslie Caron, a young European student. Fred Astaire and Leslie Caron dance elegantly around a college gym to the strains of "Something's Gotta Give," played by Ray and his orchestra. The song went on to become one of Ray's many big hits.

Ray loathed the idea of playing himself in the film. He had real ambitions of getting established as an actor. Even though he was constantly after his agency, MCA, to get him cast in dramatic roles, he only managed to play small parts as musicians and bandleaders.

We began going out every night. We hit all the L.A. nightspots: Ciro's, Mocambo, Chasen's. We had plenty of things to talk about, but there were silences too—times when we just looked into each other's eyes in a gaze that spoke more eloquently than words about how we felt about each other.

Being out on the town every night took its toll on me. Where Ray found the energy, I'll never know. Getting into bed to sleep a couple hours before racing to work at five A.M. put dark rings under my eyes and made every movement an effort. I was afraid that the studio executives who saw the rushes every day would call me on the carpet for looking so tired on-camera. I told Ray that we had to get in at a decent hour so I could get some rest.

Life with Ray was a dream. He was handsome, charming, and witty; he was urbane, while being down-to-earth; and he was a snappy dresser, though I felt his color combinations were a little gaudy.

Most of all he was sexy.

During the next few weeks I found myself walking around the U.I. lot singing to myself. It was an extremely happy time for me.

I should have been looking over my shoulder.

One day I was called into the office of one of U.I.'s top executives. A summons like that was a sure sign of trouble.

"I shouldn't even be telling you this, Mamie," the U.I. executive said in a low voice. He had shut the door of the office and it was quiet as a tomb. "This is *strictly* unofficial."

"What's the matter?" I asked.

"You can't go on seeing a married man."

"A married man? Who?"

"Who? Don't you know? Ray Anthony."

I was stunned. "His wife's back East. They're separated."

"Only by the miles, Mamie."

"He told me that he's getting a divorce," I said defensively.

"Unfortunately, he hasn't told her. She's seen the newspaper photographs back there and she's threatening to make trouble. Big trouble."

"God, I had no idea . . ."

The studio executive smiled benignly. "I didn't think you did."

Suddenly my head was spinning. I couldn't make myself think clearly. I was furious with Ray for not telling me the truth, furious with myself for believing him, and furious with the studio for meddling in my private life.

"The next time we talk about this subject, Mamie, it'll be official. And if there's a reason for the next time, the studio will be giving you your release. U.I. can't afford this kind of publicity."

"I understand," I said morosely. I walked to the door and turned. "Is that all?"

"You love him, Mamie?"

I nodded.

"Tell him to announce that he's divorcing his wife. Don't be seen around town together for a couple of weeks. The studio will have no quarrel with that."

I brightened a little. "Okay."

* * *

When I got home that afternoon, Ray was on the phone with my mother.

"Here she is now, Ray, just coming in the door," Mother said. She handed me the receiver.

"Ray, why didn't you tell me that you were not legally separated from your wife?" My voice was raspy with anger.

"Well, we're separated, Mamie," Ray answered, obviously surprised by the tone in my voice. "I'm out here and she's in New York."

"But *legally?*"

"I've told you before, honey. We've been having problems for a while. It's gotten to the stage that we're arguing over a settlement. I've been so busy working that I'm just now getting around to the legalities of the situation. What's wrong?"

"The studio doesn't want me to continue seeing you until you get a divorce from your wife."

"What business is it of theirs?"

"They put a morals clause in all our contracts. They'll drop me if we continue seeing each other while you're married. They say your wife wants to make trouble."

Ray sighed heavily. "We aren't doing anything wrong, Mamie. I *am* separated."

"I believe you. But we need to do something to make the studio happy."

"I know just what to do. I've got a good P.R. man who'll know what to say. I'll have him put out a statement that my wife and I are legally separated and that I'm going to Mexico for a quickie divorce."

"If you say that, the studio'll be watching to make sure you do it."

"Let 'em watch. I'll do it."

"You will?"

"I finish shooting *Daddy Long Legs* in just a few days and I have to leave with the band for another short tour. When I get back in a couple of weeks, I'll fly to Mexico and get the divorce. Then I'll fly back, you meet me at the airport, and we'll take the next flight out to Hawaii. How's that sound?"

"It sounds great. I love you!"

* * *

Before Ray got back from his tour, I received a phone call from Louella Parsons.

It took a moment for me to recover when I answered the phone. What could the Great Bitch want from me?

"Louella, how good to hear from you."

"I just saw the previews of your last picture. You look absolutely darling with that donkey."

I kept my voice sweetly modulated. "What a lovely thing to say. Francis sends his regards." *To a fellow ass,* I thought.

Louella managed a laugh. "Cute. Very cute." She cleared her throat and changed the subject.

"Mamie, I'll get right to the point. Is it true that you're going to marry Ray Anthony as soon as he gets a Mexican divorce from his wife?"

This was too good an opportunity to let pass.

"Well, I don't know," I said coyly.

"His press people released a statement to that effect more than a week ago. Unfortunately, Ray's out of town on tour with his band and I can't reach him."

"Things will just have to work themselves out, Louella. Musicians sometimes do wild and crazy things. But, of course, I don't need to tell you that."

Silence.

"Mamie, since this announcement comes directly from Ray's publicist, I take it that you two are about to set a date. Correct?"

"Louella, I really can't say any more at present. I'm sure you understand the position it puts me in."

"Of course, dear. Does this mean that Ray will not be seen around town in the company of an assortment of glamour girls like he has in the past?"

"I'm sure that Ray will make the right choice. Louella, I really must run now. I've enjoyed talking with you."

"You too, darling. 'Bye."

I hung up the phone and started looking for Hedda Hopper's number.

"What the hell did you think you were doing?" Sam Israel screamed. "Giving Hedda an exclusive on your engagement to Ray Anthony! Good Christ, Mamie! Do you have any idea how mad Louella is?"

Sam stopped yelling and chain-smoked while he glowered at me across his desk. Sam had replaced Al Horowitz as U.I.'s head of public relations. Before Horowitz was fired, Sam had worked for Louella Parsons. Now Sam had the hot-seat job at U.I. It looked like it was already taking a toll on him. Sam was a gray man—hair, eyes, skin, suits.

"She couldn't hate me any more than she did before," I countered.

"Wanna bet?" he snapped. "She calls you and tries to make nice and what do you do? Turn around and stab her in the back!"

"Is telling me I look nice with a donkey making nice?"

"At least she was looking at you for a change." He lit a fresh cigarette and crushed out the stub of the last one. "Mamie, I'm not going to argue with you. I'll do what I can to patch up the damage you've done. Incidentally, Hedda wants to do an interview with you for the Sunday L.A. *Times.*"

The damage turned out to be very little. If Louella's animosity didn't lessen, at least it didn't get any worse. And my little exclusive cemented a good relationship with Louella's arch rival, Hedda Hopper, who wrote about me more and more over the years and was as unfailingly nice to me as Louella was unpleasant.

Ray got back into town and immediately flew to Mexico for his divorce. When he came back, I was waiting for him at the airport, along with most of the L.A. working press. We posed for pictures. Soon the papers were plastered with stories about the "Young Man with the Golden Horn" and the "Platinum Girl" setting a date to tie the knot.

The week he got back from his tour we cut our evening short and went to his suite at the elegant Sunset Towers Hotel overlooking Sunset Boulevard. A sort of apartment hotel, the Sunset Towers was one of the "in" places to stay in Hollywood if you had achieved celebrity status but were footloose or felt that buying a house was too bourgeois. Ray took me in his arms and pulled me close. Our own ragged breathing was the only sound in the apartment over the noise of the traffic far below on Sunset. Soon we had undressed each other, and our naked flesh touched. A tingling of electricity coursed through my body. I had never wanted a man with such intensity. We threw ourselves on each other in an explosion of passion.

I was not disappointed. Ray was that combination that every woman looks for: aggressive but gentle, ardent but cool, devastatingly skilled, and handsomely equipped. I lay cradled in Ray's arms after a series of soul-shattering climaxes, and we slept like tired children.

One of our favorite places to make love was Palm Springs. We would often spend the weekend there at a small, secluded hotel. The desert sun multiplied the heat of our supercharged relationship.

One warm Saturday morning we sped down Foothill Boulevard toward Palm Springs in Ray's Cadillac convertible, we feasted on Italian bread, salami, and cheese and sipped at a bottle of wine. Ray kept one hand on the wheel and one hand on me while we alternately ate, drank, and kissed. Finally so aroused that we couldn't stand it a moment longer, we began looking for a secluded spot. The little towns on the way were all surrounded by miles of thick orange groves, and we found a turnoff in a deserted area. Ray drove down the little dirt track and parked so we were not visible from the road. For modesty's sake he put the top up and we made love in the midday heat amid the smell of orange blossoms and the sound of buzzing bees.

Just when my personal life was back on track, an old problem reared its head again in my professional life. The studio casting office had several scripts for which I was being considered, but their calls to Jimmy McHugh were not returned. They were at a loss about how to deal with me.

Ray was an astute businessman who ran his career with the kind of calm assurance I wished I had. I turned to Ray with the McHugh problem and asked his advice.

"Why don't you set up a meeting with him?" he asked. "Let's sit down and talk and see what he's got in mind for you."

We met Jimmy at his house on a Sunday afternoon. McHugh was impressed with Ray's musicianship. Ray was, of course, impressed by Jimmy's songwriting ability. Ray mentioned that he might like to record some songs of Jimmy's. Jimmy replied enthusiastically that there was nothing he'd like better.

The talk ranged over a variety of subjects, in and out of show business. Ray expressed his own desire to act in more movies and he gently probed McHugh for any plans he might have for my career.

Jimmy was vague. He told Ray that he'd been in poor health for some time with a heart condition, even though today he looked in ruddy good health, lounging by the pool, sipping champagne. He hinted that it was my fault I'd been turned down by a number of studios for loan-outs. He made it sound like advancing my career was generally a hard sell.

McHugh excused himself and went into the house. He came out carrying a handful of pictures. He handed them to Ray.

"Take a look at these," McHugh said. They were pictures of me, taken a bit over two years ago, not long before I got my U.I. contract. They were clumsily posed because I didn't know how then. My makeup and hair were overdone because I had yet to be taught the tricks of the trade by the great makeup men like the Westmores. They were not bad pictures. They were pictures of a girl trying to be someone.

"She was nothing before she met me," McHugh went on. "I made her what she is today."

Ray looked at the pictures silently. A muscle twitched along his jaw as he handed them back to Jimmy.

"She looks good to me," Ray said proudly, trying to help cover my embarrassment.

We left shortly afterward and I cried a little in the car.

"Don't worry, Mamie," Ray said, putting his arm around me tenderly. "I think he's jealous that your career is really taking off without his help."

"In spite of him. And Louella. What do you think I should do, Ray?"

"I think if there's any way you can do it, you should get out of your contract with him."

The next day I called a man that had befriended me when I was just sixteen, one of Hollywood's most high-powered lawyers—Jerry Geisler.

"How long has it been, Joan? Or should I say: Mamie?" Jerry's smooth voice drifted quietly across his dark office.

"Whatever you're comfortable with, Jerry," I replied. Jerry Geisler did not invite loud talk. The famed trial lawyer whose clients included Errol Flynn and Charlie Chaplin had all the presence of a great stage actor. And like all great trial lawyers, a great actor is precisely what he was. His slow, soft manner of speaking made every word he spoke seem important. Yet his rich voice was never so subdued that a word was missed—unless that was what he intended. You found yourself hanging on every syllable.

"I'm very comfortable with your new name. Mamie is who you are now. But there's still a trace of that brash young kid who talked her way into my office five years ago. How is your mother?"

Five years before, shortly after I had returned from New York, my mother had been critically injured when a drunk woman ran a red light and broadsided my parents' car. Mother nearly died. When she was out of danger, it became clear that there would be a serious shortage of money to pay the hospital bills. My dad started looking for a lawyer to sue the woman who hit them. I read in the newspapers that Jerry Geisler was the best lawyer in Los Angeles, and I told my dad that he was the one who should represent us. I went to Geisler's office and managed to get in to see him. Because of a streak of kindness a mile wide, Jerry took our case. And won it big.

"She's fine now, Jerry. They owe everything they have to you."

"I was paid for it."

"But nobody else could've gotten the settlement you got. And you certainly didn't have to take the case. The percentage you made off the settlement was nothing to you."

"I took the case because I liked you. You were a kid with guts. You needed a better lawyer than you could afford. Anyway"—he shifted in his chair and folded his hands on his desk—"what can I do for you now?"

I explained the situation with Jimmy McHugh. Jerry watched me through eyes squinted down to slits. It was a habit of his, part of his flawless courtroom technique. He would watch through those narrowed eyes with the air of someone who knows more about what you're saying than you suspect. Occasionally he would disconcertingly widen his eyes, piercing you with their azure sparkle. It was as if someone shone a flashlight in your face. Occasionally he stopped me to ask a question.

I handed him my contract with McHugh. He glanced at it and turned his attention back to me.

There was a long silence before Jerry spoke.

"Okay, Mamie," he said at last. "Let me look into your friend McHugh. I'll call you tomorrow afternoon and let you know what I find out."

"Thanks, Jerry."

When he rose to show me out of his office, I realized that while he was still a large, imposing figure of a man, Jerry Geisler was getting older. There was a slowness in his step that hadn't been there before. He touched my arm gently at the office door.

"How's this Ray Anthony treating you, honey?" Only a consummate actor like Geisler could put both fatherly concern and lecherous irony in that simple question.

"Not as good as you could, Jerry." I reached up and kissed him. There had never been anything more physical than that between Jerry and me, but it pleased both of us to kid and tease that there might have been. Perhaps if our ages had been a little closer together, there would have been.

He grinned and patted my arm. "I'll call you tomorrow."

Jerry got a hold of me late the next day at the studio. He said simply, "You no longer have a contract with Jimmy McHugh."

"Just like that?" I asked, surprised.

"Yes. Very simple." Jerry's voice turned professionally deliberate. "It turns out that Mr. McHugh is not registered as an artists' manager with the state of California. Consequently, the contract he has with you is worthless. Also, I noted that you were legally a minor as of the date you signed this contract and your parents did not sign it with you. I repeat: the contract is worthless."

"Jerry, you are truly wonderful."

"I consider that a very great compliment, Miss Mamie Van Doren."

"What do I do now? Do we have to go to court?"

"We do nothing. I sent a letter by messenger to Mr. McHugh this morning advising him that you are no longer under contract to him for managerial services. I hinted that if he would like to contest the matter, he could be assured of a very dicey time of it in court. Fraudulently representing himself to a minor as an artists' manager might look pretty bad in all the papers. Simply put, Mamie, I don't think he'll make a fuss.''

"Thank you, Jerry. Okay, I'm braced. How much is your fee for this?''

"Oh, it's going to be very steep, I'm afraid. This one will really cost you. How about dinner with you and that handsome trumpet player of yours?''

"You're on. Bring Ruth, of course.'' Ruth was Jerry's wife of many years. She had given him a son and a daughter late in his life.

"It's a date.''

I gave Ray a call and told him the news. Then I walked out onto the U.I. lot and looked around. There was, as always, a considerable amount of activity up and down the streets. Grips moved heavy loads of props, and gaffers rolled thickets of light stands in and out of soundstages.

There was no denying that Jimmy McHugh had helped put me here, just over two years ago. I really was, at least in part, what Jimmy had made me. And I had tried very hard to be what he said I should be. But unlike Eliza Doolittle, I did not earn the respect and affection of my Henry Higgins. In the end, in front of the man I loved, all Jimmy McHugh could manage was gloating scorn over his creation. But then Eliza and Higgins were created by George Bernard Shaw; McHugh and I were both created by Hollywood.

Chapter Twelve

Ray and I had been totally preoccupied with each other on our Hawaiian holiday. On the long flight over, passengers slept in Pullman-like berths. After dinner I slipped into a filmy nightgown and Ray climbed through the curtain and initiated me into the mile-high club. We woke to a champagne breakfast the next morning and watched the deep green Hawaiian Islands come into view as the airplane's shadow raced over the water.

Once in the islands, we were constantly hugging and nuzzling. We would no sooner settle down on the famous beach at Waikiki than we started kissing and we'd have to hurry back to our room and get it out of our systems again. No matter where we went, it seemed, there were photographers and reporters dogging our trail. It was a serious state of affairs for a couple newly and passionately in love. We found ourselves gobbling down our food and hurrying away to avoid what had become a constant annoyance.

Nonetheless, our Hawaiian idyll was all too short. Ray had to return to the mainland for the premiere of *Daddy Long Legs,* and there was another script waiting for me at U.I.

Shortly after we returned, Sam Israel called me into his office. I thought I was probably in for another chewing-out about Louella.

"Mamie, we have a very serious problem," he began.

What now? I thought.

"Mamie, *Confidential* magazine is about to print a story saying that you and your mother were prostitutes. The story is scheduled to break in their next issue."

I sat in stunned silence. When I found my voice, I had to keep it carefully under control. "That's a filthy lie."

"Only the top two men here at the studio and I know about this. I can tell you they are in a panic. You realize what this could mean to the studio if it gets printed?"

His hand shook as he put out his cigarette. I suddenly realized how frightened he was.

"Mr. Israel, that magazine is about to ruin me and my mother. Not only my career, but our good name is on the line. You and the others know this is a malicious lie."

"Mamie, of course we know it is."

"Is the studio going to stand behind me if they print the story?"

Sam remained silent.

"Or are you going to throw me to the wolves?"

"We're not going to throw you to the wolves, Mamie. We just have to . . . wait and see what happens. Someone's got it in for you. In the worst way. Our people are going to work on it from this end."

"How?" I asked.

"At this moment, I don't know."

I was so angry that the blood was pounding in my head.

"I'm going home. I need to talk to my mother. Somehow we've got to stop this."

When I broke the news to my mother, she went to pieces.

"Oh, Jo," she said through her tears. "What an awful thing! Who would tell such a horrible lie?"

"I don't know, but I know who to call to help us."

I dialed Jerry Geisler's number. His answering service informed me he was out of town. I told them it was an emergency and to have him call me no matter what time he got back.

Mother and I spent a sleepless night. I thought about how hard I had worked to get my career started. Now someone was attempting to sabotage me. If the story got out, my career was finished. Even if *Confidential* printed a retraction later— even if I got denials in every newspaper in the world—the tarnish to my reputation would never go away. And the pain it would inflict on my mother was unthinkable.

The next morning Jerry Geisler returned my call. When I explained the situation to him, even Jerry was shocked by the virulence of the attack. He said he would look into it and call me back.

It could have been no more than an hour or two before the phone rang again.

"Mamie," Jerry Geisler said, "tell your mother to go back to bed and get some sleep. The story's been pulled."

I told Mother and we both burst into tears again.

"Thanks, Jerry," I said when I was under control. "What happened?"

"It was all very simple. I got ahold of the publisher of *Confidential* and told him that he'd better have irrefutable proof of that story he was going to print about you, because if he printed it, he was going to get an opportunity to use it in court. And if he didn't prove it, which he knew and I knew he couldn't, I promised that I would first close him down, and then slap him with a judgment so large that you and your mother would be the new owners of *Confidential*."

"But they didn't come up with this story all by themselves, did they?"

"No. There was a source for the story."

"Who?"

"Mamie, it won't serve any purpose for you to know who it was."

"Jerry, who was it? Knowing could be protection for me."

Geisler hesitated a moment. "I guess you're right." He told me who it was. "Now that you know, don't go looking for revenge."

"No revenge, Jerry. I promise."

In April 1955, still tanned from our Hawaiian vacation, Ray and I went to the premiere of *Daddy Long Legs*. The crowds screamed and waved at me as we got out of our car. Ray was chagrined over the fact that he did not have a leading role in *Daddy Long Legs*. And I think the fans screaming for me planted a seed of jealousy in him.

Jealousy too often plays a part in show-business marriages. His career is down, hers is up. Hers starts to decline, his becomes ascendant. The pride and ego and selfishness that no one likes to admit to eventually surface. All too often the support that married couples outside of show business give each other goes out the window when he and she have stars on their dressing rooms. Later I would discover that I was not immune to such jealousy myself.

Ray and I weren't married, of course, though he had asked me. While it seemed like a good idea, still I hesitated. U.I. would surely not be happy. A career as a sex symbol is harder to build if the star is a married woman. So when Ray asked me, I put him off. After all, there was plenty of time for marriage. In the meantime, we were in love and having a wonderful time.

In May 1955 I went to work on my next picture, *The Second Greatest Sex*, a musical adaptation of Aristophanes' *Lysistrata* set in the Old West. Starring with me were Bert Lahr, Jeanne Crain, George Nader, and Keith Andes. True to form, I played a dumb little country blonde named Birdie Schneider who was in love with the town preacher, Keith Andes. As in Aristophanes' original plot line, the women withhold sex until the men stop fighting a war—in this case, a feud with a neighboring town.

As I began filming I did not feel well when I came to work in the mornings, though I wasn't sure why. I was a couple weeks late with my period, but I didn't think too much of it. I started bleeding on the set and went immediately to see my family physician, Dr. Wesley Wright. It turned out I had been pregnant. The blood was due to the fact that I'd had a miscarriage.

The miscarriage itself did not leave a lasting impression on me. But afterward, the potential consequences of the pregnancy frightened me. Pregnancy, even more than marriage, and particularly pregnancy *without* marriage, was a surefire way to screw up one's future at U.I. I couldn't afford it. Ray would have to do what my other lovers had done—wear a rubber.

When I first discovered the joys of sex, after my marriage to Jack Newman, I read up on pregnancy and diseases. And I learned about rubbers. Unfortunately, most of the men I encountered didn't want to use them, so they didn't carry them.

"C'mon, baby, I don't have one, but it'll be all right. I promise," was a too-common theme in my love life.

Right. An easy promise to make, and just as easy to break. The consequences were not the man's, but the woman's. Nine months of pregnancy and how many years of rearing a child? And too often the man was nowhere to be found.

So I started carrying my own rubbers.

I'll never forget one of the first times I went into a drugstore to buy rubbers before a date with Ray. I put on a makeshift disguise of sunglasses and a scarf so that no one would recognize me.

Inside the drugstore I took a deep breath and squared my shoulders.

"I'd like to buy a gross of rubbers," I said to the druggist boldly. Of course, for all my worldliness, I wasn't sure how many a gross was.

The druggist did a double-take. "You want a what?"

"I'd like a gross of rubbers, please."

"Oh, would you now?" He looked me over carefully. I was afraid for a moment he would recognize me. "Think it's going to rain, girlie?"

I smiled at him innocently. "Look, mister, they're not for me, they're for my older brother, okay? He sent me to buy him a gross of rubbers."

The druggist shrugged and reached under the counter. He came out with what looked like a large cigar box. "Is this how many you want? That's a gross—exactly one hundred and forty-four."

I stared at them for a moment in embarrassment.

"Just give me five."

That spring a new producer named Albert Zugsmith was hired by U.I. to make a "comeback" picture with Joan Crawford entitled *Female on the Beach*.

I was in the wardrobe department getting a fitting one day when Joan Crawford drove up in her white Lincoln Continental with the initials J.C. in gold script on the driver's-side door. She got out with her two chubby white miniature poodles and strode in wearing white shorts and shirt, a large bow tie, and clipping along in high ankle-strap heels. She was fashion-model-thin. Inside, she surveyed the room imperiously. It was obvious that she was checking out the new young ingenues to see who her new competition would be. I remembered vividly the night at the Photoplay Awards when she had been so obnoxiously drunk, and I shied away from her. The others began to fawn over her, when she spied me across the room.

"So you're Mamie Van Doren?" she said, coming up to me.

"Yes," I said, liking her in spite of myself.

"You have such a sweet face. You look like a doll, Mamie," she said.

"Thank you."

"Have we ever met before?" She had the poise of the great actress she was.

"Yes," I said. "At the Photoplay Awards two years ago. My real name is Joan. My mother named me after you."

"Really? That's very sweet of you to say so," Crawford said, obviously meaning it. "I'm surprised I don't remember it. I would never forget a face like yours, dear."

For all of her elegance and charm, however, Crawford was at the end of her career. *Female on the Beach* went on to be a disaster, and her comeback was over before it started. For me, young and on my way up, it was a sobering glimpse of a star on her way down. (Many years later, in early 1977, I was staying in the suite next to hers at the Ambassador East Hotel in Chicago. I wanted to call her, but decided against it. She was seldom seen outside her room, but I could hear her up at all hours of the night, watching television and moving about like a phantom. A short time later, she died.)

With the opening of *Daddy Long Legs,* Ray continued to try to land another part as an actor. He was not entirely motivated by ego. It had become increasingly difficult for him to get bookings for the band. The expenses and logistics of traveling with twenty-five musicians and four singers were becoming a nightmare.

Ray was known in the industry as a little Caesar—he would stand for no nonsense from his musicians. Any of them caught smoking pot or using other drugs was immediately dismissed. And he took a hard line on drinking, either before or during work. Ray also strongly objected to smoking while the musicians were on the bandstand. Ironically, Ray became the summer replacement for the Perry Como show on television, sponsored by Lucky Strike. Ray, who had never smoked a cigarette in his life, was forced to pose for his sponsor with a Lucky held awkwardly in his fingers.

Big bands were waning in popularity in 1955. There was a new music on the horizon, a new kind of music Ray didn't understand, best typified by Elvis Presley. It was called rock 'n' roll.

One day I found out from a columnist that Marilyn Monroe had been in the hospital with exhaustion and a bad cough, and had received two dozen roses from none other than Ray Anthony.

I was furious.

"How's Marilyn?" I asked him icily that evening.

"I don't know. Is there something wrong with her?"

"Why, there must be, Ray. Otherwise why would you send her two dozen red roses?"

His face turned red. He muttered, "Roses?"

"Yes, roses, you son of a bitch! Not only did you send flowers to another woman, but sent them to someone who's my direct competition. It's as if I decided to sleep with Harry James!"

"I didn't sleep with her!"

"How do I know that? You gave that big party for her."

Just before Ray and I started dating, he threw a party for Marilyn that was the talk of Hollywood. He also wrote a song about her called, of course, "Marilyn." To mollify me, Ray bought me a fur coat. But it was an incident that would stick in my memory for years.

When *The Second Greatest Sex* was completed, U.I. scheduled another picture for me. The film was entitled *Running Wild*, and was to be shot in black and white. It was U.I.'s answer to MGM's *Blackboard Jungle* and the rest of the emerging genre of movies about the supposedly wild, restless younger generation.

I did not want to make the film for several reasons. First, it was in black and white, a comedown for me after doing movies in color and CinemaScope. And it was a role that I thought was out of character for me—a *bad* girl. (How wrong

I would turn out to be about that!) Finally, the movie score contained that blossoming corrupter of American youth: rock 'n' roll. I was required to sing *and* dance in the picture.

Because I still did not have an agent or manager to replace McHugh, Ray agreed to act as my manager. We scheduled a meeting with the man in charge at U.I., Ed Muhl, to try to get out of doing the picture.

Ed Muhl had the eyes of a poker player. While he might smile, his eyes told you nothing. As we sat across from him in his office, Ray enumerated the reasons I should not do *Running Wild*. Occasionally Ed would nod, but he refused to back down.

Finally I vowed, "I'd rather go on suspension than do this movie."

Muhl drummed his fingers for a moment on the arm of his chair. He looked across at Ray and me and smiled.

"Well," he said, "if that's what you want. If you absolutely refuse to do *Running Wild*, Mamie, you can go on suspension."

"That doesn't seem fair, Ed," Ray put in. "There has to be a third way we can go."

"Ray, you're here because of Mamie," Muhl said patronizingly. "I respect the fact that you think you're looking out for her. But I'm here because of the studio. I have to consider the best interests of U.I. *and* the best interests of Mamie. Hopefully, the two are one and the same. Now, if she feels that strongly about not doing this movie, so be it. I feel that strongly about her doing it. Those are the alternatives. You decide."

I decided to do the picture.

In the process of making *Running Wild*, I discovered how exciting rock 'n' roll was. I starred along with John Saxon and Keenan Wynn. The bad girl I played was the girlfriend of teen gang leader Jan Merlin. The music of Bill Haley and the Comets of "Rock Around the Clock" fame was used in the film's soundtrack, and I jitterbugged to their music in the local saloon.

The doughy complacency of the fifties was being punctured by rock 'n' roll. Parents were up in arms about it and public figures spoke out on the evils of the new music. But young people kept on listening, kept on buying the records. U.I.

was one of the first studios to discover that teenagers and their music were exploitable in films. Teenagers would flock to see movies about themselves, thus making *Running Wild* and many other films like it very successful at the box office.

Another movie company that exploited the youth scene was Warner Brothers, who cast a boyish-looking actor named James Dean as a misunderstood teenager rebelling against his parents and society in the movie *Rebel Without a Cause*. Jimmy Dean was an all-too-shy young man who loved fast cars, motorcycles, and girls, though not necessarily in that order.

I ran into Jimmy at a little hangout across the street from U.I. called Eddie Keys'. The rock 'n' roll on the jukebox was loud, the drinks were liberally poured, and the customers were a wide cross section of movie people, from grips to stars.

Susan Cabot, another U.I. contract player, and I were sitting in Keys' later one afternoon when Jimmy Dean and a couple of his friends came in. They were dressed in leather motorcycle jackets, jeans and T-shirts. A cigarette dangled indolently from Jimmy's lips, and he pushed his dark glasses up on his head as he surveyed the room. His eyes came to rest on Susan and me and he grinned shyly. Susan knew Jimmy from somewhere before and struck up a conversation with him. His mumbled replies were barely audible over the din of the jukebox. Eventually he wandered back to his friends, and Susan and I finished our drinks.

As I was getting into my car in the parking lot I heard a voice behind me.

"Want to go for a ride?" the soft voice inquired.

I recognized Jimmy in the gathering darkness. "I don't think so. I'm really not dressed for it, Jimmy."

"What does that have to do with it? Get on."

There was something very appealing about Jimmy's thin-jawed, angular face. His eyes were soft and vulnerable, and their inviting gaze overcame my initial refusal.

I tucked my skirt around my legs, climbed on behind Jimmy, and put my arms around him. I could smell the mix of leather, gasoline, and hair oil as I held him tight for warmth in the chilly evening air.

We roared up through serpentine Coldwater Canyon, the

wind tugging at us and my hair streaming behind. It was frightening and thrilling. Jimmy drove the motorcycle as if demons were chasing him. In several sharp turns he leaned the bike so far over that the footpegs struck sparks on the pavement.

My heart was pounding with fear when we reached the top of Coldwater Canyon. Instead of following the road that descends the other side of the canyon into Beverly Hills, Jimmy turned off on a narrow dirt track. It was a rough ride. The rear wheel threw dirt on me and the dry brush scratched my legs. He finally stopped the bike at a clear spot and killed the engine. My ears rang from the noise for a few moments. Jimmy leaned the motorcycle on its kickstand and swung a leg over. He lit a cigarette and let the smoke out slowly.

"Whew! Some ride," I said, shaking out my hair.

"Yeah." Jimmy grinned. "I like to take it up the canyon to unwind after work." He seemed to notice for the first time that my arms were bare. "Hey, are you cold?"

I rubbed my goose-pimpled arms. "A little."

He slipped off his jacket and put it around my shoulders. As he did, he brought his face close to mine.

"You like motorcycles, Mamie?"

I nodded and he kissed me. It was a soft, awkward, adolescent kiss, tasting of cigarette smoke and beer. Jimmy cupped my breasts with his hands and we kissed again, more deeply.

"Jimmy," I breathed, "not here."

He stopped and searched in my eyes as if looking for what I really meant. "Then where?"

I explained to him that I was virtually engaged to Ray Anthony. Jimmy seemed disappointed but shrugged it off. We talked for a while and looked at the view of the L.A. basin as it grew darker and the freeways became rivers of light.

Finally we rode back down to Eddie Keys', where I picked up my car.

When I got off his motorcycle, Jimmy asked, "Can I call you sometime?"

"Sure." I gave him my phone number, but I never saw him again.

In the middle of filming *Running Wild*, U.I. received another request to loan me out. This time it came from New York and producer Jule Styne. Styne flew out to the Coast to have me read for the part of Rita Marlow in *Will Success Spoil Rock Hunter?*

The play had been written by George Axelrod as a satire of Marilyn Monroe and Hollywood's studio system. My first reaction to the play was negative. I told Bob Palmer that I wasn't interested.

"I've been to New York," I said flippantly.

"It's an unusual opportunity, Mamie," he countered. "It isn't that often we get this kind of request for an actress."

"I don't know, Bob. I want to think about it."

"Jule Styne's out here from New York now. At least have dinner with him and get acquainted. Read for the part. Take Ray along if you like."

"Can you get me a copy of the script?"

"Styne wants you to read cold."

That evening, Ray and I talked it over. He was mildly enthusiastic about it, but I could tell he was thinking the same thing I was: what would happen to us? A long separation was not what I wanted and I sensed that it was not a popular idea with Ray. With him trying to work in movies out here and me back in New York working for God knows how long in a Broadway play, the relationship might never survive. And yet it was an extraordinary opportunity. Relationships with men had taken a back seat to my career since I had signed up at U.I. Could I back away from a star role in a Broadway show because of Ray?

A few days before I was to have dinner with Jule Styne, Keenan Wynn came pounding on my dressing-room door on the *Running Wild* set.

"Mamie!" Keenan bellowed in his gravelly voice. "I've got your script."

"What script?" I asked, opening the door.

He grinned behind his walrus mustache and held the cover up to my eyes. "*Will Success Spoil Rock Hunter?* I'm up for the role of the cynical writer. I understand you're up for the lead."

"I'm supposed to meet Jule Styne and read for him this week. But I don't know if I'm interested."

"You've read the script, haven't you?"

"No. Styne wants me to read cold."

Keenan screwed up his face. "Aw, fuck that, Mamie. Here, take my script home and read through it. At least give yourself a good chance."

I thanked him and took the script home.

Ray and I met Jule Styne at a posh Beverly Hills mansion for dinner. He turned out to be a small, likable, well-dressed man, and we hit it off right away. After dinner, Styne and I went into the living room and he gave me a script.

"Read this, Mamie," he said. "I want to hear how you sound."

The beginning of the *Rock Hunter* stage script is virtually a ten-minute monologue by the character I was to play, Rita Marlow. I read the part for a few pages and Styne liked it.

"That's excellent. Very good. I'd like you to come to New York and meet George Axelrod. He'll be directing the play. And he wrote it with you in mind, Mamie."

When I left that evening I knew that Styne, who would produce the play, wanted me to star in it and that Axelrod, the director and writer, would probably like me too.

I paced the floor that night, trying to decide what I should do. On the one hand, a role in a new Broadway play; on the other, my love affair with Ray Anthony. And there was the image of Marilyn which had haunted me throughout my career. Although the play was a spoof of all the dumb blondes created by Hollywood, wasn't it making fun of me too? And what about all the work? The weeks of rehearsal, the performances for a year or two—it seemed as if I was letting myself in for an unbelievable ordeal.

In the end, I decided there were too many arguments against taking the part, and called Styne the next day to turn down the role.

Styne left for New York to continue his search for an actress to play Rita Marlow. The girl he eventually found was an unknown with very little acting experience. Her credits consisted of some shopping-center openings and an occasional small role. After she got the role in *Rock Hunter*, her star began to rise rapidly. Her name was Jayne Mansfield.

Ray and I were still passionate lovers. Unfortunately, my resolve to make him use a condom every time we made love soon evaporated. Since we were both so much in love, and Ray had asked me to marry him, I was not overly worried about getting pregnant. Before long, I missed my period. I checked with my doctor, and he confirmed what I suspected— I was pregnant again.

It was the Fourth of July and Ray was about to go on the road again with his band when I broke the news to him. But quite to my surprise he seemed not to hear me. When I repeated the news, he snapped, "I don't want to talk about it now."

I didn't hear from Ray the next day. I called his suite at the Towers but he told me he didn't have time to talk—there was too much to do getting the band ready to go on the road. It was as if he was another person.

I felt as though my heart was breaking. The man I loved and who I thought loved me was acting as though I was a stranger because I was pregnant. Was this the same man who had asked me to marry him a few months before?

Suddenly I was frantic. It seemed to me that Ray no longer had any intention of marrying me. When I could no longer hide my condition from the studio, my contract would be terminated. And hiding my condition was apt to be pretty difficult since I had already begun having violent morning sickness.

I told my parents, and they agreed to try to talk with Ray about the situation. Ray came to the house and sat at the kitchen table to talk with my mother and father. After Ray left, I came out of my room.

"Jo," my father said, "I did everything I could."

Mother put her arm around me. "Honey, I think you'd better realize that you're on your own."

"What am I going to do?" I cried. "What did he say about me?"

My father shook his head as he turned his coffee cup idly in its saucer. "He said that you were no minor. That you knew what you were doing. He doesn't want to marry you."

"He said he loved me," I sobbed.

"I know, honey," Mother comforted me. "I know."

The next day, I called Ray and begged him to see me.

"Okay, meet me in the garage in an hour. I've got to go out and I can talk to you down there."

It stung being told to meet him in the darkness of the Sunset Towers garage like some kind of hooker, but I agreed, thinking it was my last chance.

When Ray stepped out of the elevator and got into my car, I fought back my tears and tried to keep my voice level. "You act like I'm some sort of stranger. And it's not fair. I'm pregnant. With your child. If I don't get married, the studio will drop me because of the morals clause in my contract. If I do get married, who knows how long before I'll be able to work again—if ever."

"What do you want me to do?" Ray asked coldly.

"I would think that's obvious. You asked me to marry you not long ago, Ray."

He twisted the button on his sport jacket.

"Mamie, I just can't have all this on my mind right now. I have too much else to do. Do you understand?"

"No, I don't! What I suddenly have on my mind is the loss of a studio contract and a career that I have worked hard to get. I'm pregnant and, dammit, *you* participated in that little detail very cheerfully, as I recall."

The conversation deteriorated into a lot of crying and name-calling, mostly on my part. When I got home I was totally despondent. My head spun as I tried to come to grips with the sorry state of my life. In a fog, I went through the house and into the bathroom and threw up until I was collapsing with dry heaves.

My scene with Ray had played pretty badly. I could feel the child within me growing by the minute. The beat of a tiny heart echoed in my ears like a distant drumroll as I sat on the cold bathroom floor. I was without a prospective husband. My stomach would grow; the studio would discover my secret; I'd be an outcast with no career, no husband, and a child to raise.

"Honey," Mother said through the bathroom door. "Are you all right?"

"I'm so sick, Mama," I cried. She came in and cradled my head.

When I was revived and feeling better, Mother said: "Jo, an Al Zugsmith called from the studio. He wanted you to call him back about a script."

"Oh, God," I moaned. "I don't need that now."

"That's what you need now more than anything. You need to get your mind off yourself. Now, pull yourself together and give him a call back."

I had first met Albert Zugsmith in the Universal commissary while I was having lunch with Jeff Chandler and Tony Curtis. Zuggy, as I would come to call him, was a maverick producer at U.I. The straightest arrow I have ever known in the movie business, Zuggy was always absolutely candid and truthful in his dealings. And he was far too original for Universal's management. Thankfully he had a nose for what the public wanted *and* he saw possibilities for me that no one else did.

I dried my eyes, dialed Zugsmith's number, and instantly his gravelly voice was rumbling over the phone. He said, "The studio thinks that you're wrong for this part, Mamie, but I want you to test for it. The script's called *Star in the Dust*, and I have a feeling you're just what I'm looking for."

Star in the Dust was Universal's answer to *High Noon*. That was one of U.I.'s problems—they had an "answer" to everything rather than doing something original. The role Zugsmith wanted me to play was a "good" girl, a Grace Kelly part. John Agar was to play the sheriff, the man I was in love with. In the movie, he believes my brother, played by Leif Erickson, is a cattle rustler. The real rustler turns out to be someone else entirely, that perennial bad guy, Richard Boone.

Zuggy told me that I would test for the role in about a week and not to worry.

"You'll show 'em what you can do, Mamie."

About a week after Ray left for his tour, he called. I talked to him for a while and told him about the screen test. A few days later he called again, from another city. I called him back the following day to say I'd gotten the part in *Star in the Dust*.

I was more confused than ever. Ray continued to call, we continued to talk, but nothing ever seemed to change in our relationship. And sadly, I still loved him to distraction.

One evening after the first week of shooting *Star in the Dust*, I asked Mother when I got home from the studio if Ray had called again.

"No," she answered curtly. "Jo, it's time I gave you some advice. If you want Ray to marry you, you've got to stop talking to him."

"Why? If I do that, he'll just think I've lost interest. At least this way there's—"

"Listen to what I'm telling you, Jo. As long as he can call up here and talk to you, things will stay just as they are." She held up her hand to stop me from interrupting. "I know what I'm talking about. You make yourself a little more scarce and see what happens."

I started to disagree with her, but she had that same look in her eyes as the day she refused to let me see Howard Hughes.

"Okay, Mother."

The next five weeks were miserable. The phone rang at night and we finally took it off the hook. We had to put pillows over the receiver to block out the whine of the off-the-hook tone. None of us slept much. My father suffered because he had to get up early to go to work. And I was up before daylight most mornings to get to the studio for an early makeup call.

I was sick every morning and during the day I was cinched tightly into an eighteen-inch-waist dress by a corset that became my sworn enemy. I would throw up before they laced me into it, then pray that I could keep from throwing up again afterward.

Luckily, the distractions of my work helped keep my mind off my condition. The pressures of moviemaking kept my mind occupied during the day, though I was haunted by bad dreams at night.

Mother was worried about me. During one scene where I was supposed to fall off a rooftop onto a mattress, Mother came to the set to be with me. She was afraid I would hemorrhage when I fell, and bleed to death before anyone could help me.

A few days after I finished shooting *Star in the Dust* there was a knock on our door late at night. It was Ray's brother Bob.

"Is everything all right?" Bob asked when my dad opened the door.

"Yes."

"Ray's been trying to get in touch with Mamie, but the phone's not working."

"The phone's working fine," Daddy said. He's a pretty good poker player, and he suddenly felt he'd drawn a good hand. "But there's not much for Ray and Jo to talk about, I'm afraid, Bob. She doesn't want to talk to him."

"Ray's frantic. He sent me over here to see if I could get her to talk to him."

"What does he want to talk about?" Daddy wondered out loud.

We put the phone on the hook when Bob Anthony left. Within a half-hour Ray was on the phone asking for me. Mother smiled slyly. She put him through several rounds of "She really *doesn't* have anything to say to you, Ray . . ." before she handed the phone to me at last.

"Mamie, how're you doing?" Ray asked cheerily.

"Pretty good," I replied noncommittally.

"Finish the movie yet?"

"Yes."

"Why don't you catch a plane and meet me in Toledo."

"Toledo?"

"Sure. I'm playing a one-nighter there."

"I've already *been* a one-nighter."

Ray swallowed on the other end of the line.

"Look, I realize I can't live without you. These last six weeks have been hell."

"They sure haven't been any picnic for me either."

"Mamie, meet me there and let's get married."

The next morning Mother and Daddy walked me toward the gate of my departing flight. I had stopped at a ladies' room and thrown up again and my knees felt wobbly. They put me on the flight to Toledo with hugs and good wishes for Ray and me.

Early the following morning, I was married to Ray Anthony. It was August 29, 1955, and it rained in Toledo all day.

Chapter Thirteen

If I had expected Ray to be the considerate, exciting lover he had been while we were dating, I was wrong. Ray was like a different person. As any woman knows who's ever been through pregnancy, there is nothing she needs more than a loving, understanding mate. Ray was anything but.

There were times he would slip back into the role of a caring lover. For instance, he met me at the Toledo airport on the day of our marriage with a beautiful three-carat diamond ring. But more often he would recoil from me as if we were enemies, yelling at me for something inconsequential. I was so confused by the hormones coursing through my body and the erratic behavior of my new husband that it was all I could do to make it through a day without crying.

I think part of the reason Ray acted so strangely was that his mother was bitterly opposed to our marriage. Mary was the matriarch of her family. She quietly ruled her four boys and two girls with a firm hand. Divorced for many years from their father, Quino, she always lived with her children. I believe they accepted it as a matter of course that their mother would be a permanent fixture in their households and were content to remain in orbit around Mary.

At the time Ray married me, he was about to buy Mary a new house. Our marriage delayed the purchase and she blamed me for having to continue on a little longer in her house in the San Fernando Valley. This only added fuel to the fire of her opposition to me.

One day, before the baby was born, Ray announced that he had arranged a weekend for us in Las Vegas. He booked us at the Sands Hotel, Frank Sinatra's hangout, where the early members of the Rat Pack stayed. A musician and minor movie star, Ray was bucking for membership. He and Sinatra were both Capitol Records artists at that time, although Ray's records were the label's biggest sellers and Frank's were just moderately popular. Nevertheless, Ray looked up to Frank.

When Ray and I got off the plane in Vegas, I glanced at the front pages of the newspapers and discovered that James Dean had been killed in a head-on car crash the day before. His death hit me hard. The skinny, serious-faced young actor I had known had been snatched from life in the prime of his career. I remembered the thrill of our motorcycle ride a year before, and began to cry.

"What's the matter with you?" Ray snapped as we rode in a taxi to the Sands.

"Nothing," I said. "I was just thinking about poor Jimmy."

"Poor Jimmy?" Ray's voice had a rising edge to it when he got angry. Ray's jealousy had smoldered ever since I had told him about my evening ride with James Dean.

"He never really had a chance—he was just getting started."

"Hell!" Ray said loudly. He did a slow burn as we rode the rest of the way to the hotel in silence.

When we checked in and got up to our room, Ray exploded. "You went to bed with him, didn't you?"

Suddenly I felt tired. "Ray," I sighed, "nothing happened between us. Ever."

Ray kept worrying the subject as we unpacked and got changed for dinner. I tried to ignore him, but my patience was nearing the breaking point. He continued his accusations over dinner. Finally I slammed my napkin down on the table.

"Ray, you are acting like a child over this Jimmy Dean business."

"I have the right to be angry over my wife mourning one of her ex-lovers."

"He is *not* one of my ex-lovers. But I guarantee you this: you've made me damn sorry I didn't screw him right there in the grass beside his motorcycle."

I pushed my chair back and stalked out of the restaurant, leaving Ray staring after me openmouthed.

My favorite singer, Lena Horne, was playing the Sands' showroom. Ray and I barely spoke throughout Lena's closing-night show. Ray's pal Vic Damone was scheduled to open the next night. Vic's wife, Pier Angeli, had just had a son named Perry a few months before and had come to Vegas with the baby to be with Vic while he worked. Vic called Ray that evening, insisted we get together for drinks, and asked us to stay for his opening. I didn't feel like it, but I had little choice. I looked at their baby with mixed fear and wonder. I knew that soon I would be holding and caring for my own baby.

Pier was sweet, angelic, and totally dominated by her husband. She was petite, with lush dark hair, deep liquid eyes, and skin so fine it never needed makeup; I always wondered what she was thinking beneath that placid exterior. There must have been strong emotional currents hidden in the depths of those eyes, because Pier would eventually die by her own hand.

Pier had had a torrid love affair with James Dean. The gossip in Hollywood at the time had it that Jimmy was desperately in love with her until the day he died. In fact, his fabled self-destructive streak was blamed on the breakup of their romance. I heard he had stood crying outside the church the day Pier married Vic Damone.

Looking at Pier with her new baby, I wondered if she regretted the choice she had made. She had a lovely new son now, but the relationship between Pier and Vic seemed less than ideal. An ambitious and talented performer, Vic was an often harsh and tyrannical husband who drained Pier emotionally, probably without realizing it.

Choices. Those we make, and those that are made for us. In my weaker moments I thought that my choices were made for me, and the world was handing my dreams back, broken. But as I looked at Pier and Vic together, and then thought of my relationship with Ray, I realized that the choices we make are all our own.

* * *

Our son, Perry, was born six months later on March 18, 1956, in St. John's Hospital in Santa Monica. The birth was an ordeal—I spent twelve hours in labor. Because the doctor in attendance neglected to have me catheterized to evacuate my bladder before the birth, I suffered a ruptured urethra and a prolapsed bladder.

Perry was a big, squalling, strapping boy with a shock of dark hair and a big voice. Ray began to act like the father he now was, and for a few days I thought everything might turn out all right.

Ray had not worked for some time. We had been living on dwindling reserves, and the day Perry was born Ray was served a subpoena for back alimony payments by his first wife. There were hospital bills from the birth and a nurse and a maid to be hired to help me take care of Perry and the house while working. The back-alimony payment forced Ray to take his band on the road again.

Bad luck tends to come in bunches. Before I left the hospital I had a visit from a new U.I. executive, Donna Holloway. Donna had been private secretary to Harry Cohn at Columbia before she was hired away to manage the actresses at U.I. It was a painful fact that there was no one at Universal during the time I was under contract who understood how to promote the female stars. The men who ran the studio could build male stars with comparative ease, but women were a complete mystery to them. Naturally, the men in charge would never admit that they didn't know what to do with their female stars. Donna Holloway was hired to be a sort of senior den mother to us, to tell us how to floss our teeth, listen to our complaints when we had our periods (or missed them!), and try to provide liaison between us and the studio execs.

Donna arrived carrying a small package. "I brought you a little something," she crooned in a cultured voice.

"Thank you."

I opened it and held up the bright blue bottle of Charles of the Ritz perfume. It was not one that I used, but I didn't say so. "How lovely."

"I'm glad you like it. It's Marilyn Monroe's favorite."

The smile I managed could not have been very good. I set

the perfume bottle aside as Donna made herself comfortable in a chair by my bed.

"The reason I'm here, Mamie, is your contract at U.I."

It was a visit I had been expecting, now that the baby had arrived.

"The studio," she continued, "has decided that since you're now happily married and a mother, they're going to drop your contract. After all, your image in the films you've made doesn't exactly fit with this new you, does it?"

I eyed her suspiciously. "What cause does the studio have to break my contract, Donna?"

"Break? Oh, they're not *breaking* your contract, Mamie. You'll be paid for the next year, up through your contract anniversary in 1957. But your services will not be required for any movies at U.I."

"Will I be able to work at other studios?"

"Oh yes. And U.I.'s willing to make your ballet and diction lessons available to you as though you were still actively working at the studio."

In later weeks I would return to U.I.'s lot to get back into shape with ballet, and to sharpen my skills again with diction and voice lessons. But it would never be the same there for me, even though I gossiped and lunched with the same people. Suddenly I was a mother. And all at once I felt old at twenty-three.

One morning I received a script by messenger from my new agent, Maurie Gutterman. Maurie, a distinguished, well-groomed little man who looked like Adolphe Menjou, was one of the top agents in Hollywood, an associate of Charlie Feldman's Famous Artists' Agency. The script was called *The Girl in Black Stockings*. I called Maurie to tell him I thought my part looked like a pretty good role.

"Good," Maurie said. "Lex Barker is playing the lead. The director really likes you—can't wait to meet you. Guy name of Koch—Howard Koch. The producer is his partner, Aubrey Scheck. They've got plans for a few movies and they seem to know what they're doing."

"When do I meet them?"

"They start shooting in three weeks in Kanab, Utah. Why don't you fly up to meet them?"

"Okay."

As I hung up, Ray wandered into the room. We were living in a pleasant two-bedroom apartment in Beverly Hills. It was expensive, but somewhat cramped with the addition of Perry and his nurse. Yet it was all Ray could do to earn enough money to keep us going while meeting his alimony payments to his ex-wife.

When I told Ray about the movie, he replied, "Great," but without conviction. He was disgruntled because his agent at MCA had been unable to get him another part in a movie.

"Will you be in town during the shooting?" I asked. I told him the dates, but he only shrugged. "I don't want Perry to be alone," I added.

"He's got a nurse," Ray said. "That's what we pay her too much for."

"It's not the same, Ray."

"I'll be here. Don't worry. Hey!" Ray snapped his fingers. "Why don't I meet you in Vegas after you finish? I need to talk to Frank about some business—he'll be playing the Sands then."

"Okay," I said. "That might be fun."

Ray had continued to cultivate Sinatra's friendship, and while he may not have been a member of Frank's inner group, since Ray was married and didn't party with them, Ray and Frank were becoming closer, at least professionally. They recorded an album together that year for Capitol called *Melody of Love*. The album was not wildly successful, but it did well enough for them to begin plans for other projects.

Kanab, Utah, was a paradise. A small town high in the mountains with crystal-clear air and cool, quiet nights, it was used for western location shooting by all the studios, as well as independents like Scheck and Koch. It was located deep in Mormon country, which meant that at the motel where I stayed, you couldn't even get coffee with your breakfast, much less anything stronger. The cast and crew drove to the nearby Nevada border, where we stopped at the first road-house to drink and listen to rock 'n' roll on the jukebox. Carl Perkins' "Blue Suede Shoes" was the rage that year.

The Girl in Black Stockings was about a series of murders in a small western town. My costar, Lex Barker, was married to Lana Turner and she came up to keep an eye on Lex after the first few days of shooting. And not without good reason. Lex had a roving eye that took in everyone from the script girl on up. Lana kept eyeing me as if I had intentions, but I had let Lex know the first day that I was not interested. Lana was pregnant, and she and Lex kept to themselves, friendly but aloof.

My pals during the filming were Marie Windsor and Anne Bancroft. Anne (which I pronounced "Annie") was the murderer in the film. Off the set she never let a moment go by without having something outrageous to say or do. An incurable shutterbug, Annie constantly had a camera in her hand, snapping pictures of me while I did my scenes. With little else to do, Marie, Annie, and I sat by the pool at our little motel and gossiped prodigiously.

Annie initiated us into the "split-face" game, which came out of an Actors' Studio exercise. In the split-face game, you attempt to express two simultaneous, conflicting emotions with only your face.

"Okay," she would bubble, "now be afraid with your mouth and have an orgasm with your eyes." And we would dissolve into gales of laughter, grimacing and rolling our eyes.

Annie was also a very talented mimic. After hearing the story of my screen test for Ado Annie in *Oklahoma!* she stuffed chewing gum under her upper lip to imitate Gloria Grahame's protruding lip.

"Aw right, darlingsh," she said around the wad of gum to Marie and me, "let's all be Gloria." And we all laughed helplessly until the gum fell out of our bulging lips.

The shooting took only two weeks, and when we were through, I was reluctant to leave. Making a movie in Kanab was like being on vacation.

I met Ray in Vegas and we saw Sinatra's show together. But Frank had a cold and was not holding court that evening. Ray was disappointed.

After the show we went to the Riviera to watch the floorshow. My attention was suddenly caught by the sight of a familiar figure among the dancers crossing the stage in front of us, costumed in the body stockings, strategically placed sequins, and giant feathered headdresses that had been staples of the Las Vegas showgirl since I had worked there nearly seven years before. It was Danielle Cory.

We went backstage after the show. When Danni came out of the showgirls' dressing room she was met by a gorgeous little brunette. Danni kissed her fully on the mouth and slipped her arm around her in a proprietary way.

"Hi, Danni," I said.

After a moment of hesitation Danni smiled. "Joan . . . or rather, Mamie!"

"How are you?" I asked.

"Oh, just great."

There was an uncomfortable moment while we all wondered what to say next. Danni broke the silence.

"This is Brenda." The dark-haired girl nodded politely.

I introduced Ray and everyone shook hands stiffly.

"So," I said to Danni, "you're back from Paris to stay?"

"I think so. I got all I could out of the modeling world. Time to move on to other things."

"What kind of things?"

"Movies, perhaps. I'm going back to L.A. soon. I've followed your career from Europe, Mamie. You're on the covers of magazines in Paris all the time."

U.I.'s worldwide publicity campaign for me had been effective. Pictures and stories about me and the movies I was in had been featured in French, Italian, Spanish, and German movie magazines frequently over the last two years.

"Well, it hasn't always been easy."

Danni smiled. "But I knew you'd make it. I said so that day by the pool at the El Rancho."

"I remember," I said, smiling. I dug a scrap of paper and a pencil out of my purse. "Here's our number. Give me a call when you get to L.A. Maybe I can help you get started."

Before Ray and I got back in our room, he lit into me.

"I never knew you liked *girls*."

"Don't be ridiculous. Danni and I knew each other from my Las Vegas showgirl days, and back in L.A. for a while. She went to Paris to become a model."

"And you didn't know she was a lesbian?"

"Of course I knew. We were good friends. But I let her know early on that I wasn't like her."

Ray continued to rant about an "affair" until finally I barked at him: "Ray, why don't you stop being so . . . Italian!"

We continued to fight the rest of our stay in Las Vegas.

We had been back in Los Angeles only a few days before I had to leave for New York and a guest appearance on the Steve Allen show. Going on that show scared the hell out of me. Live TV was very different from my work in cinema. Unlike movies and ninety-nine percent of today's television, there was only one take—the one the folks saw out there in their living rooms. Nonetheless, the reaction to my appearance astonished me. People seemed to love me. By the time I got back to L.A., Steve's producers were already on the phone to my agent, lining up my next appearance.

When I got home, Ray announced to me that MCA had gotten him another movie. He would be playing opposite Jayne Mansfield in a picture called *The Girl Can't Help It*. I went through the roof.

"How dare you make a movie with Jayne Mansfield?" I shouted at Ray.

I was still mad at Jayne for having taken the role in *Rock Hunter* that I'd turned down, and becoming a star as a result. Besides that, she and Marilyn were my competition at the box office.

I refused to visit the set during the filming of *The Girl Can't Help It*. I was confident that Ray would make very little headway with Jayne, since her fiancé, Mickey Hargitay, that year's Mr. Universe, seldom left her side. And Jayne's taste ran to big, well-developed hunks, not diminutive bandleaders.

Coincidentally, a day or two after Ray told me about *The Girl Can't Help It*, I received an offer to do the L.A. production of *Rock Hunter*, scheduled to be performed at the Carthay Circle Theater in Beverly Hills.

Perversely, I turned it down.

"The money is great," Maurie Gutterman said. "And it's now a hit show. It's proven and you can move into it and make it yours."

"It was *written* for me," I said.

"Then now is the time for you to do it. The producer wants you and the director wants you."

I thought about it.

"No. Jayne's already put her stamp on the role."

For days after that conversation, I moped around the house.

I should have realized what that feeling of angst meant: I had twice made the *wrong* decision about the same play.

In early 1957 Chrysler Corporation signed Ray to do *The Ray Anthony Plymouth Show* on ABC-TV, and our fortunes took a turn for the better. When the contracts for Ray's show were signed, we moved from the apartment on Shirley Place in Beverly Hills to a beautiful three-story, six-bedroom Spanish-style stucco house, with swimming pool and tennis court, on La Presa Drive in Hollywood. We now had a gardener, maid, and cook, in addition to Perry's nurse. The house had a formal dining room and large bedrooms and a comfortable rumpus room with a piano and pool table.

In a flurry of activity, Ray began rehearsing a thirty-piece orchestra for his premiere show. The show was a dance-variety format built around Ray's trumpet and orchestra. Vic Damone was an early guest, as was I. But when I sang a song on Ray's show, I was made to sit on a piano so I couldn't move my body in ways the sponsors considered too suggestive.

Because of my wild and sexy screen image, I was unpopular with Chrysler and the network. The sponsors often gave parties to which I was pointedly not invited. Ray went alone, leaving me to sit at home with the baby. Finally the unfairness of it all became too much for me.

One night when Chrysler and the network people were partying it up in Trader Vic's at the Hilton, I got mad. After Ray left for the party, I put on my slinkiest gold lamé gown with all the trimmings and went to the Hilton.

Ray found out from someone at the party that I was in the bar at Trader Vic's. By the time he found me, I was drinking my second scorpion. The scorpion is a near-lethal concoction of several rums, coconut juice, pineapple juice, and God knows what else, with gardenias floating on top, served in a big bowl with two straws. Civilized folk drank them with a partner. I was feeling very uncivilized that night. I had gardenias pinned all over the front of my dress.

"Just what the hell are you trying to pull, Mamie?" he whispered furiously to me.

I smiled innocently as I tried to focus on his face. "Nothing."

"You're making me look like a fool."

"Am I? Surely you don't need my help with that." I took a pull at the long drink straw.

"What will the Chrysler people think if they find out my wife is out here drinking alone in the bar?"

"If they ask, why don't you tell them that it's because she wasn't invited to the party."

"Mamie, this party is business!" The bartender looked up from the other end of the bar. Ray caught himself before he started shouting. "These people are paying our bills, you know."

"If you ask me, I think it's shitty business." I took a long sip. The straw gurgled, signaling the end of the drink. I motioned the bartender over. "Bring me another bouquet, please." I turned back to Ray. "I think you'd better get back to the party before you're missed."

Ray furiously twisted the button on his jacket. It popped off and fell to the floor. "What about you?"

The bartender slid a fresh scorpion bowl in front of me. "Oh, I'll just stay here," I said, taking the straw on one side. "I'll see if anyone would like to suck on this other straw."

Ray growled. He grabbed me by the hand and pulled me off the bar stool. "C'mon, dammit. Just try to sober up."

He dragged me into the party in Trader Vic's. Unfortunately, by that time I was pretty well loaded. I giggled too much at every introduction. I'm sure that some of the wives had strong words for their husbands after the party, since I took every opportunity to leer at the men. It's a miracle that Ray didn't lose the show on the spot.

After making *The Girl in Black Stockings,* Howard Koch signed me to a two-picture deal. Both Ray and I were relieved when the next film I would star in came along. Sitting around the house waiting for him to come home had grown dangerously thin for both of us.

The movie, *Untamed Youth,* was a teen exploitation film in the finest tradition of teen sex, teen violence, and rock 'n' roll. The songs for the movie, some of which I would be singing, were being written by a shy young man who was a friend of Buddy Holly's—and his lead guitarist for a time—Eddie Cochran.

Howard brought Eddie and a couple of his band members

over to the house to meet me. Eddie was blue-eyed and skinny, with curly blond hair and an all-American smile that won me over right away. He brought along his guitar and we sat in the rumpus room while Eddie sang some of the songs he had in mind for me.

Ray skulked around the house that day, refusing to sit with us and listen. He hated rock 'n' roll and its surging popularity on the music scene.

Eddie came to the house a second time with the songs for the movie on demo discs so that we could rehearse them together. Ray was at a rehearsal for his show. Eddie and I worked for long hours in the rumpus room. It was obvious to me that Eddie had talent. It was also obvious that I was attracted to him. And given my strained relationship with Ray at the time, I was particularly vulnerable to the attentions of another man.

A few days later Eddie came over again to work on the songs. Again Ray was at rehearsal. After an hour or two we took a break, sitting together on the big leather couch that dominated one side of the rumpus room. All at once Eddie leaned over and kissed me. In a few moments we were in each other's arms.

Suddenly the front door slammed—Ray was back from rehearsal! Eddie and I straightened ourselves out, and I flipped on the record player with one of the demos on it. A rock-'n'-roll dance beat boomed out through the room.

Ray stuck his head into the room and wrinkled his nose. "What the hell's that?" he shouted over the din.

"One of Eddie's songs!" I yelled back. "I'm singing it in *Untamed Youth!* Don't you love it?"

His mouth became a slit and he slammed the door without saying another word.

I turned down the volume.

"I don't think your husband likes my music," Eddie said, ill-at-ease.

"Don't take it personally," I told him. "He hates all rock 'n' roll. It's putting him out of business."

Though Eddie and I saw each other frequently during the filming of *Untamed Youth*, we never got together again— partly out of shyness on Eddie's part, and partly because I was so weighed down with the responsibility of starring in the film. But if I hadn't been married, I would have done my best to overcome those obstacles.

Eddie's music helped make *Untamed Youth* a success. And while songs like "Oobala Baby!" and "Salamander" did not become rock-'n'-roll classics, by performing them I became one of the first actresses to be identified with rock 'n' roll.

It was getting harder and harder for Ray to get bookings in nightclubs. Worse yet, his record sales were declining. His Capitol Record recordings had always been the staple of his earnings as a performer. The Plymouth show boosted his record sales for a while, but Ray was smart enough to see that the times were a-changing. Even if he didn't like it, he was helpless to stop the rising tide that was rock 'n' roll.

When I finished *Untamed Youth,* I had a hiatus of several months before undertaking my next film. I spent a great deal of time with my son, and tried to patch up my relationship with Ray. It was both the best of times and the worst of times. Being with Perry was an absolute joy; Ray, however, was an impossibility.

A few months later, in late 1957, Maurie Gutterman arranged for me to star in Lou Walters' Latin Quarter Review at the Riviera Hotel. I was to close the show with a thirty-minute nightclub act. The hotel would pay me ten thousand dollars a week for a four-week run.

Performing in Las Vegas is one of the most trying, exhausting, exhilarating experiences in show business. I began hurriedly putting together a nightclub act. I selected the songs I wanted to sing and Jack Baker choreographed some movements for me. Norman Norrell, the couturier, designed gowns for the act. Before long I was in the midst of rehearsal.

By the time the act was ready, *Untamed Youth* had opened around the country. Because of the music in the movie, I became the focus of criticism by parents and church groups concerned with the morality of rock 'n' roll. Hate mail began pouring in. I kept my morale up by thinking that at least they were spelling my name right.

Flying to Las Vegas, I was a seething mass of nerves. Ray was there with me and, uncharacteristically, he was an enormous help. The day of the opening, the Latin Quarter Review's orchestra picked their way through my songs in rehearsal, and then began packing away their instruments. But Ray had other ideas.

"Wait a second, guys," he said, holding up his hand as the musicians started to get up from their chairs. "Now, you're going to play through the entire show."

There was a chorus of moans and groans. "Who the hell does this guy think he is?" somebody in the back row complained.

"I'll tell you who I am," Ray snapped. "I'm the guy that's going to make sure Mamie gets to hear how her show's going to sound. Her whole show. Now, let's get to it."

Bless his heart, they sat down obediently and played the whole show through.

One day my choreographer, Jack Baker, introduced me to Neile Adams, a featured dancer in the show that was closing at the Riviera. A perky, athletic brunette, she helped me learn new steps as Jack fitted my act to the Riviera's stage.

I saw Neile again when Ray and I had a late-night dinner at the Garden Room at the Sands Hotel. On our way out we stopped by her table and Neile introduced the handsome sandy-haired man sitting next to her as her husband, Steve McQueen. I didn't suspect that I would get to know Steve very well in the years to come.

I opened at the Riviera Hotel on October 2, 1957. The reviews the next day were very good, and Lou Walters was ecstatic.

Lou, a frail-looking, fine-boned man whose face was dominated by thick glasses and large watery eyes, was one of the premier nightclub operators in the country. His daughter, Barbara Walters, would later become famous in her own right. The Latin Quarter in New York had long been world-renowned for great entertainment. Now the Las Vegas version of the Latin Quarter Review was also a hit. For me it marked the beginning of a long and successful association with Lou Walters.

During the four-week run of the show, Perry and his nurse stayed with me in my suite. Ray returned to L.A. during the week to work on his Plymouth show, and came back to Vegas to spend the weekends.

One Thursday afternoon the phone rang. When I picked it up I heard a familiar Deep Southern drawl.

"Hi, Mamie. This is Elvis Presley."

Elvis Presley! I remembered the first time I'd seen Elvis on television. He was making an appearance on *The Tommy & Jimmy Dorsey Show.* We had a big color television (one of the first color sets around—Ray was a fanatic for new electronic toys) and I flipped. I was like one of the teenagers squirming and screaming in the audience as he gyrated and crooned his songs. I loved his voice and the way he looked. Ray, always increasingly bitter about the encroachment of rock 'n' roll on the music business, angrily left the room.

To me, Elvis was magic. I'd imitated him in *Untamed Youth,* wiggling my hips as I performed. So much so, in fact, that the censors would not give the film their seal of approval.

"Well," I said, pulling myself together, "this is a surprise."

"How're you doin', Mamie? I understand your show is great."

"Thanks, Elvis. I'm fine—the show's a lot of fun."

"I'd like to come see you tonight. But I'd like to be, like, sort of incognito, okay?"

"I'd love to have you as my guest. I'll have them reserve a table for you, okay?"

"Yeah, but tell 'em it's for Mr. Smith. I don't want anyone to know it's me."

"Sure."

"I'll call you after the show, Mamie. 'Bye."

When I hung up the phone, I could feel the blood racing in my temples. Elvis coming to see my show! The little girl from Rowena, South Dakota, had arrived.

That night, Elvis and two other men came to the show. He arrived after the showroom had darkened, and left a few minutes before the end.

Backstage, I hadn't even had a chance to get out of my gown before I heard a knock at my dressing-room door. When I asked who it was, a familiar voice responded, "Elvis."

I let Elvis in while his friends waited in the hallway. Elvis was young and virile and handsome. His dark hair was slicked back in a pompadour with a few locks hanging over his brow. He wore dark pants and shirt and dove-gray sport jacket. His eyes were a penetrating blue, and I was stunned by their power.

"Great show, Mamie!" he said.

"Thanks. I'm glad you could come."

"Oh, I wouldn't have missed you. I saw *Untamed Youth* in Memphis and I loved it. You don't happen to have a picture you could autograph for me, do you?"

Here was Elvis, the hottest new singer in the country, and he wanted *my* picture.

"I copied your wiggle in that movie," I said as I gave him a photograph of myself.

"Yeah? I like your wiggle better. Listen, Mamie, are you free to go with me and my friends to have a couple of drinks?"

"I've got another show to do."

"What about after your second show? We'll come back and get you. We'll do this town up right."

I thought about it for all of an instant. After all, Ray wouldn't be in until tomorrow night.

"Sure."

There was a shyness about Elvis, something countrified that was very charming and appealing. He smiled as he went out the door. "See you later."

The hallway outside my dressing room was in pandemonium. Word had spread quickly that Elvis was backstage. His friends had to form a flying wedge to get him through the crowd.

Elvis was alone when he picked me up after the show in his big white Cadillac. Our first stop was the Frontier Hotel, where he had worked a few months before. Elvis insisted we stop at the long bank of dollar slot machines. With a flourish he produced a one-hundred-dollar bill and got a bucketful of silver dollars. He cradled the silver dollars in the crook of his arm.

"When I was growing up, my whole family could've lived for a month on half this much money. Now I can afford to throw it away." He gestured toward the line of one-armed bandits. "C'mon, Mamie."

After we ran through the silver dollars, laughing and shouting like a couple of kids, Elvis suggested we go see Louis Prima and Keely Smith, who were headlining at the Desert Inn. Afterward we went upstairs to the Starlight Room on the roof, where we sat in a cozy corner booth and had drinks.

Driving around later, we cuddled in his Cadillac's broad front seat like teenagers.

"Mamie, can I ask you something . . . personal?"

"Sure."

"That dress you had on tonight—were you wearing anything under it?"

I had had Norman Norrell copy some sensational gowns of Marlene Dietrich's in a nude-colored see-through soufflé chiffon with strategically placed beads, and I was back-lit on stage to make the effect complete.

I smiled demurely. "No."

He hit the steering wheel with the heel of his hand. "I knew it. Damn, but you look great up there, Mamie." He pulled me closer and added, "And you look even better here at close range."

We pulled into the parking lot at the Riviera and stopped in a pool of darkness off to one side of the entrance.

"Mamie, would you like to come back to my hotel?"

I thought about Perry upstairs with his nurse and Ray back in L.A. "No, I'd better not."

Elvis kissed me softly. I responded passionately to him, barely able to hold myself back.

"Are you *sure* you don't want to go back to my place?" Elvis asked with a chuckle when our lips parted.

I took a deep breath and shook my head. "I'd better go upstairs."

"I enjoyed the evening, Mamie. I'd like to come see your show again tomorrow night and bring some friends along. Maybe we can all go out on the town again."

I thought of Ray coming from L.A., but I didn't say anything. Who knows? I thought. Maybe I can get away.

"That sounds like fun," I said, feeling a little guilty.

We were both a little tipsy, enjoying each other's company. We looked out of the windshield of the car at the desert night and Elvis started to hum "Love Me Tender" softly. We ended the night singing it together. I got into bed as the sun was coming up over the desert.

I had told myself halfheartedly that I was a married woman and a mother. And certainly Elvis must have known that. But there was a part of me that kicked myself for not succumbing to Elvis' magnetic sexuality.

Ray was in town the next evening, though he didn't attend the show that night. Just before I went onstage one of the showgirls ran up to me breathlessly and said: "Mamie, Elvis is in the audience again!"

All I had time to do was say, "Oh no!" before the orchestra started playing my intro music. I walked onto the stage and saw Elvis with at least fifteen others at a long table next to the stage.

For a moment I completely forgot the lyrics to my opening number, " 'Deed I Do." I just stood there trying to smile, wondering what to do. Finally the words came back to me and the band and I caught up with each other.

During my act the place was a madhouse. People in the audience constantly got up during the show and snapped pictures of Elvis.

Throughout the show, Elvis' eyes seemed to send an unmistakable message to me from his table. He came backstage again after the show and invited me to join him for drinks. I didn't want to say no, but I had not figured out what to tell Ray. I told Elvis I had to go upstairs and change.

Ray was watching television up in the suite. I peeled out of my sweaty gown and began to freshen up. Before I had a chance to say anything to Ray, the phone rang.

"Mamie, it's Elvis. We're all waiting for you downstairs."

"Oh, yes," I said, trying to hide who it was from Ray.

"Are you coming down or what?"

"Yes, yes. I am."

Ray asked, "Who's that?"

"Oh, it's just a friend," I said, covering the mouthpiece. "We were going to go out for a little while."

Ray looked at me suspiciously. "A friend? Who?" He grabbed the telephone out of my hand and barked into the receiver, "Who is this?"

The color drained out of his face. "Elvis who?" he croaked. He listened a moment more and slammed the phone down. "Elvis Presley said he and his friends are waiting for you downstairs. What's this all about?"

"I was going to tell you. Elvis and some of his friends invited me out to have a drink."

Ray looked at me in astonishment. "Are you out of your

mind? Mamie, you're a married woman. You've got a child right there in the other room. How can you go out with another man?"

"We weren't going *out* exactly, Ray."

"Then just what exactly did you have in mind?"

"Having a couple drinks. We might go see Louie Prima and Keely Smith at the Desert Inn—" I stopped myself just in time from saying "again."

Ray shook his head in disbelief. He walked over to the couch and sat in front of the television. "Mamie, you go on if you want. But I promise you that if you do, I will not be here when you get back." He turned and looked over the back of the couch at me.

I hung my head. Of course I knew that going out with Elvis was not exactly proper behavior. But half of America would've died for the chance. Elvis had the kind of magnetism that could derail a marriage. I tried to explain it to Ray. I think he understood at least a little. The hardest thing for Ray to understand was that I had to have my own life, my own career. I wasn't just a supporting player in a script designed by and for him. I had to be free to live my own life, without answering to someone all the time.

I did not go downstairs to meet Elvis. I opted for maintaining a stable married life on Ray's terms. For the time being, the field I was playing in had another set of ground rules. But I couldn't resist one parting shot.

"Of course, if Marilyn called and asked you to come downstairs for a drink . . . would you go?"

He began twisting a button on his shirt.

In February 1971 I was invited to Las Vegas to do the Merv Griffin show, which then originated from Ceasar's Palace. Elvis was opening at the International Hilton Hotel, and got a message to me at Ceasar's to come see his show that night. While it was not the Elvis of old onstage, his performance still retained the spine-tingling energy of the early rock-'n'-roll days. His show left me with the impression that Elvis had matured as a man and a performer—an impression that was confirmed when I saw him backstage afterward. Not yet grotesquely bloated, Elvis was thin and pale. His familiar crooked smile was unchanged, but there was a world-weariness in his eyes as he greeted me at the door of his dressing room.

Elvis and I embraced warmly. His father, Vernon, who traveled with him in the capacity of manager and confidant, showed me to a chair. While Elvis changed out of his sweat-soaked costume, Vernon and I talked about his son's comeback and career. When I complimented Elvis' show, a smile crinkled across Vernon's face. "That's mighty good to hear, Mamie. Elvis is real proud of his new show and he'd like to know how much you liked it."

When Elvis came back into the room clad in a thick terrycloth robe, he held me at arm's length. "Mamie," he said, "you're just as pretty as ever."

"You're looking good yourself, Elvis," I replied. "Your show was fabulous. I can't thank you enough for inviting me."

"Thanks for coming, Mamie," he said, the exhaustion clearly etched on his face. We chatted a few minutes before Elvis finally said, "I'd like to talk some more, Mamie, but I've got to lie down and rest before the next show. I've had a touch of the flu . . ."

I made my apologies and left.

Elvis couldn't have been sweeter to me. As always, he was powerfully attractive offstage as well as on. But there was an undercurrent of sadness about him that had not been there before, and I sensed Elvis' internal struggle with forces beyond his control.

Chapter Fourteen

W hen I returned to Los Angeles after the show closed in Vegas, Ray and I established an uneasy truce. We weren't getting along well, but we weren't at each other's throats either. Soon after I returned, I set to work on the new script that Koch had picked for me. It was called *Born Reckless,* and Koch planned to start shooting soon at Warner Brothers. Ray was kept hard at work on his television show.

Ray managed to get me a recording contract with Capitol Records to record Eddie Cochran's rock-'n'-roll numbers from *Untamed Youth.* As far as I know, I was the only actress recording rock 'n' roll in the fifties—a time when most people considered it "kids' music" and thought it was a passing fad.

With the ten thousand dollars per week I'd made in Las Vegas, as well as a nest egg I already had set aside, I decided it was time to buy a house. All my life I had been renting. My dream was to own the house I lived in. I found a house on Rising Glen Road, high in the Hollywood Hills overlooking the Sunset Strip, and set out to make it my dream house. I had it decorated in white—walls and ceilings, carpets and furniture. I wanted to fashion it after the home of my long-time idol, Jean Harlow. My neighbors included the producer Ross Hunter, Jimmy and Margie Durante, Louis Prima and Keely Smith, Bobby Darin and Sandra Dee, and Mel Torme. Though I was on friendly terms with everyone on the street,

Margie Durante quickly became my close pal and confidante. Her best friend was Martha Raye, and the two of them immediately took me under their wings. We seldom let a day go by without seeing each other for lunch, a swim, or shopping.

I put the house in my parents' name. It seemed like a smart thing to do, since Ray's ex-wife was still trying to attach anything that she could turn into money. And unfortunately, deep down, I had a feeling that our own marriage would not last.

I began shooting *Born Reckless* in early 1958. The movie was about the rodeo circuit in which I played a trick rider and country singer. It featured Tex Williams, Arthur Hunnicutt, and Jeff Richards. Little did I know that *Born Reckless* would lead to a much bigger role in yet another movie.

Ask anyone who's been in show business and he'll tell you at least one story of a coincidence that changed his life. Many of us have dozens. This particular one involved one of my favorite pastimes. Eating.

Howard Koch and I went to lunch at the Warner Brothers commissary. Because I had been late that morning and had to skip breakfast, I was starving. I loaded my plate with enough, as my Grandma Dah used to say, for thrashers. There's no telling what I must have looked like that day, shoveling food down like I'd been adrift in a lifeboat. Howard looked on in wonder.

That night Maurie Gutterman called.

I was exhausted from the day's shooting, and the next day I had to be up at four A.M. to start again.

"I hope it's good news, Maurie. I'm too tired to cope with a disaster."

"Good news? Great news! Clark Gable called and has requested you for his next picture."

"You're kidding!"

"I'm not kidding."

"My God, that's wonderful. When does it start? What's the picture about? What kind of money are we talking about? No, never mind the money—this is Clark Gable."

"Hey! Take it easy! Don't start giving away my commission so easily. All I know at the moment is that it's to be shot at Paramount and that it'll star Gable and Doris Day."

"Maurie? How in the world did Gable come up with me for this part?"

"He saw you in Warners' commissary today."

The film I was to costar in with Clark Gable was called *Teacher's Pet*. It was the story of a crusty newspaperman (Gable) who falls in love with a college professor (Doris Day). I was to play Gable's girlfriend, a blonde nightclub performer.

Shortly after Maurie had concluded the deal, Ray and I were invited to a get-acquainted bash for some of the cast of *Teacher's Pet*. Almost everyone was there when we arrived. In attendance were the producer of the film, William Perlberg, and his wife; veteran director George Seaton with his wife; and Gig Young and his wife at that time, Elizabeth Montgomery. And dominating the party simply by his presence, by his familiar voice and face, was Clark Gable, accompanied by his wife, Kay.

Our party had reserved a long T-shaped arrangement of tables in a quiet corner of Trader Vic's. We had drinks and chatted as we waited for the last guests: Doris Day and her husband, Marty Melcher. It was a long wait. The group was well-lubricated with several rounds of drinks when William Perlberg stood up from the table.

"Well, I'm going to give Doris a call and see if something's happened to them."

He was gone a few minutes. When he returned there was a look of consternation on his face. He spoke to George Seaton.

"When I asked if they were coming to the party, do you know what she told me, George? She said, 'No one invited me.' Can you beat that?"

"That's nonsense," Seaton replied. "Of course she was invited. I remember telling her myself."

"Well, let's order before we all get too drunk to talk."

The party proceeded merrily. I was seated at the end of the table, completely smitten with Gable, who was seated on my right. I monopolized conversation with him whenever possible, though he appeared not to mind. At the opposite end of the table, Ray talked with Gig, Seaton, and Perlberg, and occasionally glowered in my direction.

"I want to thank you," I finally said to Gable.

"For?" he asked.

"For asking to have me in this movie. I'm so looking forward to it."

"Me too, Mamie."

His voice went right through me. It was that gravelly, so-often-imitated "Frankly-my-dear-I-don't-give-a-damn" voice.

"You know," Gable went on, "when I saw you in the commissary that day, you reminded me of Carole."

He said it so quietly, I was the only one who heard it.

"She had that same kind of earthy, sexy quality you do, Mamie."

Many years later, my friend Dorothy Lamour said almost the same thing to me. "And you're funny like she was too, Mamie," she added. Dorothy once told me that the first time she worked with Carole Lombard, in *Swing High, Swing Low*, opposite Fred MacMurray, "I was so nervous I couldn't remember my lines. But Carole was so considerate of me, a newcomer, that every time I'd blow my lines, she'd blow hers so the director wouldn't notice the problem I was having."

When Ray and I got back into his Chrysler for the drive home, I was humming "Tara's Theme" from *Gone with the Wind*. Ray drove in silence.

Back home in our bedroom, as we were undressing, Ray asked, "What did you think of Clark Gable?" There was a faint note of challenge in his voice.

"He was . . . charming."

"What did you talk about? You two were thick as thieves all night."

"Were we?" I sighed and fell backward across the end of the bed.

"I don't think you spoke ten words to anyone else."

"He seemed to want to get acquainted with me."

Ray carefully hung his clothes in the closet. I tossed my dress, shoes, slip, bra, and panties in a pile. He came around the bed and stood in front of me.

"I was disappointed in Clark Gable," Ray said.

"Disappointed? How?"

"He was dumpy. I couldn't believe it. The man's a stump. I always thought he was taller."

"Ray, he's *not* stumpy."

"What do you call it? He's short, he's out of shape, and he's too heavy."

"He's almost sixty years old. I think he's in fabulous shape for his age."

Actually, Gable did look a bit puffy but I was not about to concede the point to Ray while he tried to punch holes in my fantasy.

"Short he can't help."

Ray leaned over me and began to caress my breasts. It was obvious he wanted to make love.

"Shut off the light, will you, Ray?"

In the dark, while Ray huffed and puffed, I buzzed along in a champagne haze and thought of Clark Gable in *Saratoga*, making love to Jean Harlow.

My first morning on the set of *Teacher's Pet* I was weak and wobbly-kneed, but not because I had been drinking the night before. I hadn't slept all night, worrying about my first scene with Clark Gable.

Actually, it was a simple scene: Gable knocks on the door of my dressing room, I open it, squeal: "Jimmsy!" throw myself into his arms, and kiss him. The problem was, he was Clark Gable. I gargled four times to make sure my breath was fresh. I imagined over and over again what it would be like to actually kiss the King. I prayed my voice wouldn't crack from nerves.

I was at the studio early, fixing my hair and makeup, fussing over the fit of the Edith Head dress I wore. Gable was on the floor and ready to shoot at nine o'clock sharp. The assistant director called me to the set.

George Seaton asked us to take our marks for the close two-shot where I kiss him. Gable held me in his arms as he must have held scores of actresses before me—Jean Harlow, Carole Lombard, Vivien Leigh. All of them were sisters with me now. I looked up into his eyes and he gave me that little so-familiar smile that off-centered Gable's mouth when he was amused.

Seaton calmly asked for quiet.

"What's that noise?" he asked.

It was the chattering of my teeth. I clamped my jaws shut, wondering if I could kiss that way.

"Let's hold it quiet, please," the assistant director said, not realizing where the sound came from. Gable pretended not to notice, although I must have looked like Bugs Bunny eating a carrot.

"We need just a little more light on Miss Van Doren's face," Seaton said to the assistant.

Quickly a technician moved a light toward me. The light caught my eye, and suddenly I remembered a night twenty years ago, when I had anxiously awaited Clark Gable's arrival.

It was the fall of 1938 at the little Sioux Falls, South Dakota, airport. There was a blinding light and a roar of aircraft engines as a plane landed. Everyone watched the airplane taxi toward us. It was the moment we had been waiting so long for in the evening chill. The airplane carried Clark Gable and Carole Lombard. Five years old, I held my father's big, callused hand while we stood in a crowd behind the fence.

For country people like us, seeing such celebrities, especially in the deep years of the Depression, was an event. It was something we would talk about for years. We had dreamed of going to Hollywood; now Hollywood was coming to us.

I could feel the excitement of the people around me, but I couldn't see. I tugged on my father's sleeve, and he lifted me, small and thin, onto his shoulders. There the view was fine above the brown hats and out toward the airplane.

The roar of the taxiing plane reached what seemed like an impossible level, then abruptly subsided. The motors stopped and my ears rang with the silence.

The plane's door opened as the boarding stairs were wheeled out, and there was an anticipatory murmur in the crowd. Several people came down carrying baggage and gun cases. I could see dozens of pheasants brought out, hanging limply, their rainbow feathers still reflecting color in the lights on the tarmac.

Finally Gable and Lombard descended. They looked small in the night. Carole Lombard, still in her khaki jodhpurs, was saying something to Gable as they descended. He was bare-headed, his dark hair ruffled by the cold wind. I could see their breath.

They were quickly hustled into the small terminal, where they would wait for a connecting flight to Omaha. Almost before I realized it, they were out of sight, photo flashes trailing like lightning in a Black Hills summer storm. I craned my neck for a last look.

Such a vast gulf of experience separated Gable and me that night. There was no way he could guess that Carole Lombard, the love of his life, would be dead in just a few years; no way for me to guess I would be shivering in his arms on a movie set twenty years later. It is, I suppose, why we thirst for God: so that we can somehow control those chance collisions decreed for us—and know where we're going.

"All right, everyone, let's settle down, please," the assistant director said.

"Okay . . . action," said George Seaton.

"Oh, Jimmsy!" I squealed. I planted a big, nervous kiss on Gable's lips and he slapped me on the butt as he was supposed to.

But when we kissed, his mustache tickled. I giggled.

Seaton said, "Cut. What's wrong, Mamie?"

"Well, uh . . . it was—"

"It was my fault, George," Gable said with a chuckle. "I was off balance and she slipped."

"That's all right. We'll take it again."

We took it again and again. Gable and Seaton were both patient with me. Finally we did a take that Seaton liked. "Print that one. Thank you. Next setup, please."

I walked back toward my dressing room as Gable walked toward his. He detoured slightly in my direction and gently took my arm.

"Good job, Mamie."

I shook my head. "I thought I'd never get it right. I can't believe I needed so many takes."

"Don't you worry, honey," he said with a wink. "This is a pretty good little script we've got here and it's worth the time to get it right. George knew you had a good take in you. He wouldn't have kept trying if he didn't." He took my hand

and sandwiched it in between his muscular hands. "Just relax. We've got a long way to go yet."

I blurted out my memory of him at the Sioux Falls airport. And how it was like a dream come true to be here.

He looked off into space for a few moments. "Carole and I loved it up there. God, the hunting was great." He smiled sadly and came back to the present. "Well," he said, turning toward his dressing room. "Time to rest up for the next shot."

As the days went by and Gable and I became more comfortable with each other, a bond developed between us. It was one of those unmistakable things that grow up between two people working together. We grew more and more interested in each other.

To be sure, there were restrictions on us—such as a husband and a wife. Kay Gable came to the set often in the afternoons and kept a proprietary eye on her husband. Ray had the good sense to take my advice and, jealous or not, stay away from *this* set because the movie was so important to me.

"Mamie," Gable said one morning as we were going back to our dressing rooms to wait for the next shot. "Come here. I want to show you something."

Most of the morning had been spent shooting a scene where Gable and I are sitting in a nightclub booth talking. As we worked our way through the scene, Gable held my hand under the table out of view. He would whisper bits of encouragement to me between takes. We worked and acted like we were old friends. But when he invited me into his dressing room, my heart jumped.

"I thought you'd like to see the pictures they took on the set over the past few days." He pointed and my eyes swept the dressing-room walls. There were perhaps a dozen pictures of Gable and me, taken by the still photographer that is always hired as part of the crew to shoot pictures on-set. "We look pretty good together."

He motioned me to a chair and sat down. Instead of sitting where he indicated, I plopped lightly on his lap. He put his arms around me and without hesitation we kissed deeply. I squirmed in his lap as we pressed close.

"Clark," I whispered when we came up for air.

There were a few moments when it could've gone either way. Then Gable spoke.

"Mamie, Mamie. What am I going to do with you?"

"I know what I hope you'll do with me."

"Yes, that would certainly be a very fine thing to do." He rubbed his face and looked thoughtfully at me. He gave me a playful little slap on the butt and stood me up. Then he sat me on the arm of the chair next to him.

"Mamie, you and I could get ourselves in a lot of trouble. You know that?"

I nodded. "Yes."

"Now, I'll tell you something that if you ever repeat while I'm alive, I'll deny: I haven't wanted anyone as much since . . . Carole died, I think. But for us—you and me—I'm afraid it's a case of too much too late."

"I don't understand, Clark."

"I'm almost sixty years old, Mamie. Now, that doesn't mean that there's not sex at sixty, but . . . well, if what I read in your eyes is correct, we could end up with big, big problems. Wife problems. Husband problems. But, ma'am, if it wasn't for that . . . it would surely be a pleasure."

He grinned. I knew he was right, but . . .

A wave of disappointment broke over me. Once again my marriage was pulling me away like a riptide from something—from someone I wanted. If it had been a happy marriage, I wouldn't have given it another thought. As it was, I was deeply disappointed.

I had looked forward to meeting Doris Day. A mutual friend of ours, Charlotte Hunter, a dance coach from Universal, told me what a warm, friendly person Doris was. Doris had always been one of my favorite singers, with hits like "It's Magic." I also became a fan of her movies after seeing *Love Me or Leave Me*, in which she played opposite James Cagney.

Nonetheless, our first meeting on the *Teacher's Pet* set was far from what I expected. Doris ignored me when we were introduced and proceeded to conduct herself like a spoiled star. George Seaton and Gable had to stoically bear her tantrums and disagreeable attitude.

Her dislike for me became most apparent when it was time

to shoot reaction shots of Doris, Gable, and Gig Young watching a dance number I did while singing "The Girl Who Invented Rock 'n' Roll." Doris failed in take after take to smile radiantly while watching me dance. Finally Seaton called for my double to be positioned off-camera so that Doris could watch someone who could produce the desired reaction. Doris' cold attitude toward me never improved, and mercifully we saw little of each other during the film.

In addition to working with Gable—the consummate professional, the helpful, fatherly, sexy, and compassionate fellow worker—there was the calm assurance of George Seaton's directorial style. No one could've been cooler and more in control than Seaton. The set was *his* set. He worked with a gentle power that commanded the respect of his entire crew. I never heard George Seaton yelling on his set. He was a director who worked closely, patiently, and deftly with his actors, talking quietly from behind the camera, encouraging them to keep trying, to do just one more take.

Edith Head insisted that my costumes in *Teacher's Pet* be white. The legendary costumer had a motherly concern for me while I was doing the film, making sure I was properly outfitted for the role, calling me sweetly her "Diamond Girl." (Sometime after the shooting of *Teacher's Pet*, Edith was asked in an interview who among the actresses she had fitted for costumes had the best figure. Her answer was Jean Wallace and Mamie Van Doren.)

I saw Gable only one more time after the filming of *Teacher's Pet*. We waved hello at the film's premiere, and sat around a long table with the rest of the cast at a party afterward in the Ambassador Hotel's Coconut Grove. Sadly, I never saw Clark Gable again.

A couple of years later, on the night of Gable's death, I filed silently with hundreds of other fans into a theater to see him in his last film, *The Misfits*.

The two weeks I spent shooting *Teacher's Pet* at Paramount were over all too quickly. The experience was one of the high points of my career.

Chapter Fifteen

I shook a red capsule from the bottle on my bedside table. I rolled it in the palm of my hand like a die, popped it in my mouth, and washed it down with a glass of water.

Ray and I had had another fight. It seemed like we fought every waking minute we were together. Now, as I took to my bed, I craved the sleep that would be reluctant to come without the urging of Seconal. Our marriage was tearing itself apart, and on top of that, the pressure of the new film I was making, *Guns, Girls, and Gangsters*—a film that I didn't really want to do—were making me unable to sleep.

The year before, in 1957, the film industry had been set on its ear by a lovely French actress named Brigitte Bardot in a film directed by her husband, Roger Vadim—*And God Created Woman*. Without the Hays office to censor their work, French filmmakers like Vadim could make films that dealt with nudity openly. Suddenly the home-grown sex goddesses were not enough. There was a new and more exotic siren on the horizon and Bardot's films began to exert pressure on the kinds of roles and films Marilyn Monroe, Jayne Mansfield, and I were offered.

I felt lucky, therefore, in 1958 when I signed a two-picture deal with Ed Small, who was making some low-budget pictures to finance some bigger films. It marked a period when I began making movies strictly for the money. *Guns, Girls, and Gangsters,* with Lee Van Cleef, in which I played a gangster's gun moll, was the first of the two films; later would come *Vice Raid.* I would net nearly one hundred thousand dollars for these two movies and they would take less than four months to shoot.

As far as my marriage was concerned, the handwriting was on the wall. It was fast going sour. The prudent thing for my son and myself was for me to do whatever movies came along and salt the money away for the time when we would need it. Luckily, 1958 would turn out to be one of the most productive years of my career.

Ray's television show had been canceled. He fell victim to the fate of so many TV shows before and since—ratings. Ray dreaded the next step: without the television show, he would have to go back on the road and play gigs around the country to make money.

Although my marriage to Ray was on the rocks, I didn't want to make the break, and apparently Ray didn't either. Instead, we hung on, tormenting each other with silences and rages. But Ray's wildly divergent mood swings, coupled with my own bowstring-taut nerves, brought out the worst in each of us.

Too often I lay tossing and turning all night, staring at the ceiling, listening to the night animal noises from the hillside behind the house.

One evening, a few days after the *Teacher's Pet* premiere, my friend Danni from Las Vegas called. She was now living in Los Angeles. We chatted on the phone for some time until Ray walked into the bedroom.

"Who's that?" he demanded.

I waved him away and kept on talking. When he figured out who was on the line, he blew up. He jerked the telephone out of my hand and slammed it back down on the receiver, hurling accusations at me about being a lesbian. Perhaps that was why we had not had sex in a long time, he insinuated. I in turn called him every name I could think of.

I don't remember now what it was he said, but something made me snap. I went after Ray with blood in my eye. I attacked him with a red patent-leather Pappagallo spike-heeled pump—a very smart weapon indeed. Ray was never particularly courageous. He took refuge where he always did—in the middle of the king-size bed, standing in his sock-feet, dodging from one side to the other. I faked in one direction, then ran around the other side of the bed and jumped up on it. He bounded off the other side, but not quickly enough. As he hit the floor, I bounced off the bed as if it were a trampoline and swung hard at his head.

I connected, and the tiny nail-size heel caught him right on top of the head. Blood spurted everywhere. Ray howled and ran into the kitchen. The maid came out of hiding and tried to stanch the bleeding. I tried to help too, but whenever I came near him he bawled, "Mamie! You stay away from me! If you come near me, I'll kill you! So help me, I'll kill you!"

"Oh, forget it," I finally said in disgust, "then bleed to death." I went into the bedroom and locked the door.

The outcome of all this was that Ray and Harold Plant, our business manager, summoned me to a meeting to issue their demands to me to save our marriage.

"Mamie, Ray wants you to know that if you want to continue being married, there are certain things you must agree to."

"What makes you think I want to continue the marriage?" I snapped.

Ray and Plant exchanged glances that seemed to say: I told you it would be like this.

"I presumed you might want to keep your marriage intact for the sake of your son," Plant said.

"How could it be any harder on him then it already is?" I asked. "We fight all the time. It's like a running free-for-all."

Plant ignored me and picked up a piece of paper.

"First, you must give up all the staff you have at home. The financial drain is too great to have a gardener, maid, cook, *and* nurse for Perry. Ray would like to cut it down to the nurse and a combination maid and cook. You can get a gardener as needed."

I shrugged. It was actually a reasonable request. There was no reason we couldn't get along nicely without all those people on the payroll.

"Second, you have to stop buying clothes."

"What . . . . ?"

"You will have to limit yourself to a minimal number of

new dresses each year. Ray says there are clothes in your closet that you've worn only once, if ever.''

"If I've worn them only once, it's because I was photographed in them. Surely Ray knows enough about show business to understand that problem.''

"Nevertheless, that's one of our conditions.''

"Did you say 'our,' Harold? I thought you were the business manager for both of us.''

"The third condition,'' he went on, "is that you will not go to Italy to do this upcoming film.''

The president of Famous Artists' Agency, Charlie Feldman, had called me just a few weeks before with the news that Nino Crissman, the Italian producer, had made an offer to me to star in a major film in Rome called *The Beautiful Legs of Sabrina*. At over sixty thousand dollars and all expenses paid for eight weeks in Europe, it was too good to turn down. It would be my first trip to the Continent and I was looking forward to it like a kid to Christmas morning.

"Ray,'' I said, glaring past Harold Plant. "Why would you want me to give up my career? First you want me to stop buying clothes; next you don't want me to make this film. Do you want me to give up my film career and be a housewife?''

"Why not?'' Ray challenged, speaking for the first time since the meeting started.

"Sure. Then you could have someone around *all* the time to abuse.''

"Please, don't start, you two,'' Harold pleaded.

There was an empty feeling in the pit of my stomach. This was really the end.

"Ray,'' I said, "if you want to end our marriage, why don't you just say so?'' I stood up and put my purse strap over my shoulder. "I'm willing to admit that I made a mistake marrying you. But I had no choice. I was carrying your son. I virtually had to force you to marry me to give him a name. Now you're not even man enough to say you want a divorce. You put your employee up to giving me an ultimatum so you can tell yourself it wasn't your fault.''

I walked to the door and turned. "Gentlemen, take your little ultimatums and shove them. I will *not* give up doing this film in Italy. It looks like I'm going to need the money. As far as I'm concerned, Ray, our marriage is over. I only ask that you not break the story to the papers until after I get back from Italy. It'll make it harder for me to work over there.''

Naturally, Ray couldn't wait to break the news to the press. On the way to Rome, I was held up in New York for several days until the producer of *The Beautiful Legs of Sabrina* deposited the money due me in an escrow account. Already there were rumbles in the papers about the impending breakup of my marriage.

When the money arrived, I took the next flight to Rome. In Rome, the paparazzi swarmed all over me, firing questions in broken English about my separation from Ray. Nino Crissman was livid over the publicity. He felt that in Italy, a Catholic country, news of my probable divorce would weaken the drawing power of the film.

The *La Dolce Vita* atmosphere persisted throughout the filming of *Sabrina*. I was mobbed by the Italian press wherever I went.

In *The Beautiful Legs of Sabrina*, a gorgeous model finds true love and excitement in Rome. My costar, Antonio Cifariello, was extremely popular in Italy after having costarred in several Sophia Loren movies. In the film he sweeps Sabrina off her feet and shows her Rome from the back of his Vespa motor scooter.

Thanks to the breakup of my marriage, I was susceptible to a Latin lover like Antonio. Before long we were involved in a torrid affair. I must say that Antonio upheld the much-publicized lovemaking abilities of Italian men, and showed me a good time out of bed as well as in it. Although our affair lasted only as long as the shooting of the film, it helped me to get over a rough time, and completely forget about Ray.

Though Antonio did not complain, I did not possess a body that, from the standpoint of the Italian film tradition, was the Italian ideal of a woman. My legs were too skinny (''Too nervous-looking!'' producer Nino Crissman exclaimed), and my butt was too flat. In all the scenes where Sabrina's beautiful legs or voluptuous rear were shown, a double was used. To my credit, however, from the waist up, I had exactly what the Italians were looking for.

Halfway through filming, I made a side trip to Taormina, Sicily, at the request of Marilyn Monroe. Marilyn got word

to me that she was to be given the Italian equivalent of the
Oscar at the Italian Film Festival. She asked if I could pick
up the award for her in Taormina, since she would be unable
to get there herself. Tired from the filming, nonetheless I
made an appearance with Gina Lollobrigida, Anna Magnani,
Vittorio DeSica, and Vittorio Gassman and picked up Marilyn's award.

After *The Beautiful Legs of Sabrina* was completed, Nino
asked me to make an appearance at the Venice Film Festival
to promote the picture. I agreed and, leaving most of my
luggage at the Excelsior Hotel in Rome, took a train to Venice with Nino and his wife.

Venice was seething with excitement over the festival. The
international motion-picture community had taken over the
picturesque old city. The paparazzi had been bad in Rome;
here they were like packs of wolves prowling the streets and
canals looking for a stray recognizable face. They followed
my *motoscafo* from the train station to the Excelsior Lido
Hotel, where the film festival took place.

One afternoon before I was scheduled to take pictures with
French film star Brigitte Bardot, I started feeling nauseated.
Soon I was throwing up, unable to walk, much less go to a
photo session. It turned out I had food poisoning. When I
didn't show up to meet with Bardot, paparazzi came pounding on my door. When I didn't answer, they broke the door
in and tried to shoot pictures of me half-naked, pale and wan
from being sick. I chased them out of the room and phoned
Nino Crissman.

"I want to get out of here, *now!*" I shrieked into the phone.

"Mamie," Nino replied, "the press thinks you were snub-
bing Bardot because you didn't appear to be photographed."

"Nino, I don't care what they think. I'm sick and I want
to get home. Get me on the next plane, bus, or train to Rome
so I can pick up the rest of my luggage and fly back to the
States."

I was particularly anxious to get back to California after a
phone conversation with my mother just after my arrival in
Venice. She told me that since I left, Ray had frequent parties
at the house, and in her opinion, my son was not being well-
cared-for by the nurse. Ray seemed totally preoccupied with
having a good time and ignored his son entirely.

When I returned to Los Angeles, my mother met me at the airport with Perry. He had lost weight, but was overjoyed to see me. Ray had moved out of the house the night before. Some of my clothing and jewelry were missing, presumably stolen by the strangers milling around the house during his parties.

There was no more avoiding the situation. I got Jerry Geisler on the phone and he began proceedings for a legal separation. As part of the settlement, he arranged a contract with Ray that would take care of Perry's college education. I asked for nothing for myself from Ray but a dollar a year for maintenance. The separation would last for more than two years. Our divorce would become final in 1961.

But that night, freshly back from Europe, I wondered if I was doing the right thing. A heavy rain was pelting the hillside. The house was empty, echoing with the rainstorm and memories of my marriage. There is in nearly every breakup that bittersweet quality of remembrance—even if the relationship had been a stormy one.

The house dark, with Perry asleep in his room and the maid in hers, I undressed in the living room. I walked out through the sliding glass doors into the darkened backyard. Below me, the lights of Hollywood were dimmed by the curtain of rain. I looked up and let the rain fall on my face, stinging my closed eyelids and tongue. With my arms outstretched, I exposed my naked body to the storm. I tried to imagine the rain washing away my problems, cleansing me in some magic way of the nagging perplexities of my life. I had plenty of energy to devote to a man or a career. I was unsure if I could spare energy enough for both. Yet, this was the freedom I had longed for.

I was afraid. Like a long-captive bird, once out of the cage I was torn between the safety behind the bars and the dangers outside of them. But I had a son to raise, and a house to take care of. Thus I was faced in 1959 with the fearful task of providing for us both entirely with my own earning power.

Sometime before, I had met a business manager named Pierre Cossette. I called him to see if he could give me a hand with my career.

One night we were having dinner at Peter Lawford's new

restaurant when the waiter brought a note to the table. The note said: "Mamie, I would very much like to meet you. Would you please join me at my table?" It was signed: "Frank Sinatra."

After Ray and I separated, he immediately became a regular at Sinatra's parties. His new freedom provided him the opportunity to finally move into Frank's Rat Pack. But Frank also had an unfortunate and well-deserved reputation for moving in on his friend's wives after they split up.

I handed the note across to Pierre, then passed it to his wife. Their eyes widened.

"What are you going to do, Mamie?"

I borrowed the waiter's pen and scribbled on the back of the note: "Sorry, I can't make it."

"You're turning down Frank Sinatra?" Pierre said in amazement. "Nobody turns down Sinatra."

"I'm not going to be another lonely separated wife for Frank to comfort."

After Ray and I separated, I began dating again. One of the first men I went out with was a then unknown actor named George Hamilton. George arrived in a chauffeured Rolls-Royce, chaperoned by his mother, and we went down to LaRue's, one of the "in" eating spots on the Sunset Strip. George was the spitting image of his mother down to the jet-black hair and a widow's peak. After dinner we went to the Crescendo, a Hollywood nightspot noted for its jazz performers.

The next time George asked me out, instead of picking me up in a chauffeured Rolls, he arrived at the wheel of a plain old Ford sedan. I was decked out in an elegant gown.

"Where's your Rolls?" I asked, eyeing the Ford skeptically.

"Well . . . this is just a car I'm using until our new one arrives," he replied sheepishly.

George turned out to be one of that group of men who turned other women on but strangely left me cold. We dated a few more times, and though no one could've been sweeter, finally called it quits.

Bob Evans, on the other hand, had very much the opposite effect on me. I'd met him while dining alone one evening and we exchanged phone numbers. At that time Bob lived in New York and had a clothing-design label—Picone and Evans—that was doing fairly well. But more than anything, Bob wanted to make it as an actor. His major role at that time had been playing the bullfighter in *The Sun Also Rises*. Later he would go on to become head of Paramount Studios, and one of the most influential men in Hollywood.

Bob and I got together again in Palm Springs. Perry and the maid and I stayed in a large bungalow at the sprawling Biltmore Hotel. Bob stayed in a bungalow that was so far away he had to drive to my room in his car.

One night after Bob left my place late and drove back to his room, the phone rang.

"Mamie," Bob said frantically, "you won't believe it. When I left your place, I saw your ex-husband hiding in the bushes outside. He looked like he had been trying to peek in the windows."

"Ray? You're kidding!" I exclaimed.

"I wish I was. He jumped in his car and followed me back to my bungalow. I'm afraid he's hiding in the bushes outside right now."

Bob sounded genuinely afraid. That was the only thing that kept me from laughing out loud. Somehow, I felt responsible. "I'm sorry, Bob."

"You don't think . . . ? He's not dangerous, is he? What do you think I should do?"

"Well, gee . . . Bob, you don't have a Pappagallo shoe around, do you?"

"A what?"

"Nothing. He's terrified of Pappagallo shoes. Especially red patent leather."

"I don't understand, Mamie."

"Never mind. I don't think he's dangerous. Go to sleep. He'll get tired and go away. Good night."

Ray continued to exhibit some very peculiar behavior after our separation. He not only followed me around when I went on dates but also acted very strangely when other men showed me attention, especially when one was his friend, the persistent Frank Sinatra.

Ray arrived at Rising Glen Road one afternoon to pick up

Perry for his visitation rights just as I came home. While he was gathering up Perry and some toys, he heard me ask the maid if there had been any messages while I was out.

"Just a call from Frank Sinatra," the maid replied.

"Frank Sinatra?" Ray exclaimed. "He's calling you?"

"Yes," I replied. "He saw me at Peter Lawford's. He wants me to go out with him."

The blood drained out of Ray's face and he rushed out of the house. I don't know if it was coincidence or not, but it was a long time before Sinatra called again.

During 1959 and 1960 I stayed busy with a variety of films, including *Vice Raid,* my second movie for Ed Small, in which I played a prostitute.

Earlier, in 1958, I had begun a long string of pictures with Al Zugsmith, my friend from Universal days, starting with *High School Confidential!* My costars were Russ Tamblyn, Jan Sterling, John Drew Barrymore, and Michael Landon. The movie was about the evils of marijuana, which it portrayed as a killer and corrupter of youth. As Russ Tamblyn's aunt, I did my part to corrupt him. In fact, my seduction of Russ barely made it past the censors. It was considered too sexy in the 1950's, though it contributed to the unexpected success of the movie.

After that successful outing, Zugsmith went on to do three more pictures for MGM. In the next, *The Beat Generation,* I starred opposite Steve Cochran. The story line had to do with a rapist (Ray Danton) who ritualistically wore black gloves to become excited enough to do his work. The movie also featured Jim Mitchum, son of Robert Mitchum, Fay Spain, and trumpet player Louis Armstrong. The film is the first I know of to chronicle the beginning of the hippie movement. The movie was also the beginning of my romance with Steve Cochran.

Steve Cochran was the rough-hewn, sexy, perennial movie tough guy. What I discovered about Steve after we had been dating for a while was that his behavior was frighteningly erratic. He had a violent temper reminiscent of my first husband. In bed, Steve became increasingly rougher, until one night he very nearly beat me up. I didn't see him for a while after that—I was plain scared.

During the filming of *Beat Generation*, Cary Grant was a frequent visitor to the set between takes of the Hitchcock-directed *North by Northwest* with Eva Marie Saint. Always very quiet and unassuming, Cary often had lunch with me in my dressing room, where we talked interminably. He asked me out many times, but his idea of a great evening was packing a picnic dinner and going to the drive-in movies in his Rolls-Royce. Attractive as Cary was, I preferred relationships with a little more pizzazz. Cary asked me several times to his Palm Springs house to spend the weekend. When I begged off because of Perry and his nurse, Cary said, "Hell, bring them along."

Cary was also an early experimenter with LSD-25. When I mentioned I was having difficulty adjusting to being newly divorced—dating again, living alone, supporting a child by myself—Cary suggested that I try LSD to help me cope. A longtime patient of psychoanalysis, Cary told me, "It all comes from way back in your subconscious, Mamie. This drug will help you to get it all out."

I told him that I knew of friends who had had bad experiences with the drug, which was then available over the counter in drugstores.

"Then come up to my house," Cary said. "My doctor will be there the entire time to help you through the experience."

I demurred again.

"Mamie, everyone is always exactly where they want to be. No one does anything they really don't want to do. If you don't want to come up to my house, or meet me in Palm Springs for the weekend, it'll be because you don't want to."

Cary was the most serious telephone addict I have ever known. It was not unusual for him to spend two or three hours talking to me on the phone during the time we were acquainted. The subjects he talked about ranged from psychoanalysis to the price of champagne and caviar at Gelson's Market. After the filming of *Beat Generation* was completed, Cary gave up calling me for a while.

Zugsmith signed Steve Cochran and me to do another picture together, *The Big Operator*, a gangland story about Jimmy Hoffa (costarring Mickey Rooney as the infamous union boss), and Steve and I started dating again. But it was short-lived. He was an exciting man in bed, partly because of the sense of impending danger he exuded. But I've never been good at a relationship the second time around.

Steve was in intimate of Mae West. Mae liked her men in all shapes and sizes, but she leaned toward the dark, burly, rough-looking ones, and Steve fit the bill completely.

Even Steve's death had that sexy Hollywood touch. Sailing on his boat in the Pacific with a dozen girls on board, he died of a heart attack. I can hear the men now saying he died with a smile on his face.

Following *Big Operator* I made *Girls Town*, a movie that was written specifically for me about a Catholic home for "bad" girls. The cast included Jim Mitchum, plus Gigi Perreau, Mel Torme, Paul Anka, and Sheila Graham as a nun. "Lonely Boy," one of Paul's songs featured in the film, became a hit. I sang another of his songs in a shower scene which was censored by none other than Cardinal Spellman. Because the film concerned the Catholic Church, Zugsmith had to take a final cut to Cardinal Spellman for approval. Even though I was seen from only the shoulders up, he ordered the shower scene removed from the film, over Zugsmith's protest. "But, your grace," Zuggy quipped, "even *bad* girls take showers." When Zugsmith returned to California after seeing Spellman, he told me with a merry twinkle in his eye, "The cardinal is *not* one of your biggest fans."

When I made *Sex Kittens Go to College* in 1960, I met a young actress that reminded me of myself. Tuesday Weld was eight or nine years younger than me but we immediately became friends. She was a wild youngster, always looking for excitement. Tuesday and I zoomed around Hollywood on the Vespa motor scooter I had bought when I came back from Italy. We went to Palm Springs and spent a few days hitting the Racquet Club and other "in" spots of the Hollywood weekend crowd.

The Private Lives of Adam and Eve brought me back home to Universal, where we shot on the back lot. Zugsmith put me together with people that I loved to work with—Tuesday Weld and Marty Milner, who played Adam. The role of Adam was originally offered to Jayne Mansfield's husband, Mickey Hargitay, but Jayne made such a fuss about him working with me that he had to turn it down. The role of the Devil, luring

Eve to get Adam to try the apple, was played by the inimitable Mickey Rooney. Mickey and I had become fast friends during the filming of *The Big Operator*. Now, as the Devil, Mickey displayed his formidable powers as a comic actor. There was seldom a time on the set with Mickey when there wasn't a lot of energy punctuated by frequent laughter.

Costuming and makeup for *Adam and Eve* presented some unique problems. In my case, three unique problems. Each day, a lifelike balloon-rubber cover had to be glued over my breasts, my hair glued down to the rubber. Then a fern had to be glued in place over my belly button, which was astonishing, since Marty Milner (like Jeff Chandler in *Yankee Pasha*) could show his chest and belly button at will.

After *Adam and Eve,* we shot yet another film at U.I., entitled *College Confidential*. We had no sooner started shooting than Cary Grant ambled onto the set to see me again.

"Mamie," he said with that unmistakable clipped accent, "let's have lunch."

Though I thoroughly enjoyed his company, I turned down once again his generous offers of quiet dinners and secluded weekends in the desert.

Difficult as it may be to believe, handsome, charming, debonair Cary Grant never really aroused my passion. Cary was perhaps never more dashing than he was then in his mid-fifties, but he was at a stage when he was looking for a young woman he could shape into a companion that suited him. She would need to live the private, at times nearly reclusive life that pleased Cary. And yet she had to be hot, sexy, kooky, glamorous, and susceptible to his distinguished, Continental, salt-and-pepper charms. Though he tried to remake me, I liked the fast lane too much for Cary's taste. I wanted to go out and see and be seen.

The other cast members of *College Confidential* were old friends of mine: Steve Allen and his wife, Jayne Meadows, both of whom I knew well from the days of doing the Steve Allen show; Walter Winchell, who not only appeared in the film as himself but also narrated the story in his familiarly compelling style; and an increasingly dear friend, Pamela Mason.

One evening at a party at Pamela Mason's I met Warren

Beatty, who was to become one of the most unusual of my many pursuers.

Warren began to come on to me at Pamela's little soiree. He had Joan Collins in tow—they had been dating for some time. Warren made a point of wandering over during the course of the evening, and we talked. Later he played the piano while I sang. Finally, when the evening was almost over, I quietly gave him my phone number.

Warren lost no time putting it to use.

I was just getting undressed after the party when the phone rang.

"Mamie, this is Warren."

"Warren?"

"Warren Beatty. We met at Pamela Mason's tonight. What're you doing?"

"Well, as a matter of fact I was just getting ready to go to bed."

"That's exactly what I had in mind. I'll be over in ten minutes—"

"Whoa! I've got to get up tomorrow and go to work."

"Believe me, Mamie, I'll make you feel like a million dollars. When I saw you tonight you really got me hot. That dress you wore—"

"I thought you were going with Joan Collins."

"Well, I am. But that's no reason that you and I can't . . . get together. Is it?"

"Perhaps it's a little old-fashioned, but I'd like to get to know you a little better before we just hop into bed."

"I will tell you my entire life story as soon as I get there, Mamie. It's fascinating . . ."

Warren didn't come over that night, but he called me again a few days later. Once again he wanted to come over. He began promising what a thrilling encounter if would be for me if I slept with him.

I don't know if my experience is unique, but I've found that the guys who promise you the most thrills before bed are usually the most dismal performers in it.

Warren talked such a good game, though, it was hard not to like him. He had a boyish, impetuous quality that made him good company—in short doses.

I finally had to tell him in no uncertain terms that I was

not going to be someone he could see on the side while he was seeing Joan Collins publicly.

"If you don't want to take me out, Warren, you can just forget about it."

"But, Mamie, *going out* shouldn't be the point of a relationship. It should be what two people can feel, what heights they can bring each other to, not where they're eating dinner that night."

"I mean it, Warren."

So our romance never developed. Nevertheless, we became good friends. Warren would think nothing of pounding on my door in the morning and barging right past the maid into my bedroom. He would often try to interest me in a little casual sex by making allusions to the size of his penis. I laughed at his advances. It was difficult for me to be interested in him. Most of the time he looked like he had just rolled out of bed and put on yesterday's clothes.

Always ambitious when it came to his career, Warren spent a lot of time trying to get the right parts. One afternoon I was driving up the hill toward home and met him coming down. He slammed on the brakes of his old Ford convertible. I stopped and he ran over to my car.

"Mamie! I was just up at your house. I had to tell you the latest. I'm up for a part in a movie with Vivien Leigh."

"Warren, that's great news!" I said.

"Yes. It's a Tennessee Williams script called *The Roman Spring of Mrs. Stone*. He's got approval of all the casting, so I've got to fly down to Florida and meet him. He wants an Italian to play the part so I've got to dye my hair jet black. It's the part of an Italian gigolo. At least they've got the right actor for it." He grinned. "Gotta run! Wish me luck!"

I waved as he trotted back to his car. "Good luck, Warren."

When Warren returned from Florida, he announced that he had gotten the part and was leaving for Rome soon. It was the beginning of his successful career as an actor, director, and producer.

It's ironic that the role for which he's best remembered, outlaw Clyde Barrow, in *Bonnie and Clyde*, was a man who was impotent. Warren was always horny and made sure I was aware that he was awesomely endowed.

His sophomoric machismo was often more amusing than sexy, however. On one of his impromptu visits to my house he charged into the bedroom and wrestled me around on my big bed for a while, but kissing Warren was like kissing a brother. We'd sometimes end up playing gin rummy.

As his fortunes improved over the years, Warren maintained suites at the Beverly Wilshire Hotel in Beverly Hills and the Regency Hotel on Park Avenue in New York. Like Cary Grant, Warren was also addicted to the telephone. He might call any hour of the day or night and talk for hours.

One warm afternoon he called from the Beverly Wilshire. A girlfriend of mine named Joyce was staying at my house at the time. Joyce was blonde and well-put-together.

"Mamie," Warren whispered, "can you get over here right away?"

It took me a moment to recognize the voice, it was so soft. "Warren? What for?"

"I'm sitting here on the balcony, suntanning in the nude, and I'm all hot and sweaty. I've been sitting here greased up with suntan oil, thinking about you, and I've worked up this big—"

My laughter cut him off in mid-sentence. "How nice for you, Warren."

"If you leave right now, you can get over here while it's still nice and stiff. I promise you won't be sorry."

"Well, that just seems too good to be true."

"It's not, Mamie. The sooner you get over here, the better."

I lowered my voice to a husky rasp. "You've talked me into it, baby. Just hold on till I get there. And give it a stroke or two for me."

I turned to Joyce after I hung up.

"How would you like to make it with Warren Beatty?"

"Would I?" Her eyes grew into saucers. "Sure."

"He's at the Beverly Wilshire Hotel." I gave her the suite number. "Just knock at the door and say you're Mamie Van Doren."

"Now?" she asked.

"He's all primed and waiting."

"Are you sure you don't want to go? He did call *you*."

"Warren's been calling me for a long time. I'm just not that interested. You go."

"I'll call you later," Joyce said, going out the door.

Men may realize it more in today's age of the liberated woman, but locker-room talk has never been confined to the *men's* locker room. Just as men have always compared notes on the attributes of whomever they've slept with or are trying to sleep with, so too do women.

While the men sit in judgment of the size, shape, and firmness of a girl's breasts or behind, discussion in the ladies' lockers is concerned with the firmness, shape, angle, and (yes, it's true, fellas) the *size* of her last night's date's penis. There would likely be a critique of his ability to bring her to a climax, his willingness to do so, his imagination in achieving this, and the duration of his enthusiasm.

When Joyce called me that evening she rated Warren's performance highly. So good, in fact, that she got a sunburn from making love on his balcony. There was some debate about whether I should have gone, but I was happy the way it worked out. I immediately called Warren.

"Well, how was I?" was the first thing I asked.

He laughed. "Damn you, Mamie. I was really ready for you when she knocked on my door. I'd left the door open, so I yelled, 'C'mon in, Mamie!' I was still lying naked on the chaise longue when she came in. I said, 'Who the hell are you?' and she said, 'Mamie Van Doren.' I tell you I laughed so hard that I lost my hard-on. But she was very cooperative in helping me get it back. So we made it right there on the chaise, then on the floor, then in the bed, then in the bathtub—"

"Warren, you can spare me the details."

"Just wanted you to know what you missed. You had the chance. It could've been you."

"I'll pine away from the loss."

"Why don't you come over now? I've still got plenty of steam left."

"Good night, Warren."

"No, seriously, Mamie."

"Give Joyce a call and get her to adjust your steam valve. Nighty-night."

At age one. Mom and Dad were beaming with pride.

At age sixteen with Grandma "Dah," who was still going strong.

A family portrait of four generations: Grandma "Dah," my mother, my great-grandfather Johnson, and me (in high chair).

In my mid-teens, displaying bare shoulders against
a black background. I was already leaning toward
a career in show business.

Songwriter Jimmy McHugh managed my career, bringing me to the attention of Universal International.
(Universal Pictures)

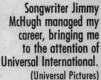

Rock Hudson and I at the Photoplay Awards. I'm wearing the infamous crinoline dress.
(Universal Pictures)

Starring opposite Tony Curtis in *The All American*.
(Universal Pictures)

With Robert Mitchum and Jane Russell in *His Kind of Woman*. I was all of sixteen, and just breaking into the business.

Marilyn Monroe, circa 1952.
(UPI/Bettmann Newsphotos)

With Francis the Talking Mule. We became friends between takes when I listened to his complaints about his agent. (Universal Pictures)

Universal was promoting me heavily as the studio's answer to Marilyn Monroe. (Universal Pictures)

The man in the center is Prince Axel of Denmark. On his left is Piper Laurie; that's me on his right. Although the prince invited me to his palace, I was more interested in my career than in a romance with royalty. (Universal Pictures)

Candidly Hollywood

A studio-arranged date with Nicky Hilton turned into a real romance. (Universal Pictures)

Mmmmm
MAMIE!

A handsome young man with a horn, bandleader Ray Anthony
entered my life and I fell deeply in love.
(Courtesy of Capitol Records, Inc.)

With my beautiful son, Perry.
He has been a source of joy
in my life since the day he
was born.

With Ray on our wedding day,
August 29, 1955.

With Walter Winchell in Palm Springs. Walter later played Cupid by introducing me to Bo Belinsky.

Ray Anthony and I with Jayne Mansfield and Mickey Hargitay at the Mocambo.
(UPI/Bettmann Newsphotos)

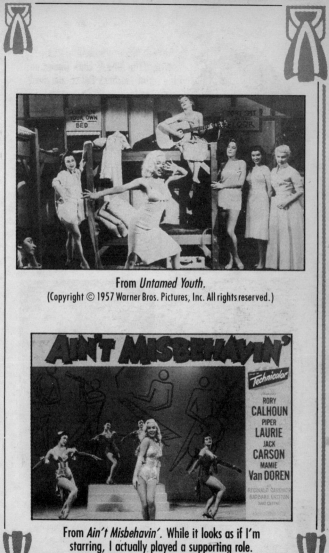

From *Untamed Youth.*

From *Ain't Misbehavin'.* While it looks as if I'm
starring, I actually played a supporting role.
(Universal Pictures)

With "The King," Clark Gable, on the set of *Teacher's Pet*. Gable lived up to his title.

Below left: As the nightclub singer in *Teacher's Pet,* singing "The Girl Who Invented Rock 'n' Roll."

Between takes Gable and I stayed close to each other. If we hadn't both been married at the time, we would have gotten closer yet.

I was working in Italy when Marilyn Monroe, who couldn't attend, asked me to accept her David award—Italy's equivalent of the Oscar—which she received for her role opposite Laurence Olivier in *The Sleeping Prince*. From left to right: me, Anna Magnani, Gina Lollobrigida and Elsa Martinelli (UPI/Bettmann Newsphotos)

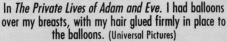

In *The Private Lives of Adam and Eve*. I had balloons over my breasts, with my hair glued firmly in place to the balloons. (Universal Pictures)

On the *Tonight* show with Johnny Carson.

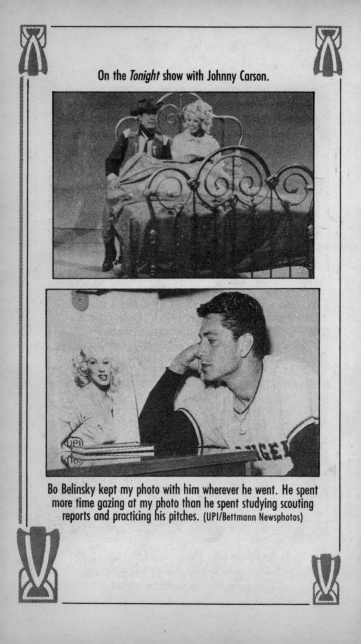

Bo Belinsky kept my photo with him wherever he went. He spent more time gazing at my photo than he spent studying scouting reports and practicing his pitches. (UPI/Bettmann Newsphotos)

Warren Beatty, one of the most obsessive, intense men I've ever known. (UPI/Bettmann Newsphotos)

Steve McQueen. Although he lived life in the fast lane, I'll never forget our time together. (UPI/Bettmann Newsphotos)

Despite his urbane charm, looks, and talent, Cary Grant did not interest me as a suitor. He made many overtures to me, but I always turned him down with an offer of genuine, uncomplicated friendship.

Lee Meyers and I were newlyweds when we posed with Johnny Carson backstage at the *Tonight* show.

Joe Namath's football skills carried him from the coal-mining hometown of Beaver Falls, Pennsylvania, to superstardom with the New York Jets. One of the spoils of his success was this Blackglama mink coat of which he was so proud. Once, during my torrid affair with Joe, we cuddled on this coat. Then, as now, I preferred sable. (UPI/Bettmann Newsphotos)

The war in Vietnam had a profound impact on my life. I lost forever a bit of my own innocence and naiveté in that scarred landscape. "In war there are only the quick and the dead," the saying goes. I shall never forget the men and women who taught me its meaning.

Thomas Dixon and I were married on June 26, 1979, in Newport Beach. My son, Perry (right), stood up for us.

What did the role call for? Vulnerability? Glamour? Cool elegance? Whatever a part required, I always tried to be ready. (Universal Pictures)

Chapter Sixteen

In 1961 I left Famous Artists' Agency to sign with artists' managers Lutz and Loeb.

Bill Loeb was in his early forties. He was a trendy dresser who always wore low-cut boots with pant legs short enough to see some of the boot top. His taste in sport jackets was on the loud side, but he cut a good figure. Loeb was also a good salesman.

Movies were becoming harder to get. For a long time Al Zugsmith had been able to get financing for his films with my name attached. But gradually that wellspring of money began drying up. That period was the beginning of the down-swing in the fortunes of all the fifties sex symbols. Marilyn's last few pictures were far from successful. While Jayne had *Will Success Spoil Rock Hunter?* to her credit, so far she had done only one movie in England and a handful in the U.S. Because of the success of the films Zugsmith and I had done together, Jayne was trying her best to get him to make a movie with her.

Because of this Bill Loeb suggested I put together a night-club act.

"I mean a *real* nightclub act, Mamie," Loeb said. "You can't go out there and do forty-five minutes of straight songs. Of course you've got to have songs, and a good voice to sing them. And you do. But you've got to have songs with first-class arrangements, a little special material, some patter and jokes. A few male dancers wouldn't hurt either. In other words, if you want to make big money, you've got to have the kind of act the clubs pay the big money for.''

Jack Brooks started by writing some jokes for the act. He put together some special material too, new lyrics to a well-known song, customizing it to my image. Then Jack Baker, my choreographer, started rehearsing the male dancers I hired with his help. I began looking around for a conductor to take on the road with me. The musical arrangements were handled by my friend, composer Johnny Mandel.

Several years later, Johnny was to write the Academy Award-winning music for a movie starring Richard Burton and Elizabeth Taylor entitled *The Sandpiper*. He called me late one night and asked, ''Mamie, I've been working on this song all night. Listen to it, will you?'' He put the phone on the piano and played ''The Shadow of Your Smile.''

''Do you like it?'' Johnny asked me after he was done.

''Yes, Johnny. It's beautiful,'' I said. ''I think it will be a hit.''

The one thing Bill Loeb had neglected to mention I would need to put my act together was money—lots of money. It seemed like everyone was on the payroll but me. It was a scary time. I watched all that money going out and nothing coming in but a lot of promises from Bill Loeb that we'd get the bookings.

After months of hard work, the act was finally ready to be tried out. Loeb booked the Chi-Chi Club in Palm Springs, a small club that would provide a good environment to iron out the kinks. I played five nights, and Johnny Mandel conducted the band himself. The reviews from *Variety* and other trade papers were good. Lou Walters of the Latin Quarter in New York booked me on the strength of the reviews and the job I had done for him four years before with the Latin Quarter Review in Las Vegas.

But before I played New York, Bill booked us into the Lotus Club, a small Chinese supper club in Washington, D.C., where Louis Prima and Keely Smith had worked. The booking served a dual purpose: it kept me working enough to pay everyone's salaries, while continuing to refine the act for New York.

There is probably no opening a performer can face that is quite as blood-chilling as a New York opening. You can tell yourself for weeks before that, yes, you'll be nervous, but, no, there's *really* nothing to worry about. After all, the people sitting out there are just people, just like the ones in Des Moines, or Dallas, or Des Plaines. Nonetheless, the reviewers from powerful newspapers and syndicates based there can control your professional fate in other parts of the world.

My opening night at the Latin Quarter was a gala event. Walter Winchell, Ed Sullivan, Earl Wilson, Louis Sobol, and Dorothy Kilgallen were some of the columnists and entertainment writers in attendance. It was the beginning of a four-week engagement, so the reviews were of great concern. They would make or break me with New York audiences and other gigs around the country.

The next morning, to my relief, the reviews were good. During the month I played there, Bill Loeb began to book me into nightclubs all over the country, getting top dollar for the act.

During the next year I would play from one end of the U.S. to the other, as well as Mexico and in Buenos Aires. For over twelve months I lived out of a suitcase in every city that had a major nightclub that could pay the freight. I had almost no time off. Perry and his nurse traveled everywhere with me.

In early 1962 I returned to Los Angeles and my house, feeling like a stranger in my own bed.

"It's ridiculous," I said vehemently one evening to Bill Loeb over coffee. "I've just spent an exhausting year out there working myself to a frazzle. But now that I'm home, I'm no better off than I was when I left. With the salaries of the dancers and conductor, commissions for you and the booking agent, air fares for everybody, and Perry's nurse, I might as well have stayed home. All I've got to show for it is blisters from dancing and a sore throat from singing."

"You've got a nightclub act to show for it," Bill put in.

"Yippee," I said morosely. "I can't keep *this* up. I'll be dead before my time."

Loeb crossed his legs and smiled. "Well, I've got an offer

for you from a dinner theater. They want you to star in *Wild-cat*.''

''The Lucille Ball musical? I don't know about doing theater, Bill. I haven't done any since before my Universal days.''

''Hell, Mamie, you did nightclubs. The show's got great songs in it and the money's five grand a week. It's not all that different from doing a club act. You sing and dance and say someone else's lines. And all you have to pay for is your food. They pay your lodging and air fare.''

''That doesn't sound too bad,'' I said.

''I'll call them this afternoon and have a script sent over. You've got plenty of time to learn it.''

After reading the script, I finally agreed to do the show.

I stayed at the Salisbury Hotel in New York while I was performing in *Wildcat*. Every afternoon a limo would pick me up and drive me to the Meadowbrook Theater in New Jersey for the perfomance, then drive me back afterward. It was my habit to eat dinner in midafternoon, take a nap, and put on most of my makeup before the car arrived. Often I ate my early dinner at the Russian Tea Room across the street from the Salisbury. The maître d' was nice enough to have a waiter serve me in the hours between lunch and dinner.

One rainy afternoon I was eating dinner in a quiet corner of the Tea Room. I had on dark glasses and no makeup, a scarf tied around my head. There were few other diners—only an occasional couple lingering late over a romantic lunch, or a businessman unlucky enough to be left out of the mainstream of the martini-lunch bunch. My usual table was in the back of the dining room, near the kitchen, and facing away from the entrance.

''Miss Van Doren,'' my waiter said quietly. ''I thought you might like to know, we're serving Miss Marilyn Monroe up at the front table.''

''Really?'' I turned around and saw a stringy-haired blonde sitting alone at a table—like me, wearing sunglasses and a scarf, and sans makeup. Her face had a hint of puffiness beneath the glasses, but her cheeks were gaunt and her mouth slack and weary.

I put my napkin on the table, pushed my glasses up onto the top of my head, and crossed the room.

"Hi, Marilyn," I said quietly. I eased into a seat opposite her. She looked at me uncomprehendingly.

"Oh, please . . . I don't feel like . . . Oh! Is it . . . Mamie? Hi!"

I reached across the table and we clasped hands. Her arm and hand felt bony. "Did you get the statue?" I asked.

There was a subtle change in her face as the lines straightened themselves; her eyes blinked behind the dark lenses. She smiled. "Oh, from Italy? Gee, you know, I think I got it. Yes . . . yes, I did."

"The people at the film festival said they'd send it to you."

"Thanks for accepting the award for me. It was the one award I wanted to pick up myself, and I was too busy." There was a rueful tone in her voice and she knocked back the vodka-rocks she had sitting in front of her. She motioned to the waiter for another. "I guess I've got plenty of time now. You heard, I suppose?"

There had been a huge amount of publicity about Marilyn's dismissal in the latter part of May from Twentieth Century-Fox and the film *Something's Got to Give*. There had been rumbles about her impending departure for some time. She was becoming increasingly hard to work with—she was late getting to the set or absent with mysterious illnesses far too often. Displays of temperament came more and more frequently, exposing the deep, raw emotional strata of Marilyn's personality. It became obvious she was unraveling, and I could sympathize with her more than the Hollywood vultures that were so anxious to criticize.

"Yes, I heard."

Her lower lip quivered and she took a long swallow of her fresh drink.

"Well," she said, "there'll be other movies." There was an almost childish challenge in her voice, as if daring me to say there wouldn't be.

I was painfully aware that there hadn't been other movies for *me* in quite a while.

Is it happening to all of us? I thought.

"Always other movies around the corner," I said as cheerfully as I could. Then, as an afterthought, I said: "If not a movie, there are theaters and nightclubs. That's what I've been doing."

"No kidding? Aren't you scared of being in front of all those people?"

"I was . . . petrified!"

"That's something I couldn't do, Mamie. It'd scare the shit out of me."

"It *did* scare the shit out of me. I used to spend an hour on the toilet before a show."

Marilyn smiled for the first time. "Yeah. I'd just die if I had to do that, I guess."

"I've got a mouth other than my own to feed. That's why I do it."

Her face really brightened and suddenly she appeared to take an interest. "Your son! Oh, I'm sorry, what's his name?"

"Perry."

"Perry! Yes, I remember seeing his picture in the paper when he was born. How old is he, Mamie?"

"He just turned six in March. Growing like the dickens."

"I envy you *so*, having a child. Who looks after him while you're gone? A nurse?"

"I left him with a nurse when Ray and I were together. Now my mother stays at my house and keeps an eye on Perry *and* the nurse. I used to take him on the road with me, but he's got to start school soon, so that's out."

"Doesn't it break your heart to leave him behind?" Marilyn leaned forward and stared intently into my eyes, as though the answer meant the end of the world to her.

"Yes," I replied, "but I need to work, so what can I do?"

"True." Marilyn nodded and looked lost in her own thoughts for a moment. When she spoke again, it sounded like an utterance in a church. "I would love to have a child. I'm trying to adopt, you know, but all the agencies look at my . . . me . . . Well, these men in blue suits say, oh so very logically: 'What kind of life would that be for a child? Marriages, divorces, the men in your life, Miss Monroe . . .' I don't know what to say to them, Mamie."

I didn't have any suggestions for her. My son had suffered through some of that already. I looked away from her.

"Perry misses his father. It's been hard on him."

"Sure. You and Ray finally got your divorce?"

There was a moment when the old jealousy flared. I wanted

to say that he was all hers, roses and all, but something stopped me. The time when I found out that he'd sent Marilyn roses in the hospital, or when I'd heard the lyrics to the song Ray had written for her, seemed very far away. My tantrums then looked childish now.

"It was a long separation. We could never reconcile."

She looked at me sheepishly for a moment, as though realizing the mention of Ray might have been painful for me.

"I divorced Arthur not long ago," she said. "No divorce is easy. You can agree to disagree all you want, but in the end each one hurts the other. Usually on purpose."

Arthur Miller had divorced Marilyn and would soon marry a photographer he had met on *The Misfits* set. That the photographer replaced her in Miller's affections was a painful memory to which Marilyn's eyes testified.

"There were times when I just wanted to die, Mamie. The pain was *so* bad."

It suddenly came home to me that Marilyn was in New York, far from L.A. and the movie colony. Was it because she was running from the pain of being sacked by Twentieth Century-Fox? Was she looking for another New York intellectual to fill the shoes of Arthur Miller? Or was there something else on the East Coast?

The jungle telegraph that operates out of Hollywood had been very specific about Marilyn's replacement for Arthur Miller. The drums echoed all the way to New York with the news that Marilyn was desperately in love with a Kennedy. There was speculation—massive speculation—about which one it was, about assignations with Jack in L.A. He was, after all, a man known, like his father, for his exotic tastes in movie actresses. Later there was the rumor about Bobby. After the President had tired of the star, some had it she was passed along, as other lovelies had been, to the little brother slaving away in the attorney general's office.

Marilyn downed her third drink since I sat down. The ice cubes clinked and she set the glass aside. She slipped off her sunglasses and looked at me hard. There appeared to be hundreds of stories flashing behind her eyes. When she spoke at last, it was a tipsy slur.

"Do your best, Mamie, not to fall in love with anybody in government. Because after they fuck you—they fuck you."

A little while later I hurried out of the Russian Tea Room and out onto Fifty-seventh Street. There was a violent thunderstorm under way and a hard, hard rain was pounding down onto the steaming hot pavement. I dashed across the street and into the entrance of the Salisbury Hotel. I would never forget my last sight of Marilyn sitting at that lonely table. In front of her on the white tablecloth were three empty glasses. A fourth stood before her, full of ice and the clear, sharp, characterless vodka that she was using to blot out her private horrors. What I couldn't tell her, because we were never close enough, intimate enough, was that it was what we all faced. When you make your living as a glamour girl, there is always, lurking around the corner, the specter of getting old, of losing your glamour.

That summer I left instructions with the Salisbury Hotel's switchboard not to disturb me with phone calls while I was sleeping. The only exception was an emergency call from my mother or father. When the telephone jolted me out of my sleep in the early morning of August 5, I frantically grabbed for the receiver.

"Mamie, this is Earl Wilson," the familiar voice on the other end said. Earl was the entertainment columnist for the New York *Post*. "Have you heard the news?"

"Heard what?" I asked groggily, the adrenaline pumping through my body.

"Marilyn killed herself this morning."

"What?" I couldn't believe it—it had only been a few months since we sat together in the Russian Tea Room. "Where?"

"In California. They found her dead in her house. It's all over the radio and TV. Can we meet to talk, Mamie?"

"Talk?"

"About Marilyn. Just for a few minutes."

"Not now, Earl. I'm . . . I just woke up. How about this afternoon, just before I go to the theater?"

"It's a date. I'll call you later."

I hung up the phone and turned on the television in my room. The *Today* show was carrying an interview with Marilyn filmed some months before. For a moment I thought someone impersonating Earl Wilson had awakened me with a cruel joke.

Then Marilyn's face disappeared and a new scene flashed onto the screen. Men rolled a white-shrouded figure on a gurney out the front door of her Brentwood home, down the steps, and unceremoniously bounced it into a coroner's-office van.

It was hard to believe that Marilyn was under that sheet.

It was all I could do to get myself together for the show that evening. I had hoped the producers might cancel the performance, but the show went on. No one at the theater spoke to me about Marilyn. I was like a zombie during the show.

That evening back in my room at the Salisbury, I watched several newscasts that gave extensive coverage to Marilyn's death. Phrases from the newscast kept looping through my thoughts: " . . . blonde sex goddess . . . rumored to be despondent . . . declining career . . . divorce from playwright Arthur Miller . . . former husband Joe DiMaggio . . ."

Divorce, devastation, decline . . . The similarities between us were frightening. I tried to keep in mind that what happened to Marilyn need not happen to me. Nonetheless, with Marilyn's death, the entire world recognized that an era was over. The days of the sex goddesses and blonde bombshells had been officially laid to rest.

Chapter Seventeen

A few weeks after Marilyn's death I was back in Los Angeles when Ray Anthony called. After we talked amiably for a few minutes, he got around to asking me if I would like to go out with a friend of his—baseball player Bo Belinsky. At the time I had no idea who Bo Belinsky, baseball's new glamour boy, was. Belinsky had become an instant celebrity in L.A. the year before when he achieved that rare baseball feat—pitching a no-hitter—in his rookie season. That summer reporters had followed him everywhere as he dated an endless procession of stars and celebrities anxious for a good time and a little free exposure. But he was a complete unknown to me, and I declined.

One day not long afterward, a man who had befriended me in my early days as a Universal starlet, Walter Winchell, gave me a call.

"Mamie, why don't you come down to the Peppermint West? There's someone here I want you to meet."

"Right now, Walter? I haven't even got any makeup on."

"That's all right. We'll wait. Come on down."

"Who's 'we'?"

"Me and my friend Bo Belinsky."

"Walter, it's kind of late—"

"Mamie, he's dying to meet you. Here, he can tell you himself."

There was the sound of Walter handing the phone over; then a younger voice came on the line.

"Mamie? Hi, this is Bo Belinsky. C'mon down! We'll have lots of fun."

"Well, I'd like to, Bo. But you see—"

"If you'd like to, then do it."

"Well . . . all right."

The Peppermint West was jammed with people. Once a sleazy little bar on Cahuenga Boulevard, it had been converted into one of the first discotheques on the West Coast. It quickly caught on in Hollywood, and became *the* place to go.

When I arrived, Walter Winchell was sitting at a table with a date, another couple, and Bo.

Bo Belinsky had the kind of charisma and sex appeal that are often found among rock stars today. He was tall and slim with a dark shock of hair, deep-set liquid eyes, a strong aquiline nose, and a leading man's smile. He was quick-witted and articulate. In a word, charming.

When Winchell introduced me to Bo, I felt a strong tug of attraction. There was that immediate ignition that I'd felt before between myself and a man. I knew this would be the beginning of something, but I didn't know what.

We danced the mashed potato endlessly that evening and had tray after tray of drinks. At one point, a group of photographers descended on us, snapping photos and babbling questions. After closing up the Peppermint West, we all went to an after-hours place, had dinner, more drinks, drove around a bit, and generally whooped it up. Baseball season was just over and Bo was celebrating the end of his rookie year. His no-hitter had made him the apple of California Angels owner Gene Autry's eye. Autry's franchise was only two years old. He saw Bo and another rookie fast-ball pitcher and Cy Young Award winner named Dean Chance as the keys to a pennant win for his club.

Bo was fun.

The next day I awoke to find our pictures in all the papers with captions to the effect that I was his new sweetheart.

That's a little premature, I thought. As it turned out, Bo had left town. It would be months before I saw him again.

* * *

Two of my closest friends during that period were Jimmy and Margie Durante, who lived across the street. We were really like a kind of extended family, going to each other's parties and visiting several times a week.

I began dating a close friend of the Durantes', dog-food magnate Clement Hirsch. Next to Howard Hughes, Clement was the richest man I'd known. At the time we were going out, he owned Kal Kan dog food, though the basis of his wealth was a large family fortune.

It was while dating Clement that I decided to get my night-club act back together and take it on the road again. Bill Loeb had come up with some lucrative bookings, and my bank account was in need of replenishment.

This time, I would tailor the act so that I could show a little more profit. There was no way I could avoid paying commission to Bill Loeb and my booking agency, MCA, so I eliminated the conductor and one of the dancers. Without the expense of their salaries and travel expenses, I would have more to show for my hard work.

First stop on the tour was Palm Springs and the Chi-Chi Club. When I was making plans for the Chi-Chi opening, my girlfriend Danni suggested that I do something different with my hair.

"I know somebody you'll like. And he lives in Joshua Tree, up in the high desert. He can come down to Palm Springs and do your hair. He's great. His name's Don Morand."

Don gave me a brand-new look, a haircut with bangs in front, curls piled on top, and barrettes pulling up each side in the back that became a style associated with the sixties. He became my closest friend and confidant for the many years during which he traveled the world with me. Unabashedly gay, he was a sensitive, artistic man, and the hairstyle he created for me was soon widely copied around town.

I opened at the Chi-Chi shortly after my thirtieth birthday in February 1963. Among the audience in the packed house that night were Frank Sinatra and his entourage. One of the numbers in my act at the time was a medley of songs that I sang while my male dancer put on several lifelike rubber masks, those of Winston Churchill, John F. Kennedy, Lyn-

don Johnson, Maurice Chevalier, Elvis Presley, and Frank
Sinatra. When I began singing "All the Way" and the dancer
came onstage with the Sinatra mask, it brought the house
down. Laughing loudest of all was Sinatra himself. At the
end of the show I introduced Frank, who smiled at the stage
and the applauding audience.

Also in the audience that night was Bo Belinsky, in Palm
Springs with the California Angels to begin spring training
after playing winter baseball in South America.

Sinatra and Belinsky both sent notes backstage after the
show. Bo sent word that he had a curfew and had to get back
to the hotel where the team was staying. (A very un-Belinsky
bit of behavior, I would find out later.) He left his number
with the request that I call him when I got up the next day.
Sinatra asked me to have dinner with him across the street at
the Ruby Dunes after the show. This time I accepted Sinatra's
invitation.

Frank's valet for many years, George, picked me up in
Frank's car and drove me the short distance to the Ruby
Dunes. When I arrived, Frank was in the midst of an argument with some men at another table. He gestured me to our
table, told me to order some dinner, and turned back to his
argument. I ordered a tray of cracked crab. He continued his
altercation during the entire time I ate my dinner. When I
finished, the waiter took the demolished tray of crab away
and Sinatra was still going strong.

I yawned discreetly. I asked the waiter for the time. Finally
I got up, told Frank good night, and walked out. He stopped
arguing only long enough to tell George to escort me back
across the street because it was late.

As I got into my car back at the Chi-Chi, I had to laugh to
myself. So much for my hot date with Frank Sinatra, I
thought.

The next morning I called Bo and we made a date to go to
the Racquet Club, the same place I had refused to meet Howard Hughes fifteen years ago.

As we sat around the club having drinks and talking, I
began to see just what a magnet Bo was with girls. They
swarmed around him. His face was well-known from his successful rookie season, and now that spring training was under

way, every Baseball Annie in the L.A. basin was out to score with Bo.

I liked him. But I could see that our future had the potential to be really rocky. He was a ladies' man fully aware of his powers and with little inclination to curb them. The sensible thing would be to just go our separate ways. But who ever said you had to be sensible when playing the field?

When I closed my show at the Chi-Chi and got back to Los Angeles it wasn't long before Bo called and asked me to come back. Enthusiastic about seeing him again, I took a room at the Riviera Hotel in Palm Springs where the Angels stayed.

After an evening of dinner and dancing, Bo and I went back to my room. I melted into his muscular arms and we kissed with growing passion. Finally we threw off our clothes and embraced. Naked, Bo was very different from the other men I had been to bed with. In the early sixties, fitness was still an uncommon preoccupation among men not involved in professional sports. The musicians and actors I had previously known were often soft and underdeveloped. Bo, on the other hand, was deep-chested, lean, and trim. As we got into bed and reached greater and greater heights of ecstasy, I felt a rekindling of desire that had been dormant in me since my relationship with Ray had started going bad.

I threw myself wholeheartedly into a romance with Bo. It's not easy to conduct a romance with a ball player during baseball season—particularly when, as an added complication, the other party is frequently on the road with a nightclub act.

As the baseball season got into full swing and we were apart, we talked for hours on the phone, especially on the nights before Bo pitched. He could never sleep the night before he had to start. He walked the floor, smoked one cigarette after another, and drank heavily. And he would do his best to have sex all night.

I've read that many athletes will not have sex before a big event—boxers, football players, marathoners, and, yes, even baseball players. And too, opera singers, ballet dancers, and one or two actors won't have sex before a big performance. Ernest Hemingway, literary godfather of machismo, cautioned writers that they might leave their best work in bed.

Bo had no such constraints. In fact, Bo left some very good

work there indeed. Making love all night was part of the ritual for him. He seemed to try to drive himself to exhaustion. His pitching performances began to show the effects of his life-style. As the season went on, it became obvious that the early promise of his pitching career was not being realized.

In retrospect it seems that the only time photographers and reporters were not swarming around us was when we were in bed. I've often been accused of doing things only for the publicity, and sometimes it's been true. But, short of Jayne Mansfield, Bo Belinsky loved publicity more than anyone I've ever met. Part of Bo's love of publicity was sheer, unbounded ego—it thrilled him to see his picture in the papers. But there was a darker side to it: a need to bolster his terrible fear of failure.

Wherever we went, from the first time we met at the Peppermint West, Bo managed to have the press there. If we had dinner at some quiet place, almost miraculously photographers appeared. If I went to see him pitch at Dodger Stadium (where the Angels played their home games before Anaheim Stadium was built), there would always be a gaggle of reporters. It was like living in a goldfish bowl. Having no private life became unnerving. But before it got better, it would get much, much worse.

Bo was haunted by his no-hitter. If he had not had the bad luck to throw that one no-hit game against the Baltimore Orioles, he might have had a longer, more fruitful career. There was just too much expected of him. Too much that he was afraid he couldn't deliver.

"If I could just find her," he mumbled one night as he paced around the room. He was scheduled to pitch the next day and his pregame nerves had him wound up like a spring.

"Find who?" I asked. My ears pricked up at the mention of another "her."

"The girl I was with the night before I pitched my no-hitter. If I could only find her again, you know, maybe I could pitch another one."

Bo had searched all over for her after the game. He even mentioned her in interviews, inviting her to call or meet him again.

"She was standing next to my car," Bo went on. He had

a gold Cadillac that was known far and wide around L.A. "She was a real looker too. She was leaning against the car with a smile on her face. We went and had a drink, then went back to my place and fucked all night. The next day I pitched the no-hitter."

"So she's your lucky charm?" I pouted. "Not me?"

He crawled back into bed and gathered me into his arms. "Haven't thrown a no-hitter yet, Mamie. But let's keep trying."

Trust was not a major component of Bo's personality. It's possible that he fell prey to my publicity much the way DiMaggio did to Marilyn's. The kind of publicity that you get when you're a so-called sex symbol is hard for any man that's serious about you to live with. There's the implication that you're always available. It's part of the image. Other men think of you as their personal property because you have so often been the object of their fantasies.

A trusting soul Bo was not. It became painfully evident late one night when Bo was on a road trip with the Angels and called me from his hotel room.

"Mamie, you're cheating on me, dammit!" he snapped.

"Cheating?" I asked incredulously. "I'm not, honey. I've been completely faithful to you."

"Bullshit!" he shot back. "Who do you know that's got a surfboard?"

"Nobody, Bo."

"That's a lie and you know it, Mamie! I happen to know that some young guy comes to your house every day with a surfboard."

My mind raced. I didn't even *know* anyone who surfed, much less have him over to my house every day. I told him so.

"Just how do you know all this, Bo? Are you having me watched?"

"Don't try to change the subject. Some guy in a blue car comes there every day and takes his surfboard out of the car and goes in your house for an hour or so. Then he comes out with his surfboard, gets in the car, and drives off."

I started to laugh, because I suddenly realized what he was talking about. I'd been continuing with my dance lessons to stay in shape for my nightclub act. One of the things I looked forward to after dancing was a good, relaxing massage. I had a standing appointment every day with a terrific Swedish masseur. He'd drive up to the house in a nondescript blue car, unload his massage table, bring it in the house, and give me a massage. It took an hour.

I explained it to Bo.

"So you'd better tell your Peeping Tom to clean his binoculars," I concluded. "That was no surfboard, it was a massage table."

"You mean you have to pay someone to come rub your ass? Or does he pay you?"

"Very funny."

"I'll do it for free, Mamie."

"How soon can you get here?"

"I'm in New York, remember?"

We talked awhile longer and made up. Just before we said good night, I couldn't resist asking: "Bo? If you thought I was having an affair with someone like that, what did you think we did with the surfboard? It's ten miles to the closest beach."

Bo proposed to me three months after we started dating, on April 1, April Fools' Day. I accepted without hesitation. I was, I believed, in love.

Bo announced to the press that we were engaged and we played, much to his glee, hide-and-seek with them for a while. After a couple of weeks Bo told me, "Mamie, I proposed to you on April Fools' Day because I thought it would make good publicity. I was going to announce it was a joke, but now I don't want to. I really want to do it."

Bo wanted to buy me a ring. "I don't want *my* fiancée walking around without a ring on. I know just the place— Marvin Hime & Company in Beverly Hills—and I know just the person to help us pick it out."

"Help us?"

"Yeah. Judy Campbell will know what to buy for you. She's got great taste."

Judy Campbell had been the wife of Universal actor Bill Campbell. She divorced Bill and went on to achieve underground notoriety as Jack Kennedy's West Coast mistress.

''Why should Judy Campbell want to go with us to buy my engagement ring?'' I asked him.

''She'll help pick it out.''

''Bo, did it occur to you that I might be perfectly capable of deciding what kind of engagement ring I want?''

''I know, Mamie. And you can cool down that jealous spark in your eyes too. There's nothing between Judy and me. She's just a friend.''

''People in love normally do *not* take along a female acquaintance of the husband-to-be when picking out a ring.''

''She just wants to meet you, okay? She says that Kennedy's interested in getting into your pants and she wants to see what you're like.''

''Why don't you just tell her how sweet and lovely I am, Bo?''

''I told her that if Jack Kennedy came sniffing around you, I'd make him real sorry.''

Bo insisted on having Judy along. It finally came out that Judy could get him a big discount on jewelry from Marvin Hime & Company because that was the store where she bought her jewelry. Apparently it was a prodigious amount of jewelry too. According to Bo, it was all charged to a secret account and paid for by the thirty-fifth President of the United States.

We finally settled on a perfectly shaped emerald-cut diamond with wonderful fire and brilliance. It was so expensive Bo had to pay for it on time—something it turned out we didn't have much of.

The announcement of our engagement brought Bo sudden and unexpected heat from the Angels' front office. Autry called him in and told him flatly that I was ruining his career. Presumably Bo did *not* tell him that was something he could do perfectly well on his own. On the other hand, perhaps there was some truth to the point. In 1962, the year before we met, Bo won ten and lost eleven and the Angels finished third in the league. The year we were together, Bo won two and lost nine, and the Angels finished in ninth place.

The Angels began a steady process of chipping away at Bo. Their releases to the press left no doubt that they did not approve of Bo seeing me, much less being engaged. Sportswriters began taking potshots at me for what I was doing to Bo.

It always bothers me when someone dislikes me but will

not just come out and say it. The two-faced attitude of smiling acceptance to my face by the Angels' management and mean-spirited disapproval behind my back always made me nauseated. They were always pleasant in my presence, whether I was waiting for Bo outside the locker room or sitting watching the game from the same rows as the Cowboy himself.

Autry would come down with his entourage and squeeze past me down the row of seats to his box. Then, every once in a while, I'd catch him looking at me, grinning from under his ten-gallon hat.

But in every other way the Angels acted as though I was single-handedly doing my best to keep Bo from pitching. Actually, I was trying to coax him into getting enough rest. Or cut down on his heavy smoking or his drinking.

Bo managed to hold out for a while against the front office's harassment. We remained engaged in the face of it all and I began to make plans. I decided to take a pretty tough string of bookings, including a stint in summer stock. These would bring in a nice chunk of money. I thought it would give us a solid foundation to live on after our marriage. We would never be able to live on Bo's salary; his career was crumbling before his eyes. Not only could he not throw another no-hitter, he could barely throw a strike.

It was obvious to me (if not to the team's management) that part of Bo's problem was that he hated baseball. He liked pitching, I think, because it gave him so much free time. He had to work only once every four or five days. And in between starts he could raise as much hell as he wanted. All the other things, the things a pitcher needs to build his career on, like running or practicing his pitches, Bo hated. He neglected all the fundamentals and did as little as he could get away with.

We had been engaged for a few months when I missed a period. My first thought was: Here we go again. I thought I was pregnant. Then I thought: No, there's no problem. Not with Bo.

Wrong.

Bo was out on the road when I told him.

"You couldn't get pregnant from me. I can't get anybody pregnant."

When we first started dating, a girl followed us around in her car one night. When I asked Bo about it, he said that she claimed she was pregnant and he was the father of the child.

"Well? Are you?" I had challenged.

"Naw," he said. "I can't get anybody pregnant."

Just his say-so didn't make a very convincing argument to me. Remembering my early problems with Ray Anthony, I felt terrible for the girl.

"If it is yours, it's your responsibility, Bo," I told him.

But the girl never filed suit. Either she was bluffing to get Bo to marry her, or she gave up.

Now Bo was pulling the same stunt with me.

"I remember you said that once before. I didn't believe it then, and I don't believe it now. I haven't made love with anyone but you."

"Oh yeah?" There was a note of suspicion in his voice that infuriated me. He was lucky we were on long distance and not in the same room.

Later that evening Bo called me back.

"Hey, Mamie, I guess I *could* have gotten you pregnant."

"You guess? Why the sudden change of heart?"

"I called up a doctor friend of mine after we talked, and he said we could check it out. He told me to jerk off into a little vial and bring it over. It was embarrassing! I had to go all the way over to his office—up the elevator, wait in the waiting room—keeping a little tube of come under my arm so it would stay warm. But it looks like I'm fertile."

Bo changed his tune completely once it began to sink in that it could be his. He insisted that we have the baby. As it turned out, I wasn't pregnant.

There were several things about Bo that were causing us problems. I have a bad allergy to cigarette smoke and his chain smoking often made me ill. His behavior was erratic due to his drinking. And his sleeping habits drove me crazy.

I'm one of those people who become basket cases if they don't get a solid eight or ten hours of sleep. Bo thought nothing of calling in the middle of the night and talking for hours. This was okay if I wasn't working, but if I was, it was disaster. Many times I had to drag myself through a second show because Bo and I had spent the night talking on the telephone.

The romance began to disintegrate several weeks later.

I was touring a summer-stock production of *Silk Stockings* with Lee Grant. We were playing Springfield, Massachusetts, when the phone woke me out of a sound sleep.

"Mamie! I'm breaking off our engagement," Bo said.

I fought my way up out of a deep sleep, trying to make sense of what he was saying.

"Breaking off . . . Why?"

"I'm tired of you being unfaithful to me."

"Bo, for the thousandth time: I'm not being unfaithful to you. Not now or ever."

"I know you've been seeing a young guy. *Really* young— like sixteen or so."

A young kid was assigned to drive me to and from the theater every night. When he picked me up at the hotel, he came upstairs and helped me with my makeup case and whatever else I might be carrying. When the show was over and he brought me back, he reversed the process and helped carry my stuff back up to my room. He was sweet and kind of gaga over being my driver, so a couple of times I had invited him to stay for a sandwich and a Coke. We talked and watched TV. Nothing could have been more innocent.

However, the fact that Bo knew about it explained some strange occurrences over the past week or so. Ever since I arrived at the hotel, odd things had been going on. One day I was suntanning on the hotel roof and got locked out when the rooftop door, which I was careful to leave open, was mysteriously closed. When I got back to my room, *that* door was open and I was positive that I had shut it. And my telephone began making funny noises when I picked up the receiver. I had the odd feeling of living with a ghost. Now I understood: Bo was having me watched again. Very closely.

"Bo," I said tearfully after explaining the young man to him, "I'm out here working so we can have a little cushion to live on. Cheating on you is the farthest thing from my mind."

He was adamant.

"Look, Mamie," he concluded, "I'm still paying on that ring. Please send it back."

When I slammed the phone down, it was daylight, I was distraught, and sleep would not return.

Lee Grant and I had become friends during the production

of *Silk Stockings*. Lee is one of the all-time great professional actresses, a woman of taste and talent who possesses down-to-earth good sense. She put me back on course. I was crying hysterically in my dressing room when Lee came in, sat in a chair in front of me, and said: "Mamie, stop punishing yourself. He's not worth it! If this is the way he treats you, be glad it's over."

I managed to straighten out and continue the show. We were finishing the *Silk Stockings* tour in Baltimore when I saw a man-in-the-street interview on a local sports show.

"What do you think Mamie Van Doren should do with Bo Belinsky's ring, now that he's broken their engagement?" the interviewer asked.

The unanimous answer was: "Keep it!"

When I stopped laughing, I looked at the ring on my finger. I really didn't want anything to do with Bo. I didn't even like the looks of the ring anymore. I grabbed an envelope from the hotel's stationery, scrawled "Bo Belinsky, Dodger Stadium, Los Angeles" on it, tossed the ring inside, and sealed it. As an afterthought, I added Bo's address on La Presa Drive, to make sure he got it.

But I couldn't forget Bo. I was so hurt by his accusation of cheating, something I had scrupulously avoided, that I felt I must speak to him again, face-to-face.

Bo lived in a top-floor apartment on La Presa Drive, not far from where Ray and I had lived when we were first married. I went to see him.

"Bo, I wanted you to know that I never cheated on you. If you wanted to end our engagement, all you had to do was say so. You didn't have to spend the money to have me followed and trump up this thing about the young kid."

The scene ended with me in tears and in Bo's arms. He delivered himself of one of the most deathless lines in the history of love affairs: "Aw, I'm a sucker for mascara."

That afternoon when we emerged from Bo's bed, we decided to get reengaged. He had at last leveled with me about the reason for breaking our engagement. The Angels had given him an ultimatum: break off with Mamie or go down to their minor-league club in Hawaii.

"Oh, well," he said with that wise-ass grin, "I've never been to Hawaii."

Bo, as advertised, had been shipped off to Hawaii and the ignominy of the minors once our engagement was revived. Then I found out he had been sleeping with other women. I also discovered he had given me the flu.

I was furious, this time with myself. I'd been a fool to try to get back together with Bo.

When I got him on the line from Hawaii, the reaction was what I expected. He denied seeing other women.

"You bastard! You weren't man enough to tell me before we went to bed, and you aren't man enough to admit it now."

There was only the sound of his breathing on the phone.

"In a way, you've done me a favor. You finally made me see what a failure you really are. I've got a lot of hard work to do on a movie soon and I won't have you around to sap my strength. I won't be rid of you completely until this flu bug is licked. But when all that virus is beaten I'll be absolutely rid of Bo Belinsky."

I should have been so lucky.

I had just signed to do a movie called *The Candidate*. It was the story of Lyndon Johnson's pal Bobby Baker and his shenanigans with Washington corruption. It starred Ted Knight in a serious role. (Robert Redford did another political movie of the same name a decade later.)

It was a good script and I was excited about doing a role that was a departure for me. I played a senator's secretary who was a Washington party girl working her way up, rather than the all-too-typical dumb blonde.

The night before I started shooting *The Candidate*, I went to bed early to be fully rested on the set the next morning.

My increasing notoriety due to my engagement and breakup with Bo made my house a frightening place to stay in alone at night. I was bothered continually with prowlers and weirdos of every stamp trying to get a glimpse of me. I asked Don Morand to stay in one of the bedrooms so at least there would be someone in the house with me.

That evening I awakened to pounding on the front door. I could hear loud voices and the sound of engines in the driveway. Red and yellow lights flashed through the windows.

In a panic I ran to the door.

"Open up!" a man's voice shouted.

"No!" I shouted back. "Who is it?"

The men on the other side answered by trying to break the door in. By this time Don was up and shouting through the door to them as well.

One of them yelled in answer, "We've had a call that Mamie Van Doren is trying to commit suicide."

"I'm fine. Go away so I can get some sleep!"

"We've got to see that you're all right."

I opened the door and was blinded by the bright lights. There were ambulances sitting in my driveway and men in white coats pushing a gurney toward me. Police cars pulled into the driveway. It was the scene I'd watched at Marilyn's house on the news a year before.

Two ambulance attendants grabbed me by the arm and pulled me toward the gurney. "Please come with us, Miss Van Doren. We'll help you."

"I don't need help. I'm fine."

Don took my other arm and pulled me back. "There's nothing wrong. Mamie's got to get up early and work tomorrow."

"We've had a call that Mamie has taken an overdose of sleeping pills because she's despondent over Bo Belinsky."

"What?" I broke up the tug-of-war and turned in fury on the ambulance attendants. They let go of my arm and backed away. So did Don. "Despondent over Bo Belinsky? I've never been so glad to be rid of anyone."

One of the police officers broke in. "Miss Van Doren, please come along quietly. You'll be just fine."

"Now, just hold it!" I barked. I took a deep breath and controlled my voice as best I could. "I did not take an overdose of pills. I am not despondent. I am especially not despondent over my breakup with Bo Belinsky."

It was late when I finally talked my way out of being carried off to have my stomach pumped. I managed to doze fitfully for an hour or so before the alarm went off.

Sometime later, Harrison Carroll, the columnist, told me that he'd had a call the same night about me. Same story—that I had taken an overdose because of unrequited love for Bo.

"Harrison, who would do such a mean prank to me?"

He only rolled his eyes and shrugged.

Who indeed.

Chapter Eighteen

At the end of the *Silk Stockings* tour in Baltimore, I received a call from Bill Loeb back in L.A.

"Mamie, can you get up to New York? Johnny Carson wants you on the *Tonight* show."

It was my second invitation to the *Tonight* show. The first had been just before I left New York at the end of the *Wildcat* production, a week or so after Marilyn's death. Jack Paar at that time was the host. Johnny had replaced Parr, bringing a breath of fresh air to the show. His rapidly rising popularity was easy to understand. He had made watching the show fun—it was like a party, with just Johnny and a few million close friends.

I took a limousine from Baltimore to New York after the last *Silk Stockings* performance. The next day I took a cab to the NBC studios at Rockefeller Plaza. I met with one of the show's writers to go over what Johnny would talk to me about. That afternoon I rehearsed the song I was to do with Skitch Henderson and the NBC orchestra. Skitch and I were old buddies from the days when he was the musical director for the Steve Allen show.

The *Tonight* show taping got under way at seven P.M. during its New York tenure. I sang my song and sat down to talk with Johnny. A retired baseball player had been invited on the show for my benefit. There were a few jokes about my broken engagement with Bo, which everyone but me thought were funny, but it was obvious that Johnny was orchestrating everything to make me look good.

During a commercial break, Johnny leaned toward me and asked: "What are you doing after the show, Mamie?"

Johnny's friendly manner had impressed me and I liked him instantly. I sensed that he liked me too. I thought he'd probably ask me out, but I didn't think it would be during a commercial.

"Oh . . . I really don't have any definite plans."

"How about dinner?"

"Sure."

We took Johnny's limousine to dinner after the show, stopping at a little out-of-the-way restaurant where the lights were low and the food was good. We toasted each other with cold beers.

Sometime during the meal we decided to go somewhere to watch the airing of the show. Johnny's penthouse overlooking the river was out of the question, since he was then married or about to be married to Joann, his second wife. The logical choice was my room at the Plaza.

Just before the limo pulled up in front of the Plaza's entrance, Johnny slipped on a pair of dark glasses. He turned to me and flashed one of his patented smiles.

"It wouldn't do for me to be recognized."

Up in my room Johnny took off his coat and loosened his tie. He flipped on the TV set and we kicked off our shoes and sat up in the big bed, pushing the pillows up against the headboard. Johnny got on the phone to room service and ordered up some champagne.

"Just wait, Mamie. I gave you top billing tonight. You'll love it."

The room-service cart arrived and Johnny paid for the champagne. He popped the champagne cork, and we were just settling down to sip our first glass as the show's familiar theme music came on, followed by the voice of Ed McMahon.

"From New York, it's the *Tonight* show, starring Johnny Carson. Tonight Johnny's guests are: Mamie Van Doren—"

"See," Johnny interrupted. "I told you."

I leaned over and gave him a kiss. "Thank you."

He kissed me back. "My pleasure."

"And now!" Ed went on after listing the rest of the guests. "Herrrrrrre's . . . Johnny!"

We stopped kissing and Johnny turned to the TV set to watch himself.

While we sat in my bed at the Plaza watching the show we'd taped earlier that evening, part of me watched Johnny too. He made comments here and there about this joke that went over, or that remark from a guest that was a bomb. He watched the show with interest, certainly because it was his livelihood, but also unmistakably because he liked it.

Johnny Carson occupies a unique place in show business. What he does—his act, so to speak—is absolutely his own. Perhaps no one will ever do it better.

Johnny is not a great actor. Nor is he a singer. He confided to me that night at the Plaza that one of the things he really *wanted* to do was sing.

"But I don't know what to do between the notes, Mamie."

As a comedian he can be funny. But he is not a comedian in the sense that Robin Williams, Richard Pryor, Jonathan Winters, or even Jack Benny, after whom he likes to pattern himself, is a comedian. He is a comedian in the tradition of Bob Hope, or, today, Joan Rivers. Johnny Carson tells jokes. He can get laughs with timing, tone, and facial expression, but he does not create comic characters or comic situations for his audience. Setup, development, punch line; many one-liners; several time-honored running jokes ("How cold *was* it?") make up Johnny's primary bag of tricks.

And then there is the part that is pure Johnny.

What Johnny creates for the viewing audience is the perfect television companion, someone you can comfortably invite into your bedroom night after night just for laughs. He is part gee-whiz Midwesterner, part New York/Hollywood sophisticate. He is the boy next door who made it big. Johnny cuts across all social boundaries, and it has made him as famous as anyone in television history.

Watching the show, I found myself wondering if I was going to go to bed with Johnny. So far, no mention of Joann had been made by either of us. It was, I assumed, some kind of convenient arrangement between them. But I wondered how convenient Johnny would have thought it was if the shoe was on the other foot and, say, he had known that Joann was lying in bed watching late-night TV, sipping champagne, and necking with Paul Newman.

I was a little tipsy from the champagne by the time the closing credits began to roll. The show was a good one, and we toasted it with the last of the champagne. Johnny turned to me and whispered softly, "You know, Mamie, you don't have to worry. I've had a vasectomy."

Quite unexpectedly, I laughed, thinking it was a joke. But I realized he was serious.

The opportunity to make love with Johnny was tempting. That boyish charm that came across the television screen seemed completely genuine up close. But despite my feeling that a new romance would be just the thing to get over the pain of my breakup with Bo, the wounds were still too fresh.

Back in Los Angeles, I spent as much time as I could with Perry. The effects of the divorce on him had been compounded by my being out of town so much and having to leave him behind. Perry clung to me constantly, demanding my attention, and I tried to make every moment with him count.

The *Tonight* show appearance with Johnny had an immediate impact on my career, as it would in the future when I appeared on the show. Bill Loeb booked me in clubs around the country, and in all too short a time I was flying off to play a week here or a week there, leaving Perry with his eyes streaming while he held his nurse's hand at the departure gate. It upset me to see him like that, but it was the only way I knew to make a living.

Then, in the fall of 1963, I signed on to do another movie. Comedian Tommy Noonan was directing a romp called *Three Nuts in Search of a Bolt*, a loosely plotted sex comedy in which Tommy also costarred. He was becoming a hot property in Hollywood. He had just finished *Promises, Promises* with Jayne Mansfield and had starred opposite Marilyn in *Gentlemen Prefer Blondes*.

It was an attractive deal for me. I would be working in town and could be with Perry, *and* was to receive a percentage of the picture. The movie's producer was L.A. Lakers owner Jerry Buss.

Tommy Noonan was a nonstop madman who ran on booze, cigarettes, pot, and crazy ideas. During the weeks of shooting the movie, it seemed like he was always in motion. In a few years he would be dead from a brain tumor, but while his candle burned, it burned brightly. One of his wild ideas was to promote the film with a nude layout of me in *Playboy*.

"Mamie, it'll be great!" Tommy promised, pacing up and down my living room, gesticulating to emphasize his point. We had just wrapped the film a few days before, and I was feeling rested. But behind his horn-rimmed glasses, Tommy's eyes were still red from lack of sleep.

"I don't know, Tommy," I responded without enthusiasm. "We're talking about taking my clothes off."

"So? It's something everyone does every night. The difference is *you* will get paid for it, you lucky girl." I grimaced at his joke and he went on in a reasonable tone. "Jayne was in *Playboy*. And Marilyn was too. Did you see those pictures from *Something's Got to Give?*"

"I saw them."

"Jayne was promoting her movie."

"Marilyn didn't have much to say about hers being in the magazine," I said.

"So?" Tommy shrugged. "Hefner's very enthusiastic about this. He wants to do a teaser issue with you fully covered by gauze and stuff. Just outlines of your body, you know? Then, just before the movie's released, another issue with you nude—in a beer bath."

"A beer bath?"

"Yeah, Mamie. Very, very sexy. But very classy. It's what this movie needs—a bath scene."

"But I thought we were through shooting."

"We were. But now we'll go back in and shoot the beer bath."

"I haven't said yes to all this, Tommy. I have some very serious reservations about being photographed nude."

"Such as?"

"For one thing, I've got a young son who's going to grow up and see those pictures. And for another, my mother and father—"

"Mamie, I promise you that these pictures will be nothing that your mother, father, or son could ever be ashamed of.

And they'll sell so many tickets to that movie! Jesus! I can see them lining up outside the theater now, their *Playboy*s clutched in their hands . . .''

"How about if I take the bath in champagne?"

"It's been done. Besides, beer is great for your skin."

I finally agreed. The pictures in *Playboy* caused a tremendous stir. In the second nude layout, Hefner featured my picture on the cover of the magazine. It was, I believe, the first time an actress appeared on the cover of *Playboy*.

A lot of people came to see the movie.

Ever since the filming of *The Beautiful Legs of Sabrina* in Italy, I had longed to return to Europe. Shortly after New Year's Day, 1964, I got my wish. Bill Loeb lined up a film for me in Germany called *The Wild, Wild West* with that country's answer to Elvis Presley, a singer-actor named Freddy Quinn.

I began a storm of preparations before departing.

I am not a light traveler. Many performers have the same affliction. It is a product of many years of being on the road for extended periods of time. There is just no substitute for having all the comforts of home along with you. If you are out there for months at a time, it's good to have plenty of your favorite soap, several jars of the *one* facial cream you adore, and a couple of big fluffy bathrobes for cuddling up in after a nice hot bath. And dozens of sets of cozy warm flannel pajamas.

This time my preparations also included someone to go along and help me. My first thought had been to take Danni. She had worked as my stand-in in *Three Nuts in Search of a Bolt*, and she had a small role in the movie. She was forceful enough to act as my secretary and bright enough to see when to run interference for me. But there were two drawbacks with Danni: one, she was involved in a romance and didn't want to leave town just then; and two, she couldn't do hair.

"Why don't you take Don along?" Danni asked when we discussed it. "He can do the secretarial stuff and do your hair too."

Don Morand had moved down from the high desert near Palm Springs and was now living in Los Angeles. Doing my hair had achieved a certain amount of notoriety for him, and other actresses became his clients too. We had become quite close, almost like brother and sister. Don was simply good company.

I asked Don, and he agreed to go.

By 1964, things were beginning to change in Hollywood and around the country. Bob Dylan's song "The Times They Are A-changin' " announced the new credo of the sixties. Down on Sunset Boulevard, the flower children marched, galvanized out of acid dreams into anti-war demonstrations. Vietnam was heating up, though not yet at its peak; young men were already returning from the war confused, shot up, or in body bags.

And blondes were no longer having more fun. Style-wise, America began to take its lead from the street, and the so-called Sixties Look began to emerge. Hair was straight and long, little makeup was worn, clothes became a loose conglomerate of American Indian, Hindu, African, and Salvation Army. Bras were out. Glamour as I had understood it in Hollywood—diamonds, furs, elegant coiffures, black tie and tails, long beaded evening gowns—began to wane.

When the times begin changing, it's not always easy to go with them, especially if the direction frightens while it fascinates, threatens to destroy while holding you in thrall.

This time, although it hurt to see Perry's tears as I disappeared through the airline gate, I was glad to be leaving behind the turmoil of change.

When we stopped over briefly in New York, I was stunned by the picture on the front page of the New York *Times* of a darkly handsome man with a cocky grin. The story underneath explained that Joe Namath had just been signed to the largest contract in professional football history with the New York Jets.

After reading all the story about Namath in the *Times*, I asked the stewardess if there were any *Sports Illustrated* issues on board. I found myself devouring all I could find on the man.

"I didn't know you were such a big football fan," Don said.

"I wasn't before today." I snuggled down in my seat with a pillow and blanket.

* * *

The Wild, Wild West was produced jointly by German and Yugoslavian companies. I spoke my lines in English; later they would be dubbed into German by another actress.

It was amusing to watch the European actors and crew tackling something as apple-pie American as a western. Freddy Quinn did a passably good job, but there were moments—like the time-honored street shoot-out—when the guttural German phrases Freddy hurled at the bad guys seemed laughably out of place.

After three weeks of shooting interiors in Berlin, we had to move the production to Dubrovnik, Yugoslavia, to film the exteriors. Our connecting flight was a twin-engine, prop-driven plane that looked like it had seen heavy service.

Three weeks in Dubrovnik felt like three months. The atmosphere was oppressive. Every waiter, porter, or hotel maid was potentially a member of the secret police.

I lost ten pounds while filming there. I couldn't eat breakfast because the eggs were so strong-smelling. Don managed to down two of them every morning to keep going, but I couldn't do it. He went down to the kitchen every morning and squeezed me a couple of quarts of fresh orange juice from tiny, almost red Italian oranges. Dinners at the hotel restaurant were fair. The lunches on location never varied much. It was a workingman's lunch: a couple of big oily sardines slapped on a hunk of local bread, washed down with large quantities of wine. Most of the time I went without lunch. And I was always thirsty. Like many Europeans, the Yugoslavians catering our lunches believed that water is meant for bathing. Wine is what you drink.

Getting to the location was an adventure in itself. We did our filming high in the mountains. The areas were accessible by what the Yugoslavians considered good roads: one-lane gravel tracks that wound up the mountain. On one side was the rock face of the mountain; on the other was a sheer drop of hundreds of feet to the sea.

The Yugoslavian men were gorgeous, built of good, sturdy stock with thick dark hair, high cheekbones, full lips, and deep soulful eyes. They are famous throughout Europe as the most handsome, most lively lovers.

But even the charms of the Yugoslavian men were not

enough to keep me there a moment longer than necessary. As soon as we were finished with *The Wild, Wild West,* Don and I hurried to the airport to catch the little airplane back to Zagreb, and on to Paris.

Paris was something I had promised myself since the trip started. I wanted to see the new fashions and spend some of my hard-earned money on new Paris dresses.

Once installed in our suite at the George V in Paris, I realized I was famished. I ordered up champagne and caviar for both of us. When the waiter came, he began dishing out spoonfuls of the shiny black beluga caviar from a one-kilo can resting on a bed of ice. Don and I gobbled down the first serving before he could put the spoon down.

"Leave the can," I mumbled through a cold, salty mouthful.

When I was full, I sent a cable to my business manager in L.A. for more money. I took a long hot bath in the suite's giant porcelain tub. I wrapped myself in one of the hooded thick terrycloth robes the George V has the good sense to provide its patrons, had a few more mouthfuls of caviar, crawled in between the bed's heavy cotton sheets, and slept. I slept for sixteen hours straight. When I woke, I ate another extravagant meal, soaked in another hot bath until I was weak, and went back to sleep.

When my eat-bathe-sleep orgy was over two days later, the money had arrived by return cable from Los Angeles.

One purpose of this Paris trip was to find a dress to wear for a commercial I had contracted to do before leaving the States. The commercial was for a new men's after-shave lotion called Aqua Velva. I wanted to find something coolly elegant, and Danni had suggested emphatically that I look in Paris.

"American designers are years behind the times," she told me. "Go to all the Paris shows. Several times a day the big fashion houses have shows in their salons. You order whatever you like and they make it up for you."

I called the concierge at the George V and got the times of the shows of the major designers. I saw shows at Pierre Cardin's and Christian Dior's, but nothing caught my eye. My next stop was Coco Chanel's.

At Chanel's salon show, the first dress down the ramp was

black and mid-calf-length, with festoons of black feathers. It was love at first sight. There were a couple of classic Chanel suits that I liked too, but the black dress was the one for the commercial.

After the show, I introduced myself to the salon's manager. I ordered the two suits and the black dress. I explained that I wanted to use the black dress for a commercial I would do in New York in two weeks' time.

"But, Miss Van Doren," the manager said. "There is no way we can have the dress ready in such a short time. We take your measurements and make up your order. Normally we cannot deliver before five or six weeks."

My face showed my disappointment. "The only reason I needed the dress was the commercial. There's no reason for me to buy it in that case. I'll just have to find something when I get back to New York."

In the midst of our conversation, the salon manager's attention was diverted to the steep flight of stairs behind us. I turned and looked. There was a woman, elegantly dressed in a black suit, climbing the stairs, a willowy young man at her elbow.

"It is Madame Chanel," the manager said quietly.

We continued to discuss the situation of the black dress. At last she rose.

"One moment, Miss Van Doren. I will check with someone about this."

She returned a few minutes later with the black dress on a hanger. Motioning me toward one of the fitting rooms, she said, "Would you step in and try this on, please?"

When I had the dress on, the salon manager took me gently by the arm.

"Madame Chanel would like to meet you, Miss Van Doren."

"And the dress?"

"Please." She gave me a knowing smile. "Come meet Madame."

I climbed the stairs and was ushered into Coco Chanel's office. It was a small, dark room, tastefully furnished with good antique pieces in quiet colors. Still, for all of its understated atmosphere, the room had a flamboyantly feminine flavor that hinted of a bordello.

Madame Chanel sat on a small couch. Deep brown hair framed her thin face. There was a pale parchment quality to her skin. She wore cascades of pearls and chains to accent the stark black of her suit and the bright white of her silk blouse. Her dark eyes piercingly evaluated the black feathered dress on me. There was a faintly roguish glint in her eyes as she swept me up and down.

Finally she said, "Ahh."

She did not rise when I shook her hand. She motioned me to a chair.

When she spoke there was a huskiness to her voice. "I understand that you like the black dress, Mamie." She pronounced my name with a soft A. It came out sounding something like "Mommy."

"It's lovely," I answered. "And I have a special use for it." I explained the Aqua Velva commercial and that people all over the United States would see her dress.

She smiled enigmatically. "My dear, people all over the United States could not tell a Chanel from a housedress. But no matter. I understand entirely."

She spoke to the salon manager.

"It needs something, I think." She made small circles over her head with a graceful hand. ". . . something on top to give her more height. Make up a small hat with . . ." She fluttered her fingers. ". . . with black feathers, like the dress. Taller. It will make her taller."

Her manager spoke rapidly in French. Madame answered quickly and quietly, with an air of finality.

I got up to leave.

"Thank you, Madame Chanel."

"Ah, the dress is lovely on you."

Downstairs again, the salon manager had a seamstress begin taking my measurements. The manager was in a dither over the situation.

"It is unheard-of, mademoiselle, this selling of a dress off a model. In the whole history of the Chanel salon, never has anyone purchased a dress in such a way."

"Believe me, I'm grateful," I said.

"It is nothing. But Madame must like very much the way the dress looks on you to do this. We have other shows to do and this dress will not be shown now. And it has been *très, très* popular.''

Before Don and I left Chanel's, Madame asked to see me again. We were taken back upstairs to her office. She was still sitting on her couch. She carefully eyed the suit I was wearing.

"This suit, Mamie," she purred. "*Do* let the hem out to just below the knee. Please?"

"Do you think I should? It's a Galanos suit that I—"

She stopped me with an imperious wave of her hand. With a look she forgave me the profanity of mentioning another designer in her presence.

"I know whose suit it is, my dear. But it is the wrong length for you."

"I'll have it let down, Madame."

"Coco. Please call me Coco. They told you when your black dress will be ready?"

"Yes, Coco. Your manager said it would be sent to the George V day after tomorrow."

"Good. The dress is perfect for you. And the suits you have chosen are too. One of them I have taken the liberty of telling them to make up in the pink wool. With your coloring . . ." She made that gesture of kissing the fingertips that so typifies the French designer. ". . . it will be stunning."

"Thank you again."

Two days later the box arrived at the hotel. Inside was the dress and the feathered hat Chanel had had made to go with it. A handwritten note inside read: "Dearest Mamie, Wear these in good health always. C.C."

When we arrived back in New York, Don and I checked into a suite in the Plaza. Perry arrived the next day feeling very grown-up at eight years after flying all the way from California to New York by himself. The New York World's Fair was in full swing and we tried to see a few of the more exciting exhibits.

The same morning that Perry arrived, the phone rang with an invitation for me to make another appearance on the *Tonight* show the following day. I said I would, and promptly went back and slept off the jet lag to get myself in shape for it.

I went to Rockefeller Center at around eleven o'clock the next day for the usual interview workup by one of the show's writers. Johnny and I rehearsed a skit that we would do and I went through a song with the orchestra.

A great deal of tired ritual has attached itself to the *Tonight* show over the years. Today, if you get to see Johnny on the show at all, there is a feeling of going through the motions. But in the early days, things seemed fresher and funnier. When Johnny went into the audience to do "Stump the Band," there was the feeling that anything might happen, and God only knew what bawdy lyrics some sweet little lady from Cincinnati might sing. When he played Art Fern in the Tea-time Movie skits, there was more snap and pizzazz to the jokes. Often it was actually impossible to keep a straight face.

Afterward, Johnny and I again had dinner and watched the show, establishing a post-show ritual that would prevail for the next nine years. This time, however, we went to Johnny's office suite after dinner to watch the show. NBC had built a private living area in his office complete with bar, a large makeup chair, and a comfortably furnished living area. Johnny, more relaxed with me than on our first date, was considerably more amorous. He pressed his body close to me as we lay on the big couch, but I begged off, saying that I was too tired. I had to get up the next day and shoot the Aqua Velva commercial.

The commercial, which ran for over a year and paid handsomely each time it did, was the beginning of Aqua Velva's public image. I purred out the slogan "There's something about an Aqua Velva man" and sang the same phrase in the soundtrack.

Perry, Don, and I flew back to L.A. when the commercial was complete. I reveled once more in getting back to my house on Rising Glen Road, sleeping in my own wide bed, and always knowing when I woke in the night that my son was safe just a few steps away down the hall.

Through the spring and summer of 1964, I started the wild nights of roaming the dance floors of the Whiskey à Go-Go and the other hot spots around town. There were not many hotter places than the Whiskey. The best of the new rock groups appeared at the Whiskey à Go-Go, from the Doors and the Yardbirds to the Mamas and the Papas and the Turtles.

On any given night you might find a couple dozen celebrities frugging and doing the swim or the mashed potato.

I met a young rock singer at the Whiskey named Johnny Rivers, who had made a hit out of Chuck Berry's "Maybelline" and was just recording a "live" album at the Whiskey à Go-Go which would feature "High on a Mountain of Love." We began seeing each other fairly regularly.

Johnny called me on his night off and asked me to go with him to the Whiskey à Go-Go—he had heard the Beatles were supposed to be there. When we arrived, the building was vibrating with excitement. A great throng of screaming teenage girls crushed against the Whiskey and spilled off the sidewalk out onto Sunset Boulevard. Johnny and I pushed our way through them to slip in the back door.

The Beatles *were* there. Paul McCartney and Ringo had left earlier, but it was easy to find the booth where John Lennon and George Harrison were sitting—it was the center of attention in the room. Jayne Mansfield was sitting with John and George.

"Hi, Jaynie," I said, walking up to the booth. Jayne lifted her head drunkenly and focused on me with some difficulty. "Mamie! How're ya? Siddown and have a drink and meet the boys."

Johnny introduced himself and turned to introduce me just as a photographer snapped another picture.

"Goddammit!" George roared. "Why the fuck don't you bloody damn vultures leave us alone?" He picked up a drink and threw it at the photographer. After several drinks, however, his aim was way off, and he drenched me with Scotch.

I wiped the drink out of my eyes and stared at him, too astonished to speak.

"What's wrong with you?" Johnny Rivers asked angrily.

George began incoherently screaming at everyone in sight. Embarrassed at the scene George had made, John Lennon tried to quiet him down, while mumbling apologetically to me. Jayne stared dully into her drink. Finally Johnny and I left in disbelief. A drunk Beatle, I'd discovered, was just a drunk.

* * *

One night as I sat at my special table with Don Morand, someone tapped me on the shoulder. When I turned I found myself looking into a familiar set of icy blue eyes.

"Hi, Mamie," said Steve McQueen. "Wanna dance?" he shouted over the music.

Although I'd turned down any number of men that evening, I slid my chair back and stood up. "You're on."

Steve turned out to be a good dancer. Dancing several fast songs, we worked up a sweat in the smoky, hot confines of the Whiskey. When the band finally took a break, we started back to my table.

"Mamie," Steve said, putting his hand on my arm. "Let's get out of here."

"Aren't you having a good time?" I asked.

"I'd like to have a better time."

"First come back to my table and meet Don. He does my hair."

"That all he does?"

"Yes—he's just a good friend."

We had another drink and talked for a while, but Steve was restless in the crowded nightclub. He radiated a kind of infectious energy and I sensed myself becoming caught up in it.

"Mamie," Steve said after some polite conversation, "are you sure you don't want to go somewhere else?"

I smiled at him. "My house."

As I climbed Sunset Plaza Drive from the Strip in my white Jaguar, Steve followed in his Ferrari. Perched on the hillside, my house had a spectacular view of the Hollywood nightscape. Climbing up into the quietness of the hills, I once again felt safe from the dangers of the restless streets below.

Steve and I made our way into the living room, and I pulled back the sliding glass doors to the evening. The night breeze was cool.

"If you squint your eyes, La Cienega Boulevard looks like a string of pearls," I told him softly, looking at the scene below.

There was the faint smell of sweat from our bodies, the result of our exertions on the dance floor. From the rate of Steve's breathing, I could tell he was looking forward to some further exertions in bed.

I circled his neck with my arm and we held each other in the pale light of the city. As we kissed I felt him growing hard against me.

Suddenly I heard a sound that made my body stiffen.

"Perry," I whispered. I left Steve standing in the darkened living room as I went down the hallway to the room where Perry slept. He had begun having frequent nightmares.

I went to his bed and put a hand on his forehead.

"Shhh, sweetheart," I said to him. "It's okay."

He mumbled something, turned over, and dived deeply back into sleep.

When I walked back into the living room my ardor had cooled considerably.

"How about a beer?" I asked Steve. I went into the kitchen and brought a bottle of Heineken back from the refrigerator.

Steve took the beer and put his arm around my waist. "Now, where were we?"

"Steve, look, can't we talk a little first?"

"Talk?" he asked incredulously. "About what?"

"I hardly know you. And you're a married man."

"I'm also very attracted to you. Let's talk in the bedroom."

I led him around the long hallway to my bedroom. Steve sat next to me as I tried to start a conversation.

"C'mon, Mamie," Steve murmured gently. He pushed me onto the bed and set his beer on the night table. Suddenly he rolled on top of me and began kissing and caressing me, his hand sliding up my side.

I pushed him away. "Steve, I'm not ready to make love yet." Turning on my side, I faced him. "You and I are so much alike. We see something we want and we go after it. But after we get it, we lose interest in what we wanted so much. I don't want that to happen to us."

Steve reached for his beer and took a long drink. "I guess you're right, Mamie. But I don't think that'll happen to us."

"That sounds suspiciously like a line, Mr. McQueen."

"Yeah, well, maybe it is." There was a twinkle in his eye as he laughed and finished his beer. "I've wanted to sleep with you since I saw you with Ray Anthony at the Sands. I want to now. Why don't we see what happens afterward, okay?"

He put his hand on my breast and kissed me hard.

"Steve, there'll be other nights." I kissed him lightly on the lips and stood up.

"Will I see you again, Mamie?" he asked before he left.

"You're married, Steve. Give me a call sometime and we'll see. . . ."

Two days later the phone rang while Don was doing my hair. It was Steve; he wanted to meet me at the Whiskey à Go-Go that evening. I told him Don and I had plans to go out.

"Bring him along," Steve said.

At the Go-Go, Steve and I danced for an hour or so before he said, "There's a party at a friend's house this evening. It sounds like a lot of fun. Are you interested?"

I was, and before long Don and I were following Steve through the winding roads of Benedict Canyon.

"Mamie," said Don as we turned into a narrow driveway, "this is Jay Sebring's house."

Jay Sebring was one of the most famous and successful hairdressers in Hollywood history. He had bought Paul Bern and Jean Harlow's old house—the Tudor mansion where Bern had shot himself soon after their marriage. (Sebring would later die tragically at the hands of the Manson Family, one of the victims of the Tate-LaBianca murders.)

The party was in full swing. There were people splashing in the pool outside; others wandered about the house drinking or smoking pot. After a while, Steve motioned me into a bathroom.

"Mamie," he said, digging in his pocket, "I've got some of the finest Sandoz sunshine acid here. Let's drop a tab or two."

I hesitated. I had heard about bad LSD trips from my friends. "I don't know, Steve. I've always been afraid of that stuff. I don't know what might happen to me."

"No bad trips on this shit. It's made by a pharmaceutical company. It's the best. It makes sex a totally new experience."

He put the pale yellow tablet in my hand. He took one himself, washing it down with a beer. I took the other one with a swallow of white wine.

For some time I didn't feel anything. We talked in the

bathroom for a few more minutes, then we went down the hall to a bedroom. It was elegantly furnished with a canopy bed. In one corner was a full-length mirror.

"You know whose room this was?" Steve asked.

"No." There was a funny buzzing sound in my ears, not unpleasant, but a strangely comforting sound. Steve's voice sounded muffled and far away.

"It was Paul Bern's and Jean Harlow's. This is the room they were in when she found out that her husband was impotent."

Steve took me in his arms and kissed my neck and face. Once again I could feel the sizable hardness of his cock against my leg.

"Thank goodness," I said, rubbing him with my hand. "At least it's not something in the room."

There was a flash of red light, like a skyrocket across the room. Following that, there was another, and another. Soon the room was crisscrossed by tracings of colored lines of light.

"I can see all these colors. What is it?"

"It's the acid. Don't worry. Just let yourself go," Steve reassured me.

We undressed each other slowly, both of us highly aroused, and lay on the big canopied bed where Paul Bern had revealed his hopeless secret.

I could feel the crinkle and crush of the bedspread beneath us as we lay in a tangle of arms and legs, creating our special tempo, our own frantic rhythms. From the haze of our love-making I could hear music in the house, guitars mimicking the beat of our bodies. My own voice, as I cried out, sounded as though it was someone else's. I was a marionette speaking in another language. I am your dancing Mamie doll. Dancing. I am your you me you you me me.

We encouraged each other to longer, more desperate fulfillments after the tidal wave of our first climax. The moments were too short, too long. We were all time, all beginning, quick thrusting, widening, our bodies each other's receptacle, and death and life were at our side. We kept on and on through the psychedelic night.

When it was over, I opened my eyes and found Steve asleep next to me. I could see everything in the room with extraordinary clarity. Every object was like the outline of a mountain against the sunrise. I propped myself up on one elbow and looked at myself in the full-length mirror across the room. Someone else with blonde tousled hair was staring at me from the mirror. But the lines were clear and sharp.

There was an object on the floor in front of the mirror. It had a vaguely pinkish color in the dim light. I knew with certainty that it was Paul Bern, dead. I stared for a moment, saddened that the last thing he had seen before blowing out his brains was his own naked body.

When I cried out, Steve woke up.

"Mamie?"

"Steve, what's that on the floor?"

He rolled out of bed naked and kicked the object in front of the mirror. It was nothing but a pile of clothing.

Steve and I continued to see each other sporadically over the six-month period during which he spent a short time in Europe filming *The Great Escape*. Though he made it clear that he had no intention of leaving Neile and his two young children, he came to my house whenever he could get away. I dated other men, and a few times I had someone else over, or was about to go out when Steve arrived unannounced, a situation which he accepted sulkily.

The attraction between Steve and me was purely sexual. He was a man of great energy and imagination who was unabashedly wonderful in bed. However, he constantly sought greater highs induced by drugs. After our lovemaking at Jay Sebring's party, I refused to take any more LSD, but Steve used it frequently. He became fond of using amyl nitrite, a prescription drug for heart patients that opens the blood vessels in the head and chest and causes a brief rush. As we were about to reach a climax, Steve would crack open one of the glass vials of amyl nitrite and inhale the vapors deeply. I tried it once at his urging, but found, like all of my drug experiences, that the loss of my normal faculties, even for a moment, was too frightening.

Not long afterward, Steve and I stopped seeing each other. It was a physical relationship that I missed when it was over, but one I could no longer countenance. I have never been one to remain in a love affair with a married man who is unwilling to leave his wife. That sort of doomed-from-the-beginning affair can only cause heartache for all concerned.

I raised a lot of hell during that summer and into the early fall. I thought I was chasing something that I needed to have. I slept until noon, got up, and started thinking about going out on the town again. I kept going faster and faster. I was afraid to stop and afraid to look back and I didn't know why.

Bill Loeb booked me to headline the Thunderbird Hotel in Las Vegas for four weeks in October, followed by a four-week stint at the Latin Quarter in New York again. Then I would have a few weeks' rest around the holidays, only to do another movie early in 1965.

"I'm glad you got these bookings," my business manager said with a worried look just before I left for Las Vegas.

"Why?" I asked.

"Well, your bank balance is okay, but with taxes coming up after the first of the year . . . you'll need them."

Chapter Nineteen

The beginning of 1965 ushered in a year when I would spend more and more time running scared. It felt like I was on thin ice—I spent all my time trying to stay on my feet while worrying about falling through.

Earlier that year I starred in a vegetarian horror about trees attacking people called *The Navy Versus the Night Monsters*. The only high point in it, outside of payday, was that my pal Pamela Mason was in it too. At least there was someone to gossip with and tell dirty jokes to.

The second movie I did in 1965 brought Jayne Mansfield and me together. It was called *The Las Vegas Hillbillys*. There was a good bit of press at the time to the effect that Jayne and I fought all the time during the filming of *Hillbillys*. The truth of the matter was that we had only one argument—a habitual one among performers: top billing. When a compromise was finally made giving us *both* top billing, Jayne and I didn't speak half a dozen words. We simply refused to be in the same room with each other if we could possibly avoid it.

Though the reasons for our unremitting hostilities are dimmed with time and death, there was one thing that I found chilling about doing this movie. I realized that Jayne and I were quickly becoming anachronisms. The era of the blondes was gone, and we seemed to be futilely trying to hold on to it. Jayne, overweight and drained from giving birth to her fifth child, appeared to live in a world midway between the fifties and sixties, holding on to the dumb-blonde persona of the fifties sex symbol while trying on the sexually liberated attitude of the love generation.

In all due respect to Jayne, I do not excuse myself from this near desperate attempt to hold on to a passing style. I was trying to keep my head above the waters that were fast closing around us in that decade. But while I saw the end coming for us all too clearly, I don't think Jayne realized what was happening.

When *The Las Vegas Hillbillys* was finished, Bill Loeb booked a series of engagements in South America in a tour that would last several months. There seemed to be little purpose left in life for me but continuing to work for as long as I could get bookings. My response was to immediately go out and buy some new clothes.

I was charmed by all of South America, and the audiences there responded to me warmly. The tour was a kaleidoscope of colors, impressions, and memories of Buenos Aires, Rio de Janeiro, Managua, Mexico City—all the romantic places I had dreamed of visiting.

That fall, passing through New York, I faithfully followed the exploits of the New York Jets and quarterback Joe Namath. Whenever I could catch a game on TV, I watched it avidly, only vaguely understanding what the game was about. But my attention was riveted to Namath as he led the Jets to the winningest season in their history.

When I got back to L.A., I stopped on impulse at the first pay phone and dialed the Western Union operator.

"I'd like to send a telegram to Joe Namath, care of the New York Jets, New York City."

"And your message please?"

"Dear Joe," I told the operator. "Good luck in this Sunday's game. Throw a long one for me. Love, Mamie Van Doren."

I charged the wire to my home phone, then told the operator to add my phone number after my name on the wire.

Well, that's that, I thought after hanging up. Of course, he may not want to give me a call. He probably gets thousands of telegrams like that one every day.

As I walked through the Los Angeles International Airport to catch a taxi for home, I didn't realize I was about to sack my first quarterback.

Early Sunday evening my telephone rang.

"Mamie? This is Joe Namath."

"Well! Hi, there, Joe."

"It's nice to meet you, even if it's by phone. Thanks for the telegram. It brought me good luck. We won."

"Good. I'm glad."

I could hear voices in the background and Joe said something to them I couldn't make out.

"Well, hey, are you interested in going out?"

"Sure. Why not? Where are you?"

"In New York right now. But we'll be out on the Coast next week to play San Diego."

"Great. Why don't you give me a call?"

"I will. I'm going to be up in L.A. on Friday to do a radio interview. Maybe we could go someplace afterward."

"That sounds like fun, Joe. Call me when you get to the radio station."

"Okay. It's a date."

There was a commotion of voices in the background again. "Aw, knock it off, you guys," he said.

"Where are you calling from anyway?"

"The locker room. Some of the guys are here. Uh, look, this really is *the* Mamie Van Doren, right?"

"You'll just have to find out on Friday."

Joe called me after his interview was over and said he didn't have a car. I volunteered to come pick him up.

It was evening when I pulled up to the curb in front of the radio station. He stepped out of a doorway and opened the car door.

"Hi, Mamie. I'm glad it's really you."

Joe's fashionably long hair was a dark mass surrounding his deeply tanned face. It was the kind of smooth, even tan that only comes from patient hours under a sun lamp. His bright green eyes had an amused twinkle and he grinned as he climbed in and closed the car door. He wore an expensive leather jacket that smelled new, and sported a large jade ring on his finger.

Joe was obviously relishing his superstar image. In fact he cultivated it. And he was, as every woman knows who has seen him up close, devastatingly handsome.

"Where can we go to have a drink?" Joe asked.

I aimed the car for the Whiskey à Go-Go while we chatted. Joe's youth showed through his newly applied facade of so-phistication. His small-town origins were obvious under-neath. He was born in a Pennsylvania coal-mining town and had grown up with a love of sports. He went to Alabama to play football with the legendary Bear Bryant. Namath became a star in college. Now, with the Jets, he was building his own legend—on and off the field. He was brash and sometimes crude; he was a young man of twenty-three on the move.

We were the first ones at the Whiskey. We had a couple of drinks and began to dance when the band finally got cranked up. Early in the evening we stumbled across football player Lance Alworth and his date, a pert little blonde who came to Hollywood to make it in the movies. After a while, we were famished, and left for dinner at an after-hours place.

It was then that I first saw a side of Joe Namath I didn't like.

When we walked in the restaurant, I saw Bo Belinsky at a booth by the door sitting with some friends. We coolly ac-knowledged each other.

A strange look came over Joe's face. He began acting very odd. At first I thought he'd had too much to drink on an empty stomach. It took me a few moments to realize that he was jealous. He wanted to leave, but the other three of us were too hungry and we talked him into staying. The service was too slow for Joe. He wanted to get up and leave again, but his dinner came just in time. Joe quickly became very caught up in his own importance in a way he hadn't at the Whiskey. He seemed to think he had to prove himself. For-tunately, Belinsky and his party left before long, Joe calmed down, and we finished our dinner. I couldn't decide if he was jealous of my old boyfriend or because he wasn't the only national sports figure in the room.

Lance and his date left us after dinner. Joe and I drove up the hill to my house.

In my bedroom, Joe proved his agility was just as great off the football field as on it. He lightly carried me to the bed and gently undressed me. When he had taken his own clothes off, I could see the white scars from his knee surgery against his dark tan. He was an impressive lover. For a man who was selfish in so many other areas of his life, Joe was singularly unselfish in bed. It was one of the contradictions that made him fun to be with.

As our passion increased, we drove ourselves on toward a climax. We called out to each other as we came together. It seemed as if we rocked the whole hillside from my bedroom overlooking Hollywood.

As we relaxed afterward, Joe and I talked. He was a private man underneath the guise of Broadway Joe, reluctant to reveal much more than the superficialities printed in the papers about him.

We made love again, this time at a slower, easier pace, each of us more familiar with the other.

As the first light began to show through the small openings between the blackout drapes in my bedroom, Joe stirred.

"I gotta get going, Mamie."

"Hmmmm?" I groaned from a half-sleep.

"I have to be down in San Diego this morning and check into the hotel where the team'll be staying."

"Okay," I said, rolling over to face him. "Good luck against the Chargers on Sunday."

Neither of us moved for a few minutes. I began to doze off again.

"Well," Joe said, sitting up in bed. "We'd better get up. I've got to catch a plane at LAX."

"We?"

"I don't have a car, remember? I need a ride to the airport."

I reached for the bedside telephone and called a taxi. After I gave them the address and hung up, I said: "There. Now you've got a ride to the airport, and I can go back to sleep after you leave."

"Why don't you come down to San Diego with me?"

I shook my head. "No. I've got some shopping to do tomorrow—make that today—for a tour I'll be doing in a few weeks. But let's arrange to see each other again, okay?"

"Okay," he said, leaning toward me.

I reached up and kissed him and pulled him down next to me.

"You've got a few more minutes before the taxi arrives."

"If I lose on Sunday, it'll be your fault."

"But just think of how heroic you'll feel if you win."

Joe and I didn't meet again until after the New Year. He was playing in the 1966 post-season Pro Bowl game, played that year at Rice Stadium in Houston. I flew in from a night-club gig in freezing Indianapolis. The warmly humid Texas air was a pleasant change and Joe and I responded to each other with even more passion than in our first meeting.

The day before the game, Joe came up to the hotel suite he had reserved for me at the Sheraton. We ordered a huge dinner from room service and stayed in bed eating and making love into the night.

When we were finally exhausted, I announced that it was time for me to go to sleep.

"Me too," Joe said, turning over and tucking the covers under his chin. "See you in the morning."

"Joe," I said after a long moment. "I can't sleep with anyone. I never have."

"What?"

"I can't sleep if there's anyone else in the bed with me."

"Yeah, but aren't you tired?"

"Sure, I am. I'm always tired after working a week of two shows a night. Sorry, Joe, but I really need to get my rest, and I won't get any if you stay in this bed."

"I promise to leave you alone, Mamie."

"That's not what I mean. I can't sleep if you stay here with me. You might as well go back to your hotel."

There was a momentary silence.

"I can't."

"Can't what?"

"I can't go back to my hotel, Mamie. Everyone's expecting me to . . . well, you know . . . spend the night."

"If you show up back at your hotel, the other players will think you struck out, right?"

"Something like that, I guess."

"Well, there's a couch out there in the living room. Why

don't you take these two pillows out there. There are probably some extra blankets in the closet. I'll go look.''

I helped Joe fix a bed on the couch in the suite's living room. He was not especially happy about it but I kissed him good night, went back into the big bedroom, and locked the door.

After the game the next day, Joe was scheduled to leave for Florida.

''C'mon and go with me, Mamie. We'll have some fun down there. I'm going to stop and see Sonny Werblin in Miami. Have you ever met him?''

I had met the Jets' owner when he was president of the giant MCA talent agency and I was considering having them represent me. I had decided not to sign with them and that was the last and only time we met.

''You can reintroduce me,'' I told Joe.

The prospect of a few days' holiday in Florida with Joe sounded good. We caught the next flight to Miami. A friend of Joe's met us with Joe's car (license plate: JET) and we drove to a small but comfortable motel outside of Miami.

We checked in and Joe's friend said, ''Joe, I've got all the papers for you.''

''Okay, good. Bring 'em in.''

Joe's friend carried stacks and stacks of newspapers into Joe's room. He put them carefully in neat piles around the floor and quietly left. They were all newspapers in which Joe had been mentioned during the season. It was a kind of giant scrapbook of newspapers from all over the country. During the time we were there, Joe carefully read all of them, scrutinizing all his press minutely for a few hours every day.

The next evening we went to see the Jets' owner. But Sonny Werblin was out of town. We let ourselves in to wander around the grounds of the giant waterfront estate. The dark water lapped against the multimillionaire's private beach as Joe and I walked hand in hand.

''I'm going to have something like this someday,'' Joe said, making a sweeping motion with his arm. ''I want to live down here somewhere and have a big spread like Sonny's.''

''There's nothing wrong with living in California. You could find a pretty nice place out there.''

"I suppose so," he agreed. "But I'm pretty much an East Coast guy. I like it down here."

I happened to be looking over Joe's shoulder one day while he read a newspaper article about his bad knees. It said that Joe was scheduled to go into the hospital after the season was over for more knee surgery.

"That's where I'm going when I leave here," he said, pointing to the name of the hospital. "Back to New York to get my knees fixed."

"Really?" I said. "Maybe I could come see you up there after the surgery."

"No, no," Joe answered quickly. "It's a private sort of thing. I don't want anyone to see me during all that."

On the same front page was an article about the latest draft call-up for Vietnam.

"At least I don't have to worry about the draft," Joe mused with a crooked grin.

"You don't?"

"My knees are too bad. The military doesn't want me."

"But you can play four quarters of football every Sunday, four months out of the year?"

"That's different than being in the service and having to fight a war, Mamie."

"Yeah. You make a lot more money in football."

We had been there four days when Joe returned from a golfing trip to Fort Lauderdale. He announced that he was going on a date that night.

"A date?" I asked in astonishment.

"Yeah. I called up a friend of mine in Lauderdale. She's a stewardess. We're going out tonight."

"Oh, sure. You just go ahead and have a good time."

That kind of treatment hurt, not that we had any strings on each other, but to announce he was going out with someone else after I had come down to Florida with him at his request—that was too much. I kept my anger under control until he left. As soon as he was out the door I threw my clothes into my suitcases, took off for the airport, and caught a plane back to L.A. I had an opening in San Francisco the next week anyway.

It would be 1968 before I saw Joe Namath again. I called him on an impulse when I was working once again in New

Jersey. He asked if he could see me right away. It was a Friday and I had the weekend shows to do, so we made a date for Monday, my day off. I still harbored some anger toward Joe but it was tempered with the knowledge that I'd let myself in for what I got.

We met at his apartment and talked over drinks about the two years since we had seen each other.

That evening we ended up in Joe's big mirrored bed with the windows looking out over the city. I can only say it was my own momentary physical need and the availability of a man to fulfill it that put me there. And it served as an exorcism.

As I walked out of the elevator on the ground floor in Namath's building the whole affair came into sharp focus for me. We had each been working out each other's fantasies. We were two people told by our press releases that we were glamorous. And for a while we believed them enough to do this dance that we felt was expected of us.

The last time I spoke to Joe was in early 1969 when I was living in Newport Beach. He called me one day from the plush La Costa resort down near San Diego and asked me to come down.

"How've you been, Mamie?"

"Not bad, Joe. You?"

"Okay. Say, how old are you now, Mamie?"

It was a question that Joe Namath asked every time we met. That and how much money I was making. He was always somehow extremely insecure about his age. He was younger than me by ten years, but the difference it made to him seemed to grow larger each time we saw each other.

"What does that have to do with anything?"

"Nothing really, I guess. I'm playing a golf match down here, Mamie. Come on down and see me. We'll have a good time."

I thought about what that might be like.

"I don't think there'd be much for me to do down there. I don't play golf, you'll recall."

"I remember. You could come down and watch me play. Meet some of the people. There'll be a lot of press. It would be good exposure for you."

"One thing I don't need is 'good exposure.' Especially the kind where I'm following you around a golf course like a puppy and looking pretty for the cameras."

"Aw, hey, Mamie. It won't be like that."

"You're damn right it won't, Joe. Bye-bye."

When I opened at Bimbo's in San Francisco, Lee Grant came over to see the show. Afterward we talked about old times on the *Silk Stockings* tour. I was feeling a little low over Namath's treatment of me in Florida, and although I didn't confide in Lee about it, her wry good humor was a boost.

After finishing the job in San Francisco, I came back to L.A. to sell my house. When I had returned from South America earlier in the year I found my home had been broken into and ransacked. Luckily, Perry was living with my mother and father while I was gone. I began having more trouble with prowlers and began keeping a loaded gun next to my bed. It was so frightening that my mother finally refused to stay in the house. Then one night I watched in terror as a man with a drawn gun prowled through the patio area of the house looking for a way to get in. I called the Foothill Patrol, but by the time they arrived, he had gone.

Heartbreaking as it was, I made up my mind to sell the lovely home I had so carefully decorated and that represented stability and independence for me. I asked Mother and Daddy to let Perry stay with them and I moved into the Shoreham Towers Hotel on Shoreham Drive, overlooking Sunset Boulevard.

Meanwhile, Perry was not having an easy time of it. Determined that he get the best education money could buy, I enrolled him in the Buckley private school. That hadn't worked out, so I took him out to Glendora to look at the Harding Military Academy. He would not have to live at the academy, but would stay with my parents, who had bought an apartment house in nearby Azusa. I told Perry that if he didn't like the military academy, he didn't have to stay. But he enjoyed the uniforms and the marching band, in which he played trumpet (like his father, of course), and the discipline was something he needed.

Sometime after that, my period was late, and I cursed myself for not using birth control. I had had a brief experiment with the pill, but I found it wasn't for me. The continual morning sickness and swelling and tenderness of my breasts was more than I could stand.

My final hope was dashed when I missed my next period. I went down to get a pregnancy test, and a couple of days later the results came back positive.

That day I sat in my apartment at the Shoreham and gazed morosely out the window over the expanse of Hollywood. Lights began flickering on as the smoggy late-afternoon glow faded in the west over Marina del Rey. I went over my options.

First, an abortion. But an abortion was one thing that I'd always sworn I would never do. If a seed wasn't strongly implanted and it later miscarried of its own accord, that was one thing. But to surgically go in and kill an unborn fetus— I could not visualize myself having that done. Abortion in 1966, while illegal, was not impossible to obtain if you could afford it. I could afford it, but there was danger. It meant in many cases turning yourself over to some butcher who was as desperate to perform an abortion as you were to get one.

Second, I could have the child out of wedlock and take my chances. Even though the times had changed since Ingrid Bergman's ostracism by Hollywood for having a child without being married, I still had an old-fashioned feeling about the child having a name.

Third, I could meet someone else, have a whirlwind courtship, get swept off my feet, get married, and announce that bingo! my new husband had taken aim and hit the mark on the first try and had gotten me pregnant. It was not a solution I felt good about, but it was workable and safer.

As if in answer to a prayer, California Angel pitcher Dean Chance called the next day.

"Mamie, how're you doin'?" Dean brayed into the telephone. "I've got somebody I want you to meet."

Prior to my breakup with Bo, the three of us—Bo, Dean, and Mamie—often went out on the town together. Lately, Dean and I hadn't seen much of each other outside of one or two lunches. Dean was like a little brother and always seemed able to cheer me up.

"Mamie, this guy wants to go out with you real bad. You

met him a couple of years ago when you were dating Bo. His name's Lee Meyers. He signed when he was seventeen as the Angels' bonus baby. Remember? Now he's all grown up at nineteen and wants to meet you.''

"Nineteen? Jesus, Dean, isn't that a little young, even for me?"

"Naw. Just meet the kid, Mamie. You might like him."

I went out with Lee Meyers and found him to be a tall, blond, gangling, and seemingly pleasant young man who was just beginning to have the veneer taken off his innocence. At least that's what I thought at first. Lee had a promising career on the horizon with the Angels as a pitcher. He had an all-American-boy quality about him that I would later discover was his way of manipulating others. After our first date, he made it obvious that he would like to see more of me.

My decision had to be made quickly. I had reached the six-week mark in my pregnancy. It would not be long before I began to show. After we'd been going together for a little over a month, I told Lee I was pregnant. With his child.

Lee and I were secretly married in early May. Since he was underage, we got married at the courthouse in Boise, Idaho, where a county judge performed the ceremony. As we walked out onto the street, I was totally preoccupied with my predicament. Without looking, I stepped off the curb into the path of an oncoming bus. Tires screeched and Lee pulled me back just in time. I broke out in a sweat and my knees went watery. Those squealing tires were like a warning to me. Pregnant or not, I realized this marriage was a mistake.

We spent our wedding night in a hotel in Boise, before Lee had to fly back and join the Angels on the road. I went back to L.A. to prepare for a production of *Gentlemen Prefer Blondes* in which I was to star that summer at the Meadowbrook Theater in New Jersey.

Once back home, though, I began to regret my plan: Lee Meyers was not the man of my dreams, but he deserved better than he was getting. I was totally at a loss for a solution to the problem, but I knew I couldn't stay on the fence about it indefinitely. I gave Danni a call and she came over to the Shoreham to talk.

I held back the information that the baby I was carrying was not Lee's.

"This isn't the way I want to start another marriage," I told her. "I'm so damned upset with myself, Danni. This is a stupid position to be in."

"Mamie, I can't understand why you don't want to go ahead and have the baby."

"Look at what kind of mother I am. I've been a rotten mother to Perry, for all that I've tried not to. I've been out of town every time he's needed me—had something else to do for every big event in his life. Why should I bring another child into the world to make miserable too?"

My eyes had filled with tears and I turned away to grab a Kleenex.

"Why don't you give the baby to me?"

"You?"

"I'll adopt it."

Danni had been having a romance with a man for some time. They were living together and thinking of getting married. She had also tried unsuccessfully to get pregnant.

"The doctor said it's impossible for me, Mamie. I can *never* have children. You can have this one and we'll secretly arrange for me to adopt it. No one will know."

There was a note of desperation in her voice. I could see from the intensity of her eyes that she meant what she said.

"I don't know if I could take that, Danni. I'd always know it was my child. We see each other so often, I just think it would be too hard."

We both stared at the floor for a long time.

Finally Danni asked the question.

"Then you're planning to have an abortion?"

"I don't know," I whispered. "Do you know of anyone?"

She shook her head. "It's not a problem I've had to confront."

"I'm sorry, Danni."

"No, *I'm* sorry, Mamie."

That night, after she left, I went down and walked on Sunset Boulevard. The sidewalk after dark was teeming with all the street people—the misguided kids, the hippies, strung out on drugs; the hustlers, pimps, and sad prostitutes; the winos; the certifiable loonies talking to their invisible demons.

And what am I? I thought. Where do I fit into this gaudy jigsaw? This was the world I would bring a child into. This was where he or she would have to survive. Why do that?

There was no answer in the night.

I sat in my girlfriend's car in front of a nondescript office building on Wilshire Boulevard. We had not spoken for several minutes. I had been sitting there staring through the windshield.

"You going in?" she asked softly.

I sighed deeply and reached for the door handle. "Yes." I felt suddenly afraid. "I'd feel a lot better if you could go up there with me."

"I know. But the doctor requested that you come alone."

"You'll wait for me?"

"Don't worry, Mamie. I'll be right here."

Inside the building the hallways were deserted and quiet. As I heard my heels clicking on the floor, I said a weak prayer for my safety and I asked the baby to forgive me.

The doctor had the pale, damp skin of a drug addict. There was a slackness around his mouth that spoke of a deep dependency on some chemical readily available to a physician.

"Get undressed," he said coldly. He was a Hungarian and had a noticeable accent.

He strapped me spread-eagled onto a table. As he stood near me to inject Pentothal into my vein, his fetid breath hit me.

"Count backwards from ten," he said.

"Ten, nine . . ."

I awoke with the sensation of choking. The doctor was slapping my face trying to bring me around. My throat was full of phlegm and as he unstrapped me, I sat up and vomited on the floor.

When I could breathe again, I looked around the room. The floor and the wall nearest the table were splattered with blood. It reminded me of the way my grandfather's barn looked back on the farm at hog-killing time.

"What . . . what was it?" I asked.

The doctor looked at me flatly, his eyes like two black marbles. I could see his hands shaking. He probably needed a fix again. He made a helpless gesture with his hands.

"A boy."

Downstairs in my girlfriend's car, I leaned back in the seat and cried as she drove away.

The decision to have an abortion is difficult for a woman to make. The decision is hers and she must live with it always. But once made, whatever the reasons, there ought to be a structure available to allow her to have it safely done. And someone there to help her through the ordeal. I guarantee it is a decision that forever makes each sunrise of your life a little dimmer.

Chapter Twenty

Lee was upset over the abortion. Callous as it sounded, I told him only that starting a marriage pregnant was something that hadn't worked for me before, and I wasn't about to try it again. I also told him that we should keep the marriage a secret for a while.

"Why?" he asked in amazement.

"To soften the blow to your career with the Angels."

"I don't understand, Mamie. The Angel organization likes me. I've gone to college at their expense, plus they've paid me a hefty bonus to pitch for them."

"That was before you got involved with me."

"Our marriage shouldn't have anything to do with it. It's my life."

"That's what you think. It shouldn't have anything to do with your career, but it will. Remember Bo Belinsky? You have no idea how small-minded the Angel organization is. Just give it a little time—wait until I get back from this show in New Jersey. Pitch this season without them finding out about us. Then you'll be established a little more."

Lee and I visited his parents in Huntington Beach, south of Los Angeles. While we were there Lee showed me some home movies of him pitching.

"Who's that?" I asked, pointing to a bunch of youngsters playing baseball on the screen.

"That's my team," Lee said. "See, there I am on the mound pitching. We won the national championship. I'll show you the trophy when we turn the lights on."

"You're kidding. How long ago were these pictures taken?"

"Just a couple of years before I signed with the Angels. What's that? Three . . . almost four years ago."

I nodded and watched the screen in disbelief.

Oh, boy, I thought. My husband the Little Leaguer.

With considerable relief I took off for New Jersey and the Meadowbrook to start rehearsals for *Gentlemen Prefer Blondes*. Just before opening I got a call from Johnny Carson asking me to be on the *Tonight* show again.

"I'll send a car for you, Mamie. We'll have dinner someplace afterward, okay?"

When the show was over that night, Johnny and I went to the rooftop Rainbow Room in Rockefeller Center. The view of New York City was breathtaking and the food was excellent. Johnny wore a gorgeous cocoa-brown suit that evening—I had told him the last time we went out that he would look good in that color. We both ordered duck in orange sauce. When the meal came, the waiter spilled the sauce on Johnny's new suit. Johnny was furious but kept his temper under control. The waiter fled in a rain of apologies while the maître d' and the restaurant manager hovered around the table dabbing at Johnny's stained jacket.

"Oh, Mr. Carson," the manager said apologetically, "what can we do? Please bring the suit to us and we'll have it cleaned."

"Cleaned? This is a *new* suit," Johnny replied levelly. "It just came from my tailor and it's the first time I've ever worn it."

The manager swallowed hard. "I . . . I'm sure we can work out something, Mr. Carson."

With Johnny mollified and the crisis over, we settled down to finish our meal. We were toasting with champagne when a new waiter brought more duck. He served me, then leaned over Johnny and spilled the orange sauce on Johnny again. Johnny jumped up from the table and angrily exclaimed that we were obviously not meant to eat duck that night.

I covered my face to keep from laughing. It had quickly become a slapstick scene worthy of the Mighty Carson Art Players, but Johnny wasn't laughing.

Wearing nearly as much of his dinner as he'd eaten, Johnny escorted me back downstairs to his office and peeled out of his ruined suit. I must say it gave him an excellent opportunity to get undressed. He flipped on the stereo and did a few reps with his exercise machine to show me the latest development of his pectorals.

We had some champagne and watched the show from his chaise longue. When the show was over, Johnny switched the set off with the remote control and put his arm around me. He kissed me and shifted a hand to cup my breast.

I was doing the *Tonight* show two or three times a year, depending on my schedule, and each time Johnny and I went through this rite of having dinner, watching the show and sipping champagne, and becoming amorous afterward. Although we had undressed each other and fondled each other, Johnny and I had still never actually been to bed. Johnny must have been getting a little frustrated by the situation. But I couldn't help it—I always felt guilty about the fact that he was married. Now that problem was doubly difficult because I was newly married and I didn't want anyone to know it.

"Johnny," I said, catching my breath after a long kiss, "I've got a confession to make."

"Whazzat?" he mumbled, nuzzling at my neck.

"I can't go to bed with you."

"Don't you want to?"

"Yes. But I can't. Please don't ask me why. I'll explain it to you someday, but I just can't right now. Okay?"

"Sure, Mamie. You . . . you don't have anything wrong with you, do you?"

"No, no, of course not. I just can't. Trust me."

"I will. More champagne?"

Lee and I were talking on the telephone one night shortly after that, when he mentioned that he told a couple of the other players that we were married. It wasn't the kind of thing he wanted to keep a secret. I, for one, didn't want it announced to the world because I felt more and more that our marriage would not be a success.

"Lee, that was a big mistake," I said.

"I don't think they even believed me."

It wasn't long before Autry's minions called Lee on the carpet and asked if the rumor going around was true. Lee must have said it was, because the Angels quickly and unceremoniously traded their erstwhile bonus baby to the Chicago Cubs.

Within a month of reporting to the Cubs, Lee announced to the newspapers that we were married. The Cubs promptly tried to take advantage of the free advertising they got as a result.

The next day it was in all the papers. The reporters descended on the house I was renting next door to the theater in New Jersey. I couldn't get out of the house and I couldn't stay in because the doorbell and phone rang every five minutes.

A wire arrived that afternoon from Johnny. It said: "Congratulations. Now I know why. Bring your new husband on the show and let's talk about your marriage."

Back home, Lee and I established a guarded relationship. I began to see another side to his personality. There was an almost Jekyll-and-Hyde quality to him that he used to advantage. A regular churchgoer, Lee could be charming and boyish publicly, but he possessed a dark interior that was troubling.

Lee's boyish charm repeatedly got him out of trouble. A wild and reckless driver, he was constantly being stopped for speeding. He relished the challenge of going before a judge and fighting the ticket. He'd smile and shrug and scuff his feet, and before long the judge would believe that the police officer had somehow made a terrible mistake.

Lee was perfectly capable of walking into a bank and convincing the manager to lend him a large amount of money. He fancied himself a wheeler-dealer and a real-estate tycoon. He was always on the lookout for "big deals" and get-rich-quick schemes.

One day while we were still living at the Shoreham Towers, Lee said, "Mamie, why the hell don't we get out of here? Let's leave this damned zoo."

"Leave?"

"Yes. Let's move out of Hollywood and live someplace where it's sane. Let's move to Orange County."

Orange County was, in 1966, the butt of many jokes of the cool, hip Southern California, L.A. types. It was conservative, it was a cultural wasteland, and there were no good delis.

"You've got to be kidding, Lee. There's nothing down there."

"Come on, I'll show you."

Lee had grown up in Huntington Beach, right next door to Newport Beach. We took a look around at a new and exclusive condominium complex being built in Newport Beach called the Balboa Bay Club. It featured adjacent tennis courts, swimming pools, saunas, gyms, and the like, with slip space for boats and a membership that would include the monied, conservative upper crust from around the world.

The Bay Club would later become the hangout for some of the more stubborn Watergate weasels of the Nixon era, but in the early days it was simply a protected haven—as long as your pedigree was right-wing enough and your bank account big enough.

I took a lovely two-bedroom apartment on the south corner of the building. The sunsets across Newport harbor alone were worth the price of admission. We were the first ones to move into the Bay Club. I took Perry out of the military academy and he came to live with us, as well. I enrolled him in a local public school and it turned out to be the best thing for Perry too. As we settled in, I felt a sense of relief from the frantic pace of Hollywood.

Lee didn't last with the Chicago Cubs and was soon traded to Charlie Finley's Oakland A's farm club. Among the players jostling along in the team bus with him through the thankless, hot minor-league season were Reggie Jackson, Dave Duncan, and Rollie Fingers.

The flamboyant Charlie Finley took a liking to me during the brief period Lee was employed by the A's. Finley took great pride in leaving his mark on the game of baseball and on many of the players who worked for him. He redesigned the uniforms for his team, giving them a little color and panache. And he invented memorable names for his players like Catfish Hunter.

One time Charlie Finley and I flew from New York together, where I had just done the *Tonight* show, to Birmingham, Alabama, where the farm club that Lee played for was based. On the flight down we were talking about the colorful names his players had.

"What about Lee, Charlie?" I asked. "What are you going to name him?"

Charlie stared at me in silence.

"Mamie," he said finally, "a ball club only needs one star. The rest of the players are just fill-ins, as long as you've got that one star out there on the field."

That was my answer about Lee's future with the A's.

In a two-year period Lee Meyers played for the California Angels, the Chicago Cubs, the Oakland A's, the Philadelphia Phillies, and the San Francisco Giants. I don't know if that is a record or not, but even Bob Uecker couldn't have moved around much more. I don't think Lee even had a chance to unpack his bags.

I think Lee lost his incentive to work at pitching when he married me. I was making a good deal of money during that period, and Lee took a lot of it. He bought himself a Ferrari and God knows what else. It was a damn sight easier than pitching.

Lee only accompanied me once when I worked on a film. The film was another sci-fi movie—a movie so bad that apparently everyone involved did it strictly for the money. The director, Peter Bogdanovich, was so worried about what the quality of the film would do to his reputation that he worked under a pseudonym. Called *Voyage to the Planet of Prehistoric Women*, the movie was shot in Malibu and featured me as the queen of a planet covered by water and populated by voluptuous women. When Lee came to visit, I noticed his eyes incessantly wandering over the other girls on the picture.

Before long, Lee got involved with drugs. One day I found a carved meerschaum pipe I had given him in a desk drawer. The pipe's bowl smelled of the sweet tarry residue of hashish. Over time his behavior became more and more erratic, and finally I became fed up enough to divorce him. Later, after a brief second marriage, Lee was arrested in Hawaii trying to smuggle hashish into the country from Southeast Asia. When a customs inspector asked if he had anything to declare, Lee started sweating profusely, talking a mile a minute, and laughing inappropriately out of the side of his mouth. When the customs people searched him they found two bricks of high-grade hashish strapped around his waist. He was arrested and charged with smuggling contraband for sale—a charge that would have netted him twelve years in prison. He was finally tried on a lesser charge, put on probation, and allowed to return to the States. It was his first offense, and as the customs inspector who arrested him said, referring to his behavior when he was caught, "This kid sure ain't no professional."

Within a few months of that arrest, Lee was killed in a high-speed automobile crash in Huntington Beach, a few miles from his parents' home. He died a few months before his twenty-sixth birthday.

Chapter Twenty-one

In the summer of 1967, before my breakup with Lee, I was again booked to do *Gentlemen Prefer Blondes*—this time in the town of Glen Cove, Long Island, at the Wedgwood Dinner Theater. Afterward I was scheduled for a ten-day engagement in Biloxi, Mississippi. I had played in Biloxi before and I was looking forward to it. Biloxi was a wild, unbuttoned place, and working there was like a paid vacation, with balmy gulf breezes and a kindly sheriff overseeing the gambling in the little casinos down near the water, and the rambunctious activities of the bordellos just outside of town.

I was due in Biloxi in July, but a complication arose. The Wedgwood Dinner Theater was doing such good business that they held *Gentlemen Prefer Blondes* over for a few extra weeks. This would overlap into my Biloxi engagement.

I was stuck. I was afraid I would have to return the money the Biloxi club had sent me and renege on my agreement.

Fortunately, Bill Loeb was able to schedule Jayne Mansfield to take my place, and reschedule me for later in the summer.

"You're off the hook. New contracts are being sent."

"The people at the club weren't mad about the change?"

"No. They're delighted—now they're getting Jayne Mansfield *and* Mamie Van Doren the same summer."

A couple of weeks later I awoke feeling groggy. It was a

stifling hot July in New York. I walked into the living room to find my hairdresser, Marquita, with newspapers spread all over the floor.

"What's all this, Marquita?"

"It's in all the newspapers. Jayne Mansfield's dead."

Below one headline there was a picture of a wrecked convertible smashed under the rear end of a truck. Jayne Mansfield had been killed the night before in a car crash on a narrow, foggy road not far from Biloxi, Mississippi. She was on her way to work a job I couldn't do.

The world suddenly slipped.

I don't remember much about the next few hours. There were phone calls from the press. I spoke to Bill Loeb. My mother called and I cried some to her. I walked around the hotel suite in a daze. I couldn't seem to think clearly. I was unable to talk sensibly for more than a minute or so before my voice trailed off and I stopped.

I began to itch with nervous tension. Large welts had appeared on my skin, first around my elbows and knees and groin, then on my arms and stomach, breasts, legs, and back. My eyes swelled nearly shut and my lips puffed up to comical size.

Somehow I managed to get through the show that evening. I had to lie on the floor of my dressing room between acts and have my body covered with calamine lotion. I must have been an odd-looking Lorelei that evening. Instead of wearing the sexy, elegant clothes I usually wore, I went through the entire show in a full-length, high-necked dress that covered virtually all of me.

That night, as I was driven back to New York in a limo, the chill of a grisly déjà vu made me shake like a newborn calf.

Damn, I thought. Are we all cursed?

Jayne's death sharply brought home the many connections in the lives of Marilyn, Jayne Mansfield, and me, the three M's. We had become identified with an era because we made more movies and lived more flamboyant lives than many of the rest. They were connections that I'd tried to push out of my mind at the time of Marilyn's death. I continued to ignore them even more when I made *The Las Vegas Hillbillys* with

Jayne Mansfield because I found it a constant reminder of how we seemed to be running out of time.

Among the connections were the men that spilled over into the lives of each of us. For example, before we began dating, Ray Anthony threw the now-famous bash for Marilyn on her birthday.

I met Joe DiMaggio the first time in 1953 when he was visiting the film set of his pal Lou Costello. We met again after Marilyn's death when I was filming a sequel to the Aqua Velva commercial in Fort Lauderdale, Florida. Joe was staying at the Yankee Clipper Hotel in Miami, and he asked me to have dinner that evening. I had to turn him down because of an early call the next morning to finish the commercial. I gave Joe my number in L.A. and told him to call the next time he was in town. He was an instantly likable man with a quiet, intelligent demeanor and a fatherly attitude.

A few months later Joe called and said he'd like to take me to dinner.

"Why don't you just come up and we'll eat here?" I asked. He agreed, and we had a delightful dinner together. After dinner we went in and watched TV propped up on pillows in my bed while eating ice cream out of cardboard containers.

Joe and I talked far into the night. He had just returned from Hawaii, where he had been vacationing with an old friend who was recuperating from a heart attack. His friend, a few years older than Joe, became ill again and had to be brought home. He died shortly after getting back to Los Angeles. The funeral had been just a few days before Joe had called me.

"I don't know, Mamie," Joe said. His voice was colored with a deep sadness. "It seems like all my friends are dying."

As we talked, I began to see how much he still loved and missed Marilyn. There was a deep void that no one would ever fill. We laughed a lot that night. It was as though we had known each other a long time, connected as we were by common memories and affection for Marilyn. I did not try to fill the void in him that night. When Joe left I gave him a sisterly kiss and waved him out of the driveway.

My path had earlier crossed that of another of Marilyn's lovers: Yves Montand. I was introduced to Yves by Pamela

Mason during a lunch we had together in the Polo Lounge at
the Beverly Hills Hotel. Yves was in town making *Let's Make
Love* with Marilyn.

It was a chilly day, so I wore a pair of suede slacks and a
mid-length suede coat. The Polo Lounge's moment of en-
lightenment had yet to arrive in 1960, and ladies were still
forbidden to wear slacks inside its sacred premises. I had to
slip into a ladies' room outside in the hotel's lobby and take
off my slacks. I stowed them rolled up in my purse, pinned
the bottom of the coat shut so it looked like a long dress, and
went in to lunch.

The other guests at the table were Yves Montand, his wife,
Simone Signoret, and Laurence Harvey. During the course of
the meal, I watched Simone's eyes carefully. The gossip
around town was that Yves and Marilyn were having a torrid
affair under Simone's very nose. She seemed to be handling
the rumors, and herself, well. Talk at the table included the
usual topics of Hollywood luncheon conversation—who's doing what picture, whose last picture was a flop, who's marriage is a flop, whose affair is a flop. There was particular
tension around the table when the conversation drifted to affairs. Simone appeared almost relieved when Yves turned his
charm in my direction.

The upshot of our lunch that day was that I dated both of
the men at the table. I went out first with Laurence Harvey,
who invited me to dinner. Afterward we returned to my place
to talk, mostly about Larry. Larry was a complete gentleman
and a fun date. My only reservation was that he was such an
actor. I've never been crazy about dating actors in general
because they're usually so madly in love with themselves. As
Marsha Mason says in Neil Simon's film *The Goodbye Girl*:
"Ask an actor where he's from and you get a list of his
credits."

I was surprised that Yves Montand asked me out shortly
after that, given that his wife was still in town and that he
was still seeing Marilyn. During dinner he scrupulously
avoided any mention of Marilyn. His European charm was
very-high-octane, but in person he was a little portly for my
taste. In attitude and manner, though, he was very much like
Joe DiMaggio.

With Jayne, too, I had connections. I recall a painful evening when Jayne drunkenly crashed a party at someone's house tucked away high up off Coldwater Canyon. There were two women within earshot making loud derisive comments about her.

"Can you *believe* her?" one hissed, inclining her chin in Jayne's direction. "She's let herself go so much."

"And that dress," the other one said. "It looks like something from Penney's."

I stood seething a few feet away. I was embarrassed for Jayne, who made it a point to rub up against every guy she got near.

I heard someone say, "She's always drunk like that, crashing every party."

Jayne suddenly performed one of her favorite party attention-getters, producing one of her pet chihuahuas from the ample bosom of her low-cut dress. The dog barked and snapped at the nearest man and Jayne laughed wildly.

"Well! I've seen it all now," the second woman said.

"But what can you expect?" the first one replied.

Finally my Swedish temper snapped. I walked over to the two catty bitches.

"At least Jayne's got the guts to do what she wants. She's not spending her time making nasty remarks behind her hand."

"My dear," one of them said condescendingly, "you're so *upset*. Have you had too much to drink?"

I looked at the glass of champagne in my hand. "Too much in the presence of pigs like you." I threw the champagne in her face and walked to the door. She was sobbing and her mascara made dark streaks down her face. Her companion stared incredulously.

I found Jayne in the driveway, leaning against the fender of a car. She was cooing drunkenly to the little dog: "It's okay, sweetie. It's okay. You're a sweet puppy."

She heard me approaching and turned.

"Hiya, Mamie."

"Hi, Jaynie. How do you feel?"

"Good question. Need a drink."

"Can you get home?"

"What'sissname in there said he would take me home. You

know, the dark-haired one with the muscles." She steadied
herself against the car. "But I sure could use another drink."

She staggered a step or two in the direction of the house.
Her heel caught on the edge of the lawn and she went sprawling in the grass. The chihuahua yelped and danced away a
few feet, only to come sniffing back to its mistress.

"Thass okay, baby," Jayne slurred. "Mama's okay."

She sat up and held the dog in her arms.

"Parties! What a drag, huh, Mamie? Wanna go down to
the Whiskey? I see you there all the time. Find ourselves a
couple of live ones? Whaddya say?"

"Not tonight, Jaynie." I helped her to her feet and we
leaned against her massive Cadillac convertible. A few more
feet and she would have parked it in our host's living room.

"So whatcha been doin' lately?" Jayne asked, peering
boozily at me.

"The usual. Nightclubs. Theaters."

"Oh, yeah? Me too. Lotsa work."

"That's good."

"An' you know what else?" She waved a finger at me for
emphasis. "Movie. Gonna do a movie in . . . in It-lee."

"No kidding? What's it called?"

"Called? Dunno. No title yet. Jus' a scrip'. Lotsa money
too. No more worries after that, Mamie."

"Right. No more worries."

"I can see you'd like to be so lucky. Like to do another
movie too, huh? Not much happenin' in movies . . . for either of us."

"Precious little. But I'm doing okay with the clubs."

"Me too. Like to do a revival of *Rock Hunter*. Get back
to Broadway. This year. Or next year. I ought to get another
drink. Hey! Bring me another . . . What was I drinking? Do
you remember?"

I shook my head.

I heard the footsteps as the broad-shouldered man came
down the sidewalk from the front door.

"Ready to go, baby?" the man asked. He was not as young
as he tried to look, but he smiled knowingly with some expensive dental work. He was an oily Latin-lover type, one
she had been seen around town with frequently.

"Yeah. Didja bring me another drinkie, honey?"

''No. You don't need another one. You'll pass out.''

She leaned against him as sensuously as she could manage.

''Honey, I never pass out.''

''Bullshit,'' he growled, pushing her away roughly. ''Are the keys in it?''

He opened the driver's side door and she flopped onto the seat. He shoved her over and started the Cadillac with a roar.

''Goddamn drunk,'' the Latin charmer said.

''Some fuckin' party. Can't even get a drink. No good parties these days, huh, Mamie?''

''Nope. Not many.''

She sat up on the back of the seat and rested her head on the edge of the windshield.

''Shitty times, huh? No fun anymore. No fun.''

I stood silently looking at her. She cuddled her dog, looking down at me with an expression of drunken childish despair on her face.

''Know what, Mamie? Sometimes I think Marilyn was lucky.''

The car roared out of the driveway. As it disappeared around the bend, Jayne was still looking over her shoulder at me.

There is a history of calamitous and violent deaths among the glamorous girls that boggles the mind and chills the blood, especially if you're one of the few survivors.

Thelma Todd, Jean Harlow, Carole Lombard, Francis Farmer, Carole Landis, Veronica Lake, Marilyn Monroe, Betty Grable, Joi Lansing, Cleo Moore, Jayne Mansfield, Barbara Ruick, Leigh Snowdon, Barbara Nichols, Barbara Peyton, Marilyn Maxwell, Marie McDonald, Marie Wilson, Diana Dors, Sharon Tate, Inger Stevens, and Dorothy Stratten were all, in varying degrees, famous, blonde, beautiful, and billed as sex goddesses of their respective eras. Most of them did not live to see fifty-five.

As young women we were told that we were infinitely desirable and beautiful, only to discover that there was always someone coming up behind who was more desirable and beautiful. Our profession is perhaps the most competitive in the world. For, to be glamorous, to be beautiful, is to be doomed eventually to be disappointed.

As my friend Dorothy Lamour, one of the most glamorous women I know, once said: "Time keeps rollin' on." She shrugged. "What're you going to do?"

If you make your living being beautiful, you've got to be willing to pay that price. You must realize that there is also something deep inside that is as beautiful as the outside; and that the beauty inside will *never* change, for as long as you live. It's too easy to try to cram so much living into your short time in the sun that like the mayfly on a warm summer's day, you flutter to the ground, spent too young.

Chapter Twenty-two

The Vietnam war is, for me, as it is for millions of others, burned indelibly into the memory. Though I was in that sad, war-torn country for only a little over ten weeks, in retrospect the time feels like a lifetime. Each moment stands out vividly, like a long row of photographs—the lush green colors of the countryside contrasting with the muted browns, blues, and greens of uniforms, often highlighted by the bright red of blood.

The first tour I made of Vietnam was in 1968. The vicious fighting of the Tet offensive that year prevented me from entertaining outside the war zone at all. Our plane touched down at Ton Son Nhut airfield near Saigon and took off again a few minutes later. But in that short time, standing on the steaming tarmac in the deep wet heat that follows the tropical rains, I could see a long line of men queued up on the back doors of a dusty C-130 transport plane.

The men stood quietly, their eyes riveted on the big clam-shell cargo doors of the giant aircraft. They were waiting to leave. Their tours completed in Nam, they waited anxiously to climb aboard for the first leg of their journey back to safety, to loved ones, to whatever private fantasy they harbored about what home would be like when they returned.

"Hey!" one shouted, pointing in my direction.

"Hey, Mamie!" yelled another.

Their heads turned in unison to watch me.

I crossed the few yards to the line of men and they crowded around. Their smell engulfed me: the flat and lonely smell of military-issue clothing mingled with their sweat and the thin, sweet odor of gun oil.

Some of the bolder ones asked for autographs; two in the long line even produced my *Playboy* beer-bath picture to be signed. The torn-out pages were dirty and creased from folding and refolding, and stained from being carried in sweaty shirt pockets.

The shy ones stood back and watched. Their eyes held mine for a moment before sliding away. The look was one I still remember—part unnameable fear; part curiosity; part sexual deprivation; part longing for the softness of a woman.

"What're you doing here, Mamie?" one soft-voiced Southern boy asked.

"I came to do some shows for you guys."

He shook his head sadly. "Don't stay here, Mamie." He hitched up the carbine slung over his shoulder and glanced up at the waiting airplane. "This is an awful place. Stay here too long, you stay forever."

There was a deep thud and the ground shook. The men nearest me jumped.

"Incoming!"

"Mortar attack!"

"Mamie!" called the steward on the Air Force jet that had brought me in. "Get back here. We're taking off. Vietcong are shelling the airfield again!"

I dashed back to my plane and up the boarding ladder. As the door closed, I could see the long line of short-timers scattering for cover. There was another thud as a mortar exploded nearby. I understood then part of that fear in the eyes of those men: the fear of dying on the steps of the plane that's taking you home.

The situation in Vietnam in 1968 caused my shows there to be canceled. However, there were officers' and enlisted men's clubs in the Philippines on my agenda. And during that part of the tour, I saw the hospitals.

Battlefield casualties, thanks to faster helicopters, could be moved quickly from the spot they were wounded. They were flown to airfields where transport planes ferried them directly to the large military hospitals at Clark and Subic bases not far from Manila.

I visited the first hospital one night between shows.

"These casualties are from all over Vietnam, Miss Van Doren," the chief nurse told me as we walked through the wide main corridor toward the wards. "Have you ever visited a military hospital before?"

"Yes," I answered. "I went to several in Germany a couple of years ago."

"But you've never been to a hospital that had battlefield casualties?"

"No."

"Then I suggest you brace yourself."

There is no way to be prepared for viewing the results of war. Nothing in the experience of the average person offers a hint about the various destructions that can be wrought on the human body by explosives and howling bits of metal. When confronted by the reality of battlefield injuries, the mind tries to reject what the eyes see.

I spoke to all the men in the long rows of beds as we worked our way through the first ward. The injuries to these men were comparatively minor. Not many were missing limbs.

The nurse was breaking me in slowly.

In the next ward there were fewer men sitting up in bed. They were flatter. The sheets bulged less in all the places where the limbs should be. Their faces were grayer, seamed in their youth with the tracks of pain. Moans and cries mingled with the "Hellos!" and "Hiya, Mamie's!" of the ones whose awareness was less deadened by painkillers. The boys tried to be men. They laughed bravely while we talked. The ones seriously wounded and maimed clung, hungry for a caress.

We continued through the hospital like a journey down through hell. There was a ward with men who had lost multiple limbs. Some had lost all of them. They stared back with the faces of old babies. Their brains swam behind their eyes, drowning in the rising horror of their plight.

Between two of the wards was a brightly lit little hallway with windows that looked out onto the tropical vegetation that grows so riotously in the Philippines. I leaned against the open window, breathing in the heavy night scent of jasmine and willing my knees not to collapse.

"Do you want to go on, Mamie?" the nurse asked gently.

"In a minute," I whispered. "How do you do it? How do you stay sane, looking at them day after day?"

She gazed out the window for a long time. Two creases appeared between her eyebrows. Finally she sighed wearily.

"I don't know. They just keep coming. Some die, some live. Some of those that die—you find you're glad they did. Some that live are in such bad shape, you start thinking that death is a gift. Our medicine is so good . . . so efficient . . . sometimes it's cruel. We save their lives much more often than we would've even five years ago. But what kind of lives are we condemning them to? What are we sending home to their wives or parents?"

She looked at me briefly and I could see the pain kept carefully hidden beneath her thick patina of nursing professionalism.

"To answer your question, Mamie, I do it day after day because it's my job. I will myself not to hurt with them. I try to relieve a little suffering, make them a little more comfortable. They're grateful, one way or another. But as to staying sane? I don't know sometimes if I am anymore, or if anyone else is either. Is any of this sane? Can anything be sane that destroys so?"

She forced a laugh and turned from the window. "I guess it doesn't make much sense, does it?"

I put my hand on hers. "It makes perfect sense."

"Are you ready to go? If you're feeling queasy, you should probably stop now. The next ones are really bad. The burn ward."

"Can they recognize me? Hear me? Are they conscious?"

"I can't promise that they're fully conscious, but even if they just hear your voice, if it becomes part of some comatose dream, it can help them."

"Then let's do it."

It was cool and dark inside the burn ward. I could hear the metallic click of the apparatus that aided their breathing and the soft whoosh of oxygen. I had a short conversation with each conscious man; I leaned down and spoke softly to the unconscious ones; told them that I loved them; tried to enter their private twilight world.

When we left, I brushed away the tears while we stood in the hallway.

"I think I've had enough for today. Sorry."

"It's okay, Mamie," the nurse said. "You can't imagine what you've done for them."

"And you don't know what you've done for me," I told her. "Your courage is some example."

She was not the only woman with iron courage and determination I saw in Southeast Asia. Little is said about the women in the war zone when there is talk about Vietnam veterans, and more credit ought to be given them for their bravery and ability to cope with the massive human tragedy they witnessed daily.

I made many more visits to the hospitals during my stay. There seemed never to be enough time to do what needed to be done. Often I performed my first show, went directly to spend some time visiting the men in a hospital, then returned to do my second show.

My 1968 tour also included visits to Okinawa, Hong Kong, Taiwan, Tokyo, and Bangkok. I played dates in nightclubs as well as service clubs. I became intimately acquainted with the Orient. But I told myself that for all its beauty and fascination, I wouldn't go back there until the war ended.

When I returned to the States later that year, the fighting still raged in Vietnam, while violent protests erupted at home. While the protesters marched, the memories were still nightmarishly fresh to me of the young men—our young men—lying helplessly in hospitals.

But back in Newport Beach, as I watched twelve-year-old Perry putt-putting around the bay in his little boat, I thought long and hard about how the war was dragging on. It would be less than six years before Perry was eligible for the draft. Surely the war would be over by then, but . . .

"Please, God," I prayed. "Please stop the war."

By 1971 my prayers had not been answered. The country still writhed in the grip of the war while President Nixon's Vietnamization program slowly disengaged us. But many Americans were still there and many died each week.

When I was approached to do another tour of Vietnam, at first I rejected the idea. But I was at a strange and dangerous juncture in my life when everyday things made no sense and the most bizarre ideas seemed logical. And because of all the clutter in my mind, I could not see clearly where I was going.

I had recognized before Jayne Mansfield's death that there was less and less work coming my way. After her tragic death and Marilyn's controversial suicide before it, I felt like an embarrassing reminder that beauty is perishable.

I began to be jealous of Jayne and Marilyn in an odd way. Interviewers invariably asked me about them. It was as if *they* had won the beauty contest and *I* was the runner-up. They were dead and therefore frozen in time—the stuff of legends. I was a face still alive, trying to earn a living, making mistakes in front of everyone.

I stared out over the Pacific from the deck of the little outboard cabin cruiser I had bought when Lee and I were first married. I thought I would sell the boat soon because I seldom had time to use it, and this solo cruise out the mouth of Newport Bay was a kind of farewell.

As the boat rocked gently in the swell, I looked westward past the dim outline of Catalina, out toward the open ocean. A feeling of peace settled over me as I listened to the water lapping at the hull. I watched my distorted reflection in the blue water as the boat drifted.

"All I need to do is stay here," I said to myself. "Just drift on this big ocean until I get to where I want to go."

I'd always been looking for the big rock-candy mountain, but I hadn't found it yet. I'd always had so much fun, but happiness eluded me. Happy ladies do not go on solo cruises and drop tears into the already salty Pacific.

Looking into the depths, I thought: When I get tired of the cruise, I can go over the side. Make a long dive down to where it's cool and dark.

I remembered an incident when I was a little girl, newly arrived in California, splashing and frolicking in the heavy Pacific surf. I had gone out too far in the water and a large wave broke over me. Before I could stop coughing and spitting up water, an undertow from the next wave pulled me down. I looked up at the retreating surface and felt a numbing weariness pervade my body.

"Enough!" I shouted, jarring myself back to the present. I wasn't ready to give up on life yet. Not for *me* to wash up somewhere like a discarded beach toy.

I pushed the electric starter on the cruiser's big outboard and pointed the bow back toward the Wedge, the jetty that marked the entrance to the Newport channel. I decided to put the boat up for sale. I would not be needing it. I was going back to Vietnam.

Not long afterward, I sat in the first-class section of a Japan Airlines 747, clutching a leather-bound Bible and dabbing at my tears with a Kleenex. I had just said a tearful good-bye to Perry and my mother. I checked again in my purse to make sure I had the letter sent to me by President Nixon thanking me for volunteering to go to Vietnam.

My first stop on the tour was Thailand, and it was even more beautiful than I remembered. My opening engagement was at Bangkok's lovely Rama Hilton Hotel. A week later, I traveled by car to the far northeastern corner of the country to entertain at the Ubon air base near the Laotian border.

At a party and reception after my officers'-club show, I met a young pilot named Dan. He was tall and good-looking with sun-streaked blonde hair and a rakish mustache.

Dan and I made a tour of Ubon city that night in a jeep he finagled for the night. We ate aromatic hot Thai dishes washed down with local beer at a tiny lantern-bedecked restaurant that catered to the servicemen.

After dinner we roared off into the night with the warm wind blowing in our faces.

"Before I take you home, you've got to see my plane!" he shouted over the wind.

"Tonight?"

"Sure!"

As we sped down the flight line of Phantom jets, the men working on the planes looked up and stared in astonishment.

"Nice night for a drive, Major," one of them quipped loud enough for us to hear.

"Hey, Mamie!" another shouted.

Stripped to the waist, the men glistened with sweat. They struggled with missiles and bombs to be attached to the undersides of the airplanes. Large hoses snaked across the tarmac, providing power and fuel to some of the aircraft. In the yellowish illumination from the airfield lights the scene had an eerie unreality.

We stopped in front of one of the gleaming airplanes and Dan said fondly, "There she is."

Towering over us, the Phantom possessed a deadly grandeur.

After the visit to his airplane, Dan drove me back to my hotel, a seedy little place grandiosely named the Sands. We were both quiet during the drive back and when we stopped outside the hotel, illuminated by the wash of color from the gaudy neon sign bearing its name, we stared into each other's eyes.

"Well, this has been fun, Mamie," Dan said expectantly.

I leaned toward him and received his good-night kiss.

"Coming upstairs, Major?"

I drifted up from sleep as I felt Dan stir. It was still night and the interior of the room was dimly lit by the reflection from the perimeter lights that surrounded the airfield just behind the hotel. In the shadowy light, Dan's body looked lean and strong as he searched quietly for his clothes.

"You go back to sleep and I'll be back in a few hours."

"Where are you going?"

He shrugged into his flight suit.

"We're scheduled to make a little unexpected delivery over the North. You'll hear the seven of us take off in about thirty minutes. The runway's just half a mile away over there." He pointed out the window to the open space enclosed by a chain-link fence behind the hotel. "Around six A.M. start listening for us to come back."

He kissed me and I could feel the cotton of his flight suit against my breasts.

"I'll be waiting," I promised.

I dozed fitfully through the dark early-morning hours, dreaming alternately of being in the arms of a faceless man, watching a jet plane streaming smoke spiraling in to crash, and flying over the South Dakota countryside with my arms outstretched like a bird.

The little bronze Tiffany travel clock I always carry woke me with its jingling. It showed six A.M. I went to the window and gazed out across the fence into the Ubon air base's emptiness, listening for the distant roar of jets.

There was a faint gray spreading over the warm black night when I heard the roar of the first one. I strained to look into the early-morning light, but the source of the sound remained invisible. The roar grew louder and I heard the faint sound of tortured tires hitting the runway. The first three landed in quick succession; then four and five, then six.

"Come on, Dan, come on, number seven," I said out loud, fiercely gripping the windowsill. "I hardly know you, but I don't want to be the last love affair of some hotshot pilot." I was answered by silence.

I was positive I had counted six. My heart pounded as I stood in terror, grief clutching my throat.

Then I heard something. At first I thought it was the rasp of my own breathing. I listened more carefully, holding my breath. It was there! A soft growl that quickly turned to a rumble, then into a deafening roar. Number seven! I breathed a sigh of relief as the squeal of the tires hitting the runway drifted toward me.

Within an hour, Dan was discreetly tapping on my door.

"Have a tough day at the office, dear?"

"Not so bad," he said with a half-smile. "Did you listen for us?"

I nodded.

Dan said, "Everybody got back okay this time. There was some antiaircraft fire, but only two surface-to-air missiles. Practically a milk run."

Back in bed we lost ourselves in each other. The sun rose and we sweated in the tropical humidity. As we dozed off, finally exhausted, Dan murmured in my ear: "War is hell."

When I left Thailand for Vietnam, Dan and I communicated as best we could, looking forward to a rendezvous we planned in Pleiku. But once inside Vietnam, I looked back on the war that Dan fought from his safe haven in Thailand as the country-club war. The dangers faced by the men flying missions over enemy territory seemed remote compared to the threat of death from so many quarters encountered twenty-four hours a day by the infantry grunts. What GI knew when he might be blown up by a bomb while having a drink in some Saigon bar? Or shot by a young girl in some outlying village? Or dismembered by a booby trap in the bush?

Inside Vietnam the war was no longer faceless and obscure. It was there at arm's reach, ugly and menacing.

Both my Vietnam tours were booked in the U.S. through Associated Booking Corporation by a talent agency in Thailand owned by two Italian-American brothers. In 1971 the two brothers began using an agent based in Saigon to book shows for officers' and enlisted men's clubs throughout the country.

After I was installed at the Embassy Hotel in Saigon, I met with the booking agent from whom my weekly paycheck would come.

My compensation for the tour was barely enough to cover my expenses and those of the conductor and secretary I hired to go with me. With the addition of the Saigon-based agent, whom I'll call Vince, problems arose.

Vince was puffy and gray, belying the fact that he was only in his fifties. His skin had that pasty transparence often possessed by heroin addicts. The fingers of his left hand were yellowed by chain-smoking cigarettes. His voice was a pitched whine that vibrated unpleasantly in my ears. It was true of Vince as it was many other civilians on the fringes of the war, that one of the reasons they stayed on in Vietnam was the easy availability of cheap, high-quality heroin. And one of the secret tragedies of the war was that many of our servicemen got caught up with the drug as well.

After my meeting with Vince, I came away with an uneasy feeling about this whole project. But I was in it up to my ears, and in no position to back out now. I threw myself into it with all my strength.

Vince had laid out an impossible schedule for me. Unlike the USO shows (including Bob Hope's shows), I would be entertaining the troops in the field at small fire stations and outposts in the bush. While most of the places I was to work were considered pacified, there were many that could never be fully declared safe. Often I made do with a truck bed or the back of a tank for a stage. My little five-piece Filipino band would be wailing away while I sang through the mike of our hastily connected sound system. More than once we were warned that we'd have to helicopter out immediately after the show because "Charlie" would attack upon hearing the music.

We flew to the DMZ in two Huey helicopters, and landed at the fire station near the border village of Quang Tri. This was where the danger was. The motto of the men at Quang Tri was: "We Walk the Line." There were North Vietnamese troops just over the border of the demilitarized zone and they were tough and fast. Quang Tri, which sat on a little plateau commanding a view of the DMZ, had had to defend itself practically to the last man more than once.

It was a sizable complement of men that defended Quang Tri and they cheered lustily when I came onstage to do my show. When the show was over there was a party and I sat down to a steak dinner with the general in charge of the area, the junior officers, and the guest of honor next to me, an enlisted man named Charlie.

Charlie, the general informed me, was going out the next day to "Walk the Line"—a scouting mission that would take him into the wild back country of the DMZ, often in close proximity to the North Vietnamese.

There was plenty of wine and the steaks were thick and the general laughed and joked with his cronies. Charlie was subdued, however. It was as though there was a curtain between him and the rest of us—as if he was singled out in a spotlight and unable to see those around him in the shadows. He was a shy young man, not much more than a boy really, in his early twenties, with that hard, lean, narrow face you find in the hollows and backwoods of Virginia and the Carolinas. He talked only a little, telling me about his family back home, showing me a fingered photograph of the girl who wore his ring.

By the time the party was over, Charlie was a little drunk. He wandered off with his buddies amid lots of back-slapping and laughing.

I went back to the little trailer they provided for my accommodations, took a shower, and got ready for bed. There was a tentative knock on the door and I opened it to find Charlie standing there. He was trying to hold himself very straight and sober, but wove slightly as he spoke.

"Good evenin', Mamie," he said carefully.

"Charlie, good evening. Don't you think you ought to get some sleep? You've got a big day tomorrow."

"Such a beautiful night, thought I'd come see if you wanted to go for a walk."

"Walk?"

"Yeah. Just out here near your trailer. I just wanted to talk to you a little. Seems like it's been so long since I talked to a woman—I mean a real lady like you."

"Sure. It looks like a nice night for a walk."

We stood in front of the little trailer and talked for several minutes about where he was from and how long it would be before he would go home.

I looked at Charlie with all his youth, with his enthusiasm for his mission, and I suddenly felt very tired. I wanted to run away from all this wasted youth being spent in the service of war that was barely understood by the government running it, much less by the boys whose deadly job it was to fight it.

"Mamie, I don't want you to take this wrong, but could you . . . could I just hold you for a minute? Nothing else, mind you. I just haven't held a woman for so long and I—"

I put my arms around Charlie and held him close. His breathing grew hoarse. His hands pressed into my back and I could feel the heat from his palms. At last he relaxed his hold on me and I looked up into his eyes.

"Thank you, Mamie, so much."

"It . . . it was a pleasure to be of service."

"Could I give you something to remember me by, Mamie?"

"I'll never forget you, Charlie. You don't have to give me anything."

"Here," he said, reaching into his pocket. "Take this." He held out a shiny Zippo cigarette lighter.

"I couldn't, Charlie, really—"

"Please take it. See, it's got our motto on it: 'I Walk the Line.' If you take it, I know it'll bring me good luck."

I took the lighter, thumbed the top open, and spun the

wheel. The wick caught and a big blue flame lit our faces. I closed it and kissed Charlie on the cheek.

If it was a budding death wish that led me to Vietnam, the wish came to full flower at the fire stations down near the Mekong Delta. In honor of Ho Chi Minh's birthday, fighting had been sporadically heavy throughout the Mekong Delta, a region of rich lowlands where the Mekong River spills into the South China Sea. It is an area of labyrinthine waterways and ever-changing floating islands not far from the Cambodian border, providing many hiding places for the infiltrating Vietcong forces. Some of the areas were so hot, I managed to get there to entertain only by overcoming the better judgment of some high-ranking officers with my own stubborn insistence.

I was increasingly tired because of the breakneck schedule that sent me racing around the country doing several shows a day. There seemed never to be quite enough time to sleep, and when I did, it was fitfully. My appetite was poor, and I was starting to lose weight. I was being bothered frequently by stomach cramps, nausea, and diarrhea.

After one of my performances at a delta firebase, I was allowed, against Army regulations, to ride back to Saigon in the fast, heavily armed helicopter gunship known as the Cobra.

When we took off, the Cobra made a low moan and as the lights from the helipad swept away behind us, we were swallowed up in the great dark belly of the night. I sat up ahead of the pilot, a young lieutenant named Bo. There was no sensation of speed as we banked and angled back toward Saigon. Bo talked to me gently through the intercom, pointing out the few landmarks that could be seen in the pitch-black world below us.

This is your trial by fire, I thought. If you're supposed to die over here, now is when it will happen.

Out ahead of us a few miles we could see the glow of a firefight in the jungle. As we skirted far around it, we watched the rocket flashes as helicopter gunships mounted a counterattack on Vietcong guerrillas trying to overrun a firebase. We listened to the frightened, uncertain, cautious, heartened, and finally triumphant radio chatter from the scene of the battle. When we landed I was drenched in sweat. But I felt somehow washed clean by the power and speed of the Cobra. As I regained the use of my watery legs, Lieutenant Bo walked me away from his sleek ship, and I thought: Maybe I'll make it through this after all.

My odd relationship with Major Kilgore, another helicopter pilot who ferried me around, began to develop as my health began to deteriorate rapidly. Unlike Dan, the major was a father figure that I clung to as I felt more and more physically run-down.

Major Kilgore somehow managed to get permission to fly me around the Delta to locations where I performed my shows. As I grew weaker, his comforting presence grew in importance for me. Before long a romance of sorts developed between us, and as it did, the major's idiosyncrasies became more apparent.

Major Kilgore was very particular about his appearance. He affected a cavalry officer's flat-brimmed hat and highly polished boots. His jumper was festooned with medals and he walked with a ramrod-straight swagger.

He was a devout Southern Baptist who kept a list of his dead soldiers in the breast pocket of his shirt.

"They're my boys," he'd say emotionally. "As much as if they were my own sons. When I get back to the States, I'm going to try to see the families of all of them."

Several times I asked the major if he was married. Each time his grave reply was, "No, ma'am."

Before long, Major Kilgore asked in his most Southern-gentlemanly way for my hand in marriage. I told him definitely: Maybe.

Major Kilgore took me out in Saigon, but even in the city there was danger. Once, coming out of our favorite restaurant, La Cave, we surprised some children trying to booby-trap our jeep with a grenade. Had we stayed for dessert that night, I would not be writing this book.

On our way to dinner another night, I saw a young American staggering in the street. He was thin and frail-looking and even in the dark I could see the sickly ivory pallor of his skin and the burning coals of his eyes. He disappeared like a wraith into an alley. Kilgore shook his head sadly and continued driving.

"Shouldn't we stop and help him?" I asked.

"There is no help for him," Kilgore replied through clenched teeth. In the reflection of the gaudy lights of Saigon's main thoroughfare I could see his jaw twitching. "He's one of the dope addicts. The stuff's so easy to get over here, Mamie. These kids get hooked before they know what's happening."

"Can't the military stop them from selling to the soldiers?"

"How? The military can't even think straight enough to win the war. How could they stop something as deep underground as dope dealing? I admit it. There's no way to stop these kids from getting dope if they want it. And they come over here wanting it more and more. There's some kind of moral breakdown going on back home, Mamie. I can see it in the kids they're sending us."

"What are they getting hooked on?"

"The worst. Heroin. It's cheap, pure, and available everywhere. Look up ahead here, I'll show you."

He pointed to a street corner as we approached it. "Look there. The old woman in rags. Watch her."

The old woman plied her trade with efficient professionalism. She held out a withered old hand to an approaching GI. He gave her money which she quickly tucked away in the voluminous folds of the rags she wore. The young soldier pushed up his sleeve and she quickly jabbed him with a shot of heroin. His legs went suddenly rubbery and nearly buckled under his weight. His buddies helped steady him as the old woman turned away and prepared another shot for the next customer. As we drove slowly past, I saw her shoot up several men from the same needle, sending them reeling on their way down the crowded street.

"Two dollars a shot," Major Kilgore said hoarsely. "One-stop happiness. And if the MPs arrest her, there'll be another one there an hour later."

I tasted bile in my throat. "Could we just go back to the hotel? I'm not very hungry now."

Eventually my illness reached the stage that I could no longer get out of bed. Major Kilgore used some influence to get me admitted to the Field A hospital in Saigon. Kilgore had taken care of me as best he could, but my dysentery was now out of control and the doctors at the hospital feared after examining me that it was amoebic in origin and that my liver was involved.

Major Kilgore's final tour of duty was coming to a close and he was leaving the country. The Army was dithering around about putting me on a Medevac flight out, so the major left ahead of me, promising that we'd meet in Hawaii.

There were endless delays in getting me out of the country. The Army brass wanted to get me well at the Field A hospital so I could leave Vietnam under my own power. But as the weeks dragged by, I didn't get any better. I begged and cajoled to be put on a Medevac plane to Tripler Hospital in Hawaii. I was caught in my own catch-22. The Field A hospital didn't want me to leave until I was well, but they didn't have the sophisticated equipment to do a liver scan to determine the course of my treatment to get me well. To civilians the stupidity of this situation is obvious, but to an organization like the Army it is a perfectly logical, normal delay.

Finally I managed to collar a major who was the chief of internal medicine. In exasperation I played my last card. I handed him my letter from President Nixon giving me his blessing to entertain the troops in Vietnam.

"I want you to show that letter to whoever's in charge of this hospital. You tell him that if I don't get on a Medevac flight out of here, I'm going to call the President personally and tell him what a comedy of errors this little hospital stay of mine has been."

"Now, Mamie, we've tried everything—"

"You tell him, dammit!" I said, setting my jaw.

The following week there was magically a space for me on a Medevac flight to Hawaii. When the doors of the big C-130 transport closed on me and the rest of the sad, wounded, silent passengers lying on cots in the cargo bay, I finally breathed a sigh of relief.

My mother and son met me in Hawaii and as they leaned over the gurney on which I was being rolled into the hospital, we all murmured our thanks that I was home safely.

After the testing at Tripler Hospital, it was determined that my liver was free of amoeba and my treatment proceeded rapidly. In a week or so I was released (much to the Army's relief, I think), and I took a room in the Royal Hawaiian Hotel, free to enjoy the warm, healing atmosphere of Honolulu.

Major Kilgore arrived from the mainland and we did the town as best we could while I regained my strength. The newspapers were after me to tell them what it was like in Vietnam, so I had a small press conference and answered questions. One of those questions was: Who was that handsome major you were constantly seen with around the island? My answer: My fiancé, Major Bill Kilgore.

The next morning I was headed for the beach and an early lunch when I stopped by the major's room and found him packing.

"I've got to go," he said nervously. "Gotta get back home to Albany."

"Why?" I asked. "I thought we'd have a few more days here and then go back to L.A. together."

"Did you see this?" He gestured to the Waikiki newspaper spread out on the bed. There was a huge headline over a long UPI story about us. The headline read: "MAMIE VAN DOREN TO WED MAJOR WILLIAM KILGORE."

I shrugged and smiled at him. "Well, you *did* ask me."

He flew out the same day.

Later that evening as I was puzzling over his behavior, my mother asked, "Honey, did it occur to you that he might be married?"

"Yes," I said. "But he told me he wasn't. He was so religious, how could I not believe him?"

After a few days I decided to find out the mysterious answer to Major Kilgore. He had left no phone number where I could reach him, but had given me dozens of religious newspapers his aunt sent him in Vietnam. They had her name and an Albany, Georgia, address on them. It took no time at all for the operator to get her number.

"No, Billy's not here," she said in a thick Jaw-jah drawl when I asked for him. "But I believe he's down at his house. Hold the line till I get my glasses and I'll give you his number."

When I called the number she gave me, a woman answered

the phone. When I asked to speak to Bill Kilgore, she asked who I was. I told her.

"And who's this?" I asked in return.

"I'm Mrs. Bill Kilgore."

There was a silence while I let that one sink in.

"Oh, I *am* sorry," I said. "I didn't know. He never told me he had a wife."

"And four sons," she added.

"Oh, boy."

For a moment I was really at a loss for words. I felt a kinship for the woman on the other end of the line. I wanted to comfort her, but I didn't know what to say.

"It's not the first time this has happened," she continued. It sounded like she was speaking of a wayward son instead of a philandering husband. "He never tells his . . . friends about the rest of his personal life. Bill's standing right here. Do you want to hear it from him?"

"Oh, I believe you, Mrs. Kilgore."

"I'll put him on anyway. Good-bye, Mamie."

"Hello," the major said dully. He sounded like a man utterly defeated.

"Is all of what she said true?"

"Yes."

"Why didn't you tell me?"

There was a long pause while I suppose he tried to come up with an answer. Finally he said, "I don't know. I honestly don't."

After some reflection, I felt a sense of relief over the loss of Major Kilgore. As it turned out, it was good not to have a relationship that was a constant reminder of the war.

Now I could put the war behind me. Except that like everyone else who came in contact with Vietnam, I could never leave it nor would it ever leave me. The memories were always waiting there, in the dark.

One of the finest tributes made about the show that I and others put on for the troops in Vietnam came from Robert Sawyer. It's a letter I'll never forget:

"I spent the better part of twenty-six years on radar sites. We never saw the Bob Hopes, the George Jessels, or Marilyn Monroes. We certainly saw and will forever be thankful for

Mamie Van Doren and others, such as Ina Balin, who put small groups together and came to small stations. Yes, I finally did get to see Ms. Van Doren in Vietnam; I get older—she gets more beautiful.''

I'm lucky to have many, many friends among the veterans around the country, particularly the ones who served in Vietnam. When I make appearances, more often than not someone will say: ''Mamie, I saw your show in Chu Lai.'' Or, ''Remember when you got me up onstage and danced with me in Quang Tri?'' And we always have a few good, warm moments of remembering.

Chapter Twenty-three

I was dashing to get ready. I was due at the taping of the Johnny Carson show in a few minutes and it would take God knew how long to get there by taxi. I finished my make-up, threw some things in my bag to make repairs later, and bounded down the hall toward the Pierre Hotel's slow, stately elevators. I threw myself headlong into a cab, told the driver Rockefeller Center, and settled back with closed eyes for the ride through New York City's surly, exhaust-smelling, honking rush hour.

The jet lag was still acute because I had arrived from London only the day before. But it was a relief to be back. After my experience in Vietnam, I had opted for a complete change of scenery to recuperate. I moved to England with the idea of working in English theater or films after I was sufficiently rested. However, I quickly found that those avenues were sewn up by English actors. (A disproportionate number of English actors deprive American actors of work every year. However, none but the most persistent and well-connected Americans may work in Great Britain.) Terrific, I told myself, now that you can't work, you can sit here and stare at the four walls while the mildew grows.

In March 1972, after six months of trying to adjust to the cold and damp of the English climate, I gave up and boarded a jet for New York. As always when I was in New York, I called the *Tonight* show and I was looking forward to seeing my old pal Johnny.

In the *Tonight* show's green room the guests had the usual pre-show nerves: an actor and actress who claim to have violent fits of stage fright, and who flood it with copious quantities of vodka; a comic who continually adjusts his crotch while standing in front of me; a funny little man who collects gadgets; and the writer of a Washington political exposé.

When the show started, I huddled in a chair, wrapped in my sable coat against the air-conditioned chill of the green room. As the time neared for me to do my song, I got up and checked my makeup, then made my way to the area behind the main stage. I was to make a dramatic entrance down a flight of stairs for the start of my song and I got myself in position for the stage manager to cue me. My song was to be right after the next commercial break. I took some deep breaths and felt the pleasant rush of nervous energy that comes before a performance.

But something was wrong. They came back from the commercial break and I could hear Johnny talking to someone in the chair next to him. No cue was forthcoming for my song. The show swung into its final ten minutes, then five, then Johnny was saying good night.

The stage manager shook his head at me and made a helpless gesture with his hands. "Sorry, Mamie," he whispered. "We ran out of time."

I walked back to my dressing room in a daze. The tears were just beginning to come. I expected any moment to hear Johnny or one of his producers at the door, apologizing profusely and making another date for me to be on the show. But no one came. Everyone averted his eyes from me as I left the theater.

While I taxied morosely back to the Pierre, I remembered an incident a few years ago that was the precise opposite of this one.

I came to New Jersey to do what I thought was a nightclub engagement, booked for me by my manager, Bill Loeb. When I arrived, I found myself booked into a burlesque house—leading the bill with a bunch of strippers. It was the most humiliating moment of my life and I was the angriest I've ever been. I got on the phone to Loeb and told him to do whatever he had to do to get me out of this gig. Unfortunately, I had signed play-or-pay contracts and the management of the theater made it clear that they would sue me for the hefty ten-thousand-dollar weekly salary, plus losses incurred by my not going on. Backed into a corner, I reluctantly worked the job.

In a day or two, Johnny Carson heard I was working nearby and called me. I poured out my heart to him on the phone about this rat hole of a burlesque house, whose name I have today mercifully forgotten. I was inconsolable. I was positive that this would ruin me.

"Aw, hell, Mamie," Johnny said gently. "Don't cry. Look, come on the show and let's talk about it."

"Talk about it?" I sobbed.

"Sure. We'll make fun of it. Make something light out of it. It'll be all right."

"Do you really think so?"

"Damn right. I *do* have a little influence in this town, Mamie. If we get it all out in the open on the show, no one will think twice about it."

And he had been right. Johnny threw his weight on my side and helped me through the rottenest time I've known as a performer. It was a truly friendly, gallant gesture.

But now this! Once inside my hotel room, I threw myself on the bed and cried. People were bumped from the *Tonight* show all the time because they ran overtime. But it had never happened to me before and I had never seen it happen to anyone else without some explanation or the merest apology afterward. The message was clear. It was, I realized, the end of the friendship between Johnny and me, an attachment that had lasted for more than a decade.

After a couple of days of shopping, the phone rang.

"Mamie?" asked a familiar voice. "This is Burt Reynolds. I know we've never met, but I'd like to take you out."

"Would you now? How'd you know I was in town?"

"Jim Hampton told me. I hope you don't mind that I called you."

In 1971 at the Arlington Dinner Theater in Chicago, I had finally starred in *Will Success Spoil Rock Hunter?* The key role opposite me, George MacCauley, was played by a pal of Burt's, James Hampton. I had spoken to Hampton a few days earlier about touring *Rock Hunter,* and he mentioned that Burt wanted to meet me.

"Not at all, Burt. It's nice to meet you, even if it's by phone."

"Great! Well, I'd like to meet you in person. Here's what I had in mind: I'm shooting a movie over in Brooklyn, and after lunch tomorrow I'm supposed to do a really exciting stunt where I do a dive through a window. So I could send a car over for you and you could watch me do the stunt and then I don't have any more shots for the rest of the day, so we could go have an early dinner and do whatever else strikes our fancy. Shall I send the car for you tomorrow afternoon?"

"I'm looking forward to it."

Burt Reynolds was then on the upswing of his popularity, shortly after his nude foldout in *Cosmopolitan.* I was singing a little tune of anticipation the next day as I got ready for the ride to his set in Brooklyn. After all, Burt Reynolds was Mr. Cool.

The set of *Shamus* (which also starred Dyan Cannon) was the usual confusion of a movie on location. Burt and I said a quick hello and he told an assistant director to take me to a seat where I could have a good view of his shot. Someone brought me a cup of tea and I settled into a canvas chair to wait for the excitement.

I should confess here, if I haven't made it clear before, that the day-to-day business of moviemaking is about as exciting as trimming your toenails. It can be massively dull when, after long hours of waiting for a shot, you do ten seconds of filming, then endure another interminable wait while the crew sets up the next shot. It requires the relaxation abilities of a house cat on a hearth, as well as the concentration and attention to detail of an artist, all the while maintaining your own sanity by not taking the whole thing too seriously. Eighteen hours a day of that and you don't feel too damn glamorous.

There was a great deal of fussing about setting up Burt's stunt. And even if it looked to me like a rather minor stunt, the Star was doing his *own* stunt, something that has always sent a tickle up the spines of movie audiences. Burt began his career in the movies as a stuntman, so presumably he knew what he was doing. There was a final check of camera angles, sound check, and a check to make sure the ambulance crew and doctor were standing close by.

"All right, everyone, let's have quiet please," the assistant director said through his bullhorn.

"Everyone in their places?" asked the director. "Roll 'em."

"Slate it," the assistant said quietly. There was the harsh clack of the slate and the slate man called out the scene and shot numbers.

"Speed," the soundman said.

"And . . . action."

Burt took a running start and launched himself through the glassed upper half of a door. He crashed through on the side facing the camera, did a quick little roll when he hit the ground, and bounced up onto his feet.

The set broke into applause and cheers. Burt got to his feet grinning and smoothed down his hair. Two or three people began brushing him off while the director and producer crowded around him to shake his hand.

In a few moments Burt came over to my chair.

"What did you think, Mamie?"

"Terrific, Burt. Wonderful."

"Exciting, huh?"

My mind flashed quickly back to Vietnam and the sounds of a mortar attack near my trailer. That had been real excitement. This was tame by comparison.

"Oh, sure. Really exciting."

"Well, I'm done for the day, Mamie. I'm starved. How about you? I know this cozy little place."

"Burt, you are talking to one hungry lady. Lead on."

"I just have to get changed and get out of this makeup. Won't take a minute."

We ate at a dark little Italian place with checkered tablecloths and sauces that made everything taste the same. Burt was an extremely funny date. He had more funny things to say then even Johnny Carson. But as he waxed romantic, he came on a little strong.

He looked at me with bedroom eyes as we toasted with champagne. "You're an Aquarian, aren't you?"

"Yes."

"Ah . . . Aquarians. I'm an Aquarian too, you know."

"Really?"

"Oh, yes." He smiled a wise, understanding smile. "I know exactly what you want, Mamie. I know exactly how to please you."

"You do?"

He nodded. "You know, Mamie. You get the *feel* sometimes when it's the start of something."

"How's that, Burt?"

"Just the *feel*. It's the beginning of a relationship, a great love affair that will last and last. Don't you think?"

"Last and last, huh? Really think so?"

"One of the great ones. No doubt about it. It's something that happens only a few times in a person's life. There's no question that this is one of them."

Well, I told myself, you wanted to go out with Burt Reynolds. Your head is swimming with champagne of questionable vintage, and it's so damn dark in here you're practically falling asleep, and it's not often lately that you've been quite this deep in such oozy bullshit, but, what the hell, Mamie, how bad could it be? This *is* Burt Reynolds, star of stage, screen, TV, and minor stunts. Why not live it up a little?

Burt suggested that we go to Candice Bergen's apartment, where he was staying while working in New York. Burt's driver dropped us at the Park Avenue address, with Burt cracking jokes a mile a minute. But I was enveloped in my own little champagne fog. The whole scene had a totally unreal quality about it. It was as though I was watching a movie in which I was starring.

Burt and I were holding hands as we made our way to the apartment, laughing merrily at Burt's jokes. Burt was laughing harder than I.

"I tell you, Mamie," he said huskily as he opened the door, "this is the start of something big."

I was too tipsy to remember my own advice about the guys with the biggest hype being the guys who deliver the least.

"I hope you're right, Burt," I slurred. "Champagne always makes me so . . . so . . . amorous."

"I'm glad we had that extra bottle. Did I ever tell you, Mamie, that I consider myself the male Mamie Van Doren?"

I recall trying very hard to focus at that point. "No, you never told me that."

He proceeded to give me a list of reasons why he thought of himself as the male me. It is certainly the most unusual statement that has ever been made to me before I went to bed with someone.

As we undressed there was a windstorm of clothing flying through the air, fluttering to the floor like tired birds. We didn't speak—there was only the sound of our breathing as we revealed ourselves to each other. A few caresses and Burt and I were between the sheets. At last we came together and from somewhere came the sounds of waves crashing. I looked up into Burt's eyes.

I was beginning to get into the spirit of the moment when Burt began to thrash wildly. His sound and movements betrayed an immediacy that I had hoped would not arrive for some time yet.

"Ohhhh!" Burt moaned. "Ohhhh! Judy! Juuuudddyyyy!"

And that was it. Out, out, brief candle. Fade to black.

Well, I thought. Could this be the American heartthrob? Mr. Cool? What happened to the burning, thrusting, penetrating desires of something big? And who was Judy? (Later I realized that he must have been calling out his former wife's name—Judy Carne from *Laugh-in*.)

"Burt?" I whispered. "Burt? Are you there?"

The sound of soft snoring echoed through the apartment. I suddenly felt very clearheaded and sober. I was brought abruptly to my senses by the coldest of showers—corked-up, unsatisfied passion.

I hopped out of bed and grabbed my clothes. After dressing in the bathroom, I went downstairs and caught a cab back to the Pierre.

My brief romance with Burt, the start of something big, was analogous to passing through a major city and having dinner in only one restaurant—and that a fast-food joint high on jive but low on substance.

When asked later what I thought of Burt's nude layout in *Cosmopolitan*, with a hat discreetly covering his crotch, I could only laugh.

"An exaggeration," I said. "A cigar could have covered it nicely."

* * *

Back in L.A. that year, because of the friendly personal communications I had from President Nixon prior to my last visit to Vietnam, I got involved in Republican politics. Newport Beach, California, buried deep in Orange County, is a stronghold of Republicanism and the home of some astonishingly wealthy folks who like to put their money where their political convictions are. A few Newport Beach residents, including John Wayne, drafted me into helping the Committee to Reelect the President (known, with malice and some justification, as CREEP) raise money for the upcoming 1972 Presidential campaign. In retrospect, it's difficult to believe the Republicans felt any sort of a threat from George McGovern's candidacy (I think it was Kurt Vonnegut who said that McGovern was the brunt of an elaborate political joke), but feel it they did, and they mobilized me and some other Newport Beach residents to beat the bushes for contributions.

I made a number of appearances around Southern California—some parades, a luncheon or two—and before long began to make contact with the Republican power brokers in the area.

As spring moved into summer I became increasingly active. I was invited to a fund-raiser in Dallas, where we took in well over a million dollars to finance Campaign '72.

In St. Louis I was being interviewed by an editor of one of the major newspapers in town and we got on the subject of politics.

"I understand," he said after the interview was over, "that you've worked for President Nixon's reelection. He's a close friend of mine. Would you like to talk to him? I'll see if I can arrange it."

I was skeptical but I kept it to myself. "I'm sure he's awfully busy. If you can get me a personally autographed picture, that would be fine."

It turned out that the President *was* too busy to talk, but, the editor told me, I would get a call the next morning from a Jeb Magruder and if I wanted an autographed picture of the President, that could be easily arranged and I should just give him an address to mail it. Sure enough, a few weeks later, an autographed picture arrived at home.

Later, I decided on impulse to send him an autographed picture of myself. I mailed it and promptly forgot about it.

Then one day an envelope came in the mail with the White House letterhead on it. I tore it open to find a letter from the President thanking me for the picture.

One of the men in the upper echelon of CREEP told me after returning from a trip to Washington that he saw my picture in the President's office.

"Of course, he doesn't keep it on top of his desk," the man told me. "But I swear to you, Mamie, that he keeps it in the bottom-left-hand drawer."

In mid-June I received an invitation to a celebrity breakfast with John and Martha Mitchell in Pacific Palisades at the home of a prominent L.A. Republican. I accepted.

Saturday morning, June 17, 1972, in the big house overlooking the Pacific, a group of us gathered to meet with John Mitchell, chat with Martha, and in general be stroked by the hierarchy of CREEP for our good works thus far, and encouraged to do more between then and the election in November. Among those gathered were Terry Moore, Chad Everett, Pat Boone with two daughters in tow, Maureen Reagan, and me. I recall there was a lot of lofty talk about the Nixon reelection and some scoffing at the opposition.

Oddly enough, Martha Mitchell and I hit it off. She was nursing a hangover with a little hair of the dog, and gabbing away a mile a minute about how much she enjoyed herself in Southern California and how about if we got together for lunch in a day or two?

As the breakfast got under way in our host's large sunny living room, John Mitchell began to speak to us about the progress the campaign was making and what a grand mandate the President would get in November from a voting public grateful for the way he was handling the country.

Partway through the speech an aide hurried into the room, went directly to Mitchell, and whispered something in his ear. His half-raised coffee cup clattered back onto its saucer. His eyes made a quick circuit of the room and he looked up at the aide and said softly, "Are you sure?"

Mitchell talked on for a few moments more, but his heart was no longer in it. He quickly wrapped up his little speech. The color had drained out of his face, and his skin, which had been rosy and healthy a short while before, now looked waxy and sallow.

Two or three conversations had sprung up when he stopped talking, and I could not hear what else he was saying to his aide. They talked animatedly for a time. The aide walked quickly out of the room. Mitchell rose from his chair and took Martha's arm.

"Come on, Martha. We have to go."

"Go? What's the matter? I haven't even finished eating yet."

"Nothing. But we've got to go," Mitchell snapped.

With hardly a word to any of us, Mitchell turned and walked out of the room while one of his aides helped Martha unceremoniously out of her chair.

I don't think any of the other guests really noticed that Mitchell and his entourage had left under such mysterious circumstances. I thought to myself: Something's going on there that we don't know about.

It wasn't until months later that I realized I had witnessed Mitchell getting the first word about the Watergate break-in. Men he had hired to burglarize Larry O'Brian's office in the Democratic National Headquarters had been caught, and for him, as well as for the Nixon administration, the end had already begun.

Sometime later, I participated in a fund-raiser disguised as a boat parade. A flotilla of boats went honking up and down Newport Harbor flying banners proclaiming that we reelect the President. I was embarked for the afternoon, smiling and waving at the crowds lining the shore, in a prominent Newport Beach matron's yacht along with John Wayne (deep into bourbon and branch water that day) and several other movers and shakers of the GOP in Southern California.

"Mamie," the lady who owned the boat gushed, "I know someone who desperately wants to meet you."

I tried to mask my dismay as I glanced around the boat at the dubious prospects sailing with us.

"Oh, really?" I asked weakly. "Who's that?"

"Welllll, he's not with us today. He had a very important meeting at his company, Fluor Corporation, this afternoon or he would have been here. Understand, it's not really *his* company—of course, it's Bob Fluor's—but he's the executive

vice-president. His name's Ross McClintock and he's positively *dying* to meet you, Mamie.''

Before too many more days had passed I was "fixed up"
with Ross. We began dating pretty regularly and he made a
concerted effort to court me. After a few weeks it became
clear that Ross wanted me to marry him. Over dinner in a
restaurant one night, Ross gave me a gorgeous ring of im-
perial jade surrounded by diamonds, and formally asked me
to marry him. I said yes. Unfortunately, I did not love Ross.
I looked at my marriage to him as one of convenience and
companionship. He lived well and moved in a circle of important friends. I thought that was what I wanted.

My marriage to Ross was the only time I ever postponed
having sex with my spouse-to-be until after we tied the knot.
The experience lives in my memory as a terrific recommen-
dation for premarital sex.

We were married in Las Vegas after flying there in Fluor's
corporate plane, a four-engine jet with full complement of
pilot, copilot, and stewardess. The pilot and copilot stood up
for us at the ceremony.

Ross insisted on waiting until after the wedding to consummate our relationship, a move which, given his physical attributes, was a mountain of wisdom on his part. Confronted
with a man of his rotund dimensions, I discovered that passion was not going to be a part of our marriage. I went through
the motions and rushed the deed to a mercifully quick conclusion.

From the wedding night on it was a situation doomed to
failure, not only because of the physical part of the marriage
but also because I discovered some of my chief functions as
a wife. Ross's idea of a good wife was one who played tennis
at the right club, bridge with the right people, and was there
when he came home. She was also one who provided the
maximum decoration and charm at all functions of Fluor
Corporation, toadied to the wives of the one or two people
in the company who outranked him, and set a grand example
for the wives of the men below him. Needless to say, it was
not the kind of thing I was used to. It went completely against
the free-spirit side of me.

The climax came when I was in Omaha playing a gig that
I had contracted to do before marrying Ross. The company

plane flew me there and went back to California. A week later it brought Ross back to pick me up and fly on to New Orleans for a meeting with some oil people.

When Ross returned he was hopping mad. He tossed a magazine in front of me.

"What's this?" he snapped.

It was a pinup magazine containing some nude photos of me that the publisher had purchased some months before. It was now actually a couple of months old and no longer on sale on the newsstands. I explained to him that the magazine had paid handsomely for the photos and that the whole thing occurred before we were engaged.

"It's unbelievable," he growled. "Don't you have any idea how a thing like this makes me look?"

"Ross, did you think you were marrying the Virgin Mary?"

"No, but flaunting your body for everyone to see is—"

"Flaunting is what I have done for a living for just about twenty years."

"Not anymore!"

He threw the magazine across the room and it fluttered to the floor behind a chair. I hadn't been overjoyed about the picture layout either, but I felt that Ross's outburst was uncalled-for.

After my last show that night, we flew on to New Orleans in the company plane. For Ross, the storm about my magazine layout seemed to have subsided, but inside I was seething. One of the things I am the worst at is taking orders. To give me an order is to guarantee that I will do the opposite.

Back home in Newport Beach, on a day when Ross had to leave town on business, I moved all my things out and rented a penthouse at the posh Versailles apartment complex.

In the spring of 1973, while the divorce was being prepared for court, I accepted an invitation to a party given in honor of German Chancellor Willy Brandt at the White House. Nixon was, to his credit, not shy about paying back debts owed to those who helped him get elected, and while being invited to a White House dinner party was not exactly like a patronage job, it seemed like a nice payback for the little bit I'd helped. It was also novel and exciting enough to send me rushing out to buy a new gown.

In Washington that spring, the cherry blossoms were co-operating beautifully in making the District of Columbia festive. Arriving at the White House that evening, I experienced the thrill that must possess anyone not given over totally to cynicism, of being in the place where the greatest power in the world is wielded.

This party was, I'm told, the standard-issue White House dinner party: cocktails first, then everyone is herded in to a seven-course dinner; after dinner, in a different room, after-dinner drinks are served and everyone goes through the reception line to meet the President and First Lady and the guest of honor, in this case Chancellor and Mrs. Willy Brandt; finally the party moves into another room for the entertainment—this evening, the Carpenters.

My old friend and former beau Bob Evans was there and we chatted over drinks about old times and acquaintances. An aide came and showed us to our table. There were eight to a table, and I've forgotten some of the people we sat with, but I was sandwiched in between Bob Evans and his pal, my date for the evening, Henry Kissinger. On the other side of Kissinger was Mrs. Rockefeller.

Henry Kissinger was then acquiring a reputation as a ladies' man. He made the papers with Jill St. John and was often seen cavorting discreetly with the beautiful people in New York and L.A. He had tried to take me out the year before, using a couple of the West Coast CREEPs as his Cyrano, but I had declined, because I was working. Now, in effect tricked into my date with Kissinger, I settled back to enjoy it in such glamorous surroundings.

We listened while the President introduced Chancellor Brandt and made some remarks about German-American relations. While he spoke I felt a gentle pressure under the table against my leg. I looked at Henry and he was watching the President with rapt attention. The pressure continued for a while, then changed to a slow rhythmic rubbing.

After the President's speech, Henry was at his most charming as the conversation moved around the table.

"You know, Mamie," Kissinger said after disengaging from a long conversation with Mrs. Rockefeller, "I've been looking forward to meeting you for a long, long time."

"And I you, Dr. Kissinger."

"Oh, please, call me Henry," he said in those rich, rolling tones of the Rhineland.

"Henry."

"Good." He gave my arm an affectionate pat. "You know, you are even more attractive in person that you are on the screen. Often ladies on the screen are a disappointment in person, but not you."

He asked me about my trip to Vietnam and listened intently while I told him. It is perhaps what makes Kissinger such an effective negotiator—his ability to listen to what you are saying and give the feeling that it is vastly important. He told me about his trips to Paris and the peace talks that were going on there, and offered interesting insights into the personality of his opposite number at Paris, Li Duc Tho.

When the dessert came, Henry leaned toward me and said softly, "The press will be waiting for us when we leave this room, Mamie. They will want to know what I was like as a dinner date."

"Well, you certainly couldn't have been more charming," I replied.

"Thank you. Is that what you're going to tell them?"

"I guess so. Did you have something in mind for me to say?"

"Oh, no. Say whatever you like. Just so it's something devastating."

Just as he said, the reporters were waiting for us outside the dining room. Several of them cornered me and inquired about my date for the evening.

"He's absolutely devastating," I said.

When we went through the reception line and met the President, I was surprised to find him warmly cordial. He made definite eye contact when he spoke and had something personal to say to everyone as he shook hands.

Mrs. Nixon was the biggest surprise to me, however. She had the same warmth as her husband and seemed downright friendly. She was not the kind of woman who stared me up and down in an appraising way. We spoke for thirty seconds and she made me feel truly welcome in her home.

After the reception, we were herded toward the East Room, where the Carpenters performed. On the way I made a quick stop in the ladies' room. By the time I came out, the guests were all seated. As I hurried down the right-hand aisle, the Marine Band began playing "Hail to the Chief." I looked around in surprise and saw President Nixon making his entrance down the other aisle. I hurried to my seat next to Kissinger and tried to look inconspicuous. He smiled and I smiled back sheepishly.

Midway through the concert, probably in the midst of the gooey strains of "We've Only Just Begun," Henry whispered in my ear, "Would you like to take a tour of the White House afterward?"

"Sure," I whispered.

After the Carpenters had finished, Henry guided me through the hallways and pointed out some of the historical sights in the White House. We ended the tour at the Oval Office. Henry opened the door and pulled the ropes aside that kept tourists from entering.

The room was smaller than I had thought it would be, but it was impressive in atmosphere. This was where the President ran the country.

"Would you like to sit in the President's chair?" Henry asked.

"Could I?"

He held the chair for me and I sat in it. I swiveled back and forth in front of the immaculately clean expanse of his desk.

It occurred to me that the little girl from Rowena had come a long way to sit in the President's chair in the Oval Office. I remembered my Pa Bennett ranting and raving about the fools in Washington and how he'd campaigned for Republican Wendell Willkie. Now here I was sitting in the chair of a Republican President.

We left the Oval Office and walked back down the hall.

"Would you like to come over to my place, Mamie?"

"Sure. I have a car and driver waiting for me outside. I'll give him the address and he can take me there."

"Nonsense. Dismiss him. We can go in my car. And my driver can take you home whenever you like."

We rode in the back seat of Kissinger's big government Chrysler, his driver and Secret Service man in front. He mentioned that some Russian friends were in town and he was having lunch with one tomorrow.

"I would be very happy if you would join us, Mamie."

I thought about it for a moment. "I'd have to stay over a day, but, yes, I'd like to have lunch with you."

"Fine," he said, genuinely pleased. "It's a date." He laughed heartily. "The Russians believe I am a sex maniac. Every time I visit the Soviet Union they have two or three husky Russian girls waiting for me when I get off the plane."

"And do you ever take advantage of these . . . welcoming gifts, Henry?"

He looked at me sideways and his eyes squinted to little amused slits. He grinned wolfishly.

"Mamie, we must all serve our country in whatever ways we can."

We stopped on a quiet street in Georgetown and the Secret Service man opened the car doors. We went up the steps to his town house, Henry unlocked the door, and we went inside.

"You'll have to pardon the mess," Henry said as he reached around the doorjamb and turned on a light in the foyer. "I just returned from China and I haven't had time to get my clothes sent to the cleaners."

In one corner of the darkened living room was a huge mound of clothing, and there was the unmistakable smell of dirty socks in the air.

"Excuse me a moment," he said dramatically, "I must call the President."

He went to the phone and dialed a number. "Mr. President," he began deferentially, "I believe the party was a success. Yes. I'm sure Chancellor Brandt must be very impressed. Well, he told me that . . ."

As he talked on, it occurred to me that, at nearly two A.M., it was late even for Henry Kissinger to be calling the President. I wondered idly as I looked around the room at some Chinese sculpture and pottery if it was really a call to the President or just a ruse to impress me. For all I knew, he had picked up the phone and called Dial-a-Prayer.

"Well, good night, Mr. President," he said in conclusion. "I'll speak to you tomorrow."

Henry's rooms were frugally furnished, giving testimony to the fact that he spent much of his time in the far corners of the world. But if the other rooms contained only the bare essentials, the bedroom was positively Spartan. There was a table and a lamp and a small unmade bed that looked like a cot out of a military barracks.

I sat on the bed while we talked some more. When I started to get up, Henry pushed me back onto the bed again. I managed to get up and sidestep him, but he took me by the arms and pinned me gently against the wall. At such close range, the smell of dirty socks was overpowered by his denture breath.

"Mamie, you don't need to go already, do you?"

"Well, I really should," I said. I wanted to at least kiss Henry good night, but the power of his breath held me at bay. "It's been a long trip for me and I really need to get a good night's sleep to be at my best."

He looked at me with shrewd eyes. "Mamie, you are a very *smart* woman. It is something that I didn't expect, but it is pleasantly surprising. I'll see you back to your hotel."

The next morning around eleven o'clock, as I was getting ready for our luncheon date, Henry called.

'I'm sorry, Mamie," he rumbled into the phone. "I have to cancel our lunch. Something unexpected has come up and I have to fly to . . . Well, suffice to say, something has come up to interfere."

We agreed to make it another time and he rang off.

The next time I heard from the White House was a few months later when I received an invitation to the Nixons' San Clemente home for a small party in honor of Soviet First Secretary Brezhnev. I was told he wanted to meet a sexy actress and a cowboy and they asked me and Chuck Conners. I was working somewhere in Ohio and could not get out of the contract at the club I was playing and so had to turn it down. I always thought that Kissinger was behind that one, and imagined him waiting for me down there in a guestroom with a rumpled little bed, his socks in the laundry, and teeth soaking in Polident in the bathroom.

Chapter Twenty-four

I went to New York after the party in Washington, expecting to hear in a few days that the divorce from Ross had been finalized. Much to my surprise, I learned from my attorney that the case had gone before an Orange County judge apparently sympathetic to McClintock's cause and he was granted an annulment. At first it was kind of a shock to learn that our marriage had never been consummated, but then, when I thought about it, it had been consummated damned little.

When I came back to California there were a number of strange phone calls which would lead me in some new directions.

One was from an agent asking if I would play a benefit in Palm Springs for the chief of police there. I would be working with Sammy Davis Jr., as an opening act for his show. I agreed to play the gig.

The show was at the Riviera Hotel in Palm Springs. Although she was ill with a middle-ear infection, my mother went with me and we took a suite there. When the show was over, Sammy came to my dressing room.

"Hey, Mamie! Great show, love," he said, waving his bejeweled hands around. "Far-out show. Listen, why don't you come over to Frank's with me? He's invited a bunch of us over for a little get-together after the show, and he said to make sure Mamie comes along. Okay?''

Naturally, he could mean only one ''Frank'' in Palm Springs, and I thought to myself: Oh boy, here we go again, another Frank Sinatra scene. Frank was in the midst of one of his periodic semipermanent retirements and spending most of his time entertaining show-business people and politicians.

It's difficult to understand Frank Sinatra unless you see him on his own turf. As Jane Goodall had to observe wild chimpanzees to discover their real behavior, so too you must see Sinatra in his own lair to know what makes him tick.

Sinatra, like many powerful men, surrounds himself with people that tell him what he wants to hear. In this way, through controlling who comes in contact with him, he controls his environment and molds it to fit his image of himself. Consequently, to come into Frank Sinatra's orbit is to come very literally into *his* world. In fact, when you pass through the driveway gates on the grounds of his estate, you hear Frank Sinatra records being played everywhere.

The party was getting under way when we arrived at his sprawling home on, of course, Frank Sinatra Drive, one of Palm Springs' many concessions to its most famous resident. Frank greeted Sammy with a certain coolness, but said hello to me in the ritualized Hollywood manner with elaborate huggings and kissings. Frank immediately took me in tow and introduced me to the hangers-on already in attendance. He called to someone to get me some champagne.

''Get the Dom Perignon for Mamie. And plenty of it,'' he added. ''Nothing but the best for her. Look at how she looks. Gorgeous!''

I wore a white satin gown that evening with a white orchid in my hair. Against the dark suntan that I always try to maintain, I looked, if I do say so myself, very fetching.

The champagne came and I sipped it gratefully. This bubbly product of a little abbey in France is my one true vice (with the possible exception of shopping), and it is the one alcoholic beverage with a taste that I actually *like*.

''Hey, Frank,'' Sammy said, ''Mamie did a great job opening the show for me tonight. You know, I've got that four weeks to do at the Sands in Vegas in October. What do you think about Mamie opening the show for me there?''

Frank broke into a broad grin. "Great idea, Sammy! Do it! She'd be perfect to open the show."

"Right on! Cool!" Sammy turned to me. "Are you free, Mamie? Can you make it in October?"

A little astonished at this sudden turn, I collected my wits as best I could and said, "Sure. I can make it."

"Then you're on, baby!"

Frank and Sammy drifted away in opposite directions and I began to circulate around the party. I fell into conversation with a handsome French film director. He exuded the gentle Continental charm that the best European men exhibit. It occurred to me that here was another product of France that could rapidly achieve the status of vice.

Someone came up to me and said, "Mamie, do you know where Frank is right now?"

"No. He was here a few minutes ago."

"He's out in the kitchen cooking lasagna, telling everybody that he wants Mamie to have some real Italian lasagna the way it should be cooked."

"Well, that's very nice—"

"Nice? It's unheard-of."

We all went into dinner that night and made appropriate sounds of delight over Frank's homemade lasagna served on his best Russian Fabergé china. To Frank's credit, it was really very good, particularly when washed down with glasses of Dom Perignon.

When dinner was over and all the guests were wandering around stuffed, Sammy Cahn started noodling on the piano. He announced loudly: "Hey, everyone, Frank's going to sing!"

Sinatra made his way casually to the piano amid the applause of his guests and launched into a slightly ragged but recognizable version of "My Way."

He finished the song with its dramatic final lyrics about doing it his way. There was really enthusiastic applause.

Sammy Davis Jr. was standing next to me during the performance. I turned to him and asked, "Is Frank coming out of retirement?"

Sammy shook his head. "I don't think so. He's having too much fun doing what he's doing. No, I don't think he'll ever come out of retirement."

"Well," I said skeptically, "he certainly sang that song like he meant business."

"That's Frank."

As the party broke up that evening and I was getting ready to go back to the Riviera, Frank took me aside.

"Mamie, we're all going out to eat at the Cask & Cleaver tomorrow night and then come back here for a movie. Why don't you come along?"

"Gee, I'd like to, Frank, but my mother's not feeling well and I think I should get her back home."

He seemed genuinely concerned. "What's the problem?"

I explained the middle-ear infection and in true Sinatra fashion, he took charge.

"Let me send my doctor over, Mamie. He's the best in California."

"Oh, thanks, Frank, but I couldn't—"

"No, Mamie. You let him come take a look at her first thing in the morning and prescribe something to help. And meanwhile, you plan on coming with us tomorrow night for dinner."

The doctor came and saw Mother the next morning and gave her some antibiotics. Mother felt better in a few hours and said she would be fine at the hotel while I went to Sinatra's again that night.

About ten of us gathered at Frank's home for drinks before going to the restaurant. Among them were bandleader Morton Downey and his wife and the French film director I had met the night before.

Frank was behind his bar pouring the Dom Perignon into my glass while his longtime girlfriend, soon-to-be-wife, Barbara Marx, sat next to me. Years before, I had known Barbara when she had been a showgirl in Las Vegas. Then each of us was beating the bushes in our own way to find Mr. Right. Barbara had found hers first, comedian Zeppo Marx, whom she later divorced.

Tonight Barbara was understandably miffed at Frank because he was paying such an untoward amount of attention to me. It was embarrassing for me, but there was little I could do to stop it without being downright impolite. And Barbara was sitting at the only other free seat at the bar, preventing my Frenchman from sitting next to me. She kept turning her back on me and facing out into the room while Frank chattered away and kept pouring.

When Barbara finally got up, my Frenchman came and sat down. Sinatra came out from behind the bar, walked up behind him, and, in the guise of a hearty hello, hit the man on the back as hard as he could. The Frenchman pitched forward and fell off the stool and it was easy to see from the look on his face that the blow hurt.

Sinatra turned and walked away as though nothing had happened. I helped my friend to his feet. He slowly regained his composure but there was anger smoldering that he could barely keep in check.

He went looking for Sinatra and repaid the favor. While Frank was deep in conversation with someone, the French film director pounded him on the back as hard as he could. Frank spilled his drink and had to catch himself on a nearby chair.

There was immediately an electric tension in the air. The Frenchman stood his ground as Frank straightened up painfully and looked at him. For a moment it could have gone either way, but Frank finally turned away.

When we left to go eat, we selected two cars from Frank's stable of Rolls-Royces, and all ten of us piled in, Frank driving one and Barbara Marx driving the other. I rode with Frank and the Frenchman and someone else. Barbara took the rest.

We endured a long, starving wait at the Cask & Cleaver during which Frank was very un-Frank-like—patient and understanding that the restaurant took so long to seat us.

After dinner, back at Frank's, we sat down to a movie in his private theater. He had retreated into a surly silence. By this time there was no question in my mind about the outcome of what was developing between the French film director and myself. In fact there was probably no question in anyone's mind about it since the two of us were hanging on each other throughout the movie.

We walked through the grounds toward his bungalow later. I made a wrong turn on the maze of paths and walked up to the door of the wrong bungalow. In the dim light that illuminated the path, I could see a brass nameplate on the door engraved with the name ''Spiro Agnew.''

Earlier I had noticed some other things around the place

engraved with Vice-President Agnew's name and I had asked our host about it.

"Oh, he's a good friend of mine," Frank said expansively. "Comes here all the time to play golf and visit. His pilot lands the helicopter right on my helipad."

My little French film director and I finally found his bungalow and settled in for the evening amid a tangle of sheets and vows of eternal love. After the next morning, I never saw him again. He was the first and last Frenchman I ever went to bed with and he honorably upheld the traditions of the French. They should hire him out as an advertisement for the country.

The other phone calls started about the time I moved into the Versailles apartment complex. In fact, before my phone was even hooked up, the first day I was there, the gate guard came running up to my penthouse.

"Miss Van Doren, there's a call for you at the front gate."

"Who is it? My mother? Nobody even knows I'm here."

"It's a man. He didn't say who he was."

When I got down to the guard shack and answered the phone it was a man's voice that I recognized from the first time he'd called me. He claimed to be involved with a public-relations firm that worked for CREEP. He'd gotten hold of me through my mother when I was working somewhere in the Midwest just a few weeks before. But I didn't want to hear what he had to say.

"What did you say your name was?" It was Steve. "I told you last month, Steve, I'm not interested in sleeping with a man I don't even know. Period."

"But, Mamie, you have to understand that this man is very, very high up in the government. If you don't do this, it'll be my ass! And that's no lie."

"And if I do it, it'll be mine!"

"Look, it's not such a tough thing to do."

"Then you do it, Steve."

"All the man wants you to do is be there when he arrives."

"I know. You've told me all that. I'm not interested."

"Mamie, I'm begging you. Just be at the Regency Hotel in New York, wear black stockings and a black garter belt, and be ready when the man arrives. He's prepared to pay a great deal of money for your . . . time.''

"Who is this man, Steve?"

"I can't tell you that. But you'll certainly find out in due course.''

"You could be anybody. I'm not going anywhere, doing anything, or even talking to you again until you tell me who the hell we're talking about. Got it, Steve?''

There was a long silence. Steve's voice became a hoarse whisper. "I can't tell you that here. These phone lines may be tapped. Where can I call you later?''

"My phone won't be installed for another week, but if you've got a pencil, I'll give you the number.''

"Your phone will be installed tomorrow. And don't worry about the number, I'll get it.''

"It's unlisted.''

"No problem. Talk to you tomorrow.''

The next morning, before nine o'clock, the telephone man arrived to install my phone.

"I thought it was supposed to be next week before you put my phone in.''

"I don't know anything about that, lady. Your installation order was on the top of my stack this morning.''

Not half an hour after the telephone man left, my phone rang. It was mysterious Steve.

"I see your phone's working okay," he said smugly.

"How did you do that?" I asked.

"That sort of thing is easy, believe me. Now look, either you're going to do this or you're not, okay?''

"I'm not even listening to anything else until I find out who I'm supposed to be meeting at the Regency Hotel.''

"Okay.''

"Okay what?''

"Okay I'll tell you. It's the Vice-President.''

"Agnew?''

"Is there more than one?''

"You must be crazy.''

Steve cleared his throat. "Now, you'll do it, won't you?''

"Hell no, Steve. Good-bye.''

I was convinced the whole thing was some kind of hoax— a practical joke from someone I knew. Whoever it was would eventually surface and we'd have a big laugh over the whole thing. The business of the phone was disturbing, but I put it out of my mind. Then, when I was out working a couple of weeks later, Steve located me again.

"Mamie, this is positively your last chance. If I don't get you to do this, I don't know what I'll do. Will you please meet him at the Regency? You name the time when you can make it. I'll coordinate the whole thing with the man."

"All right, all right," I said. "I'll play along with this stupid thing and see where it goes. Put your money where your mouth is and send me a first-class round-trip ticket from L.A. to New York."

"I can't buy your ticket from this end, Mamie. It would be traceable. But I'll send the cash to buy your ticket, plus some expenses. Does this mean you'll do it?"

"If and when I get the money, I'll let you know."

"Don't play games with this, Mamie. They're really serious. Where should I send the money?"

"I'm out on the road for the next couple weeks. Send it to my parents' address."

I really didn't think too much about the whole thing for the next couple of days. I figured the worst that could happen would be something coming in the mail that would be the punch line for this hoax.

I got a frantic call from my mother one night.

"Jo, honey, this envelope came for you and Daddy opened it. It's full of money . . ." I heard Daddy's voice in the background, then Mother said, "He says it's over two thousand dollars. What's it all about?"

I explained the situation to her from the beginning. She remembered telling the man where I was staying while I was on the road.

"Jo," Mother said sternly, "you can't keep that money."

"I know," I agreed. "Tell Daddy I said send it back."

Later that night the phone rang.

"Did your parents get the money?" Steve asked.

"They got it," I answered. "But I've told them to send it back."

"You what?"

"I don't know what all this is about, Steve, or whatever your name really is, but I want nothing more to do with it. I thought this was some kind of a joke, and I went along with it, but I see from all that money that you've got some kind of serious scam going here. Now, the money's on its way back to you. Don't try to call me anymore and don't bother my parents anymore. I'm not going to meet anyone anywhere anytime, no matter how much you send, is that clear?''

"Yes, it's clear.''

"If you try to contact me or my family again, I'm going to call the FBI.''

He laughed dryly. "Okay, Mamie, I won't call anymore. But the FBI? Do you think if he really wanted you he'd let a little thing like that get in his way?''

I didn't hear from mysterious Steve again. I still don't know if the story he gave me was true or not, but I know that the money that showed up was very real. In the summer of 1973 Vice-President Agnew's troubles began to grow by leaps and bounds. On October 10, 1973, he resigned because of indictments on income-tax evasion.

In March 1974 I was scheduled to begin an extensive tour of *Will Success Spoil Rock Hunter?* in St. Petersburg, Florida. James Hampton was unavailable to play the young writer, George MacCauley, as he had in Chicago three years before, so the director was casting locally for the role.

The director called me a few days before I left.

"Mamie, I've found George MacCauley.''

"Really? Who'd you get?''

"His name's Thomas Dixon. He's a local actor.''

"Oh, swell,'' I said without enthusiasm.

"I know, I know. But don't judge too quickly. I think you'll love him.''

When we started doing *Rock Hunter*, I discovered the director was right. Thomas did such a fine job with the role that I asked him to go on the rest of the tour. Though he was married at the time, and thirteen years my junior, he and I became steadily closer. Before long we became lovers. After he divorced his wife later that year, Thomas and I began living together in Newport Beach. We were married on June 26, 1979.

Thomas and I worked together for many years in theaters and nightclubs before he gave up acting for writing. The things we have in common are the things that have held us together over the years—something neither of us had been able to accomplish with our previous mates. We share a love of animals, of laughing, and of being together; a love of silences, and of each other's privacy. We live at the beach, comforted by the sound of distant surf, warmed by a mutual respect, and fed on the promise of the next sunrise.

Epilogue

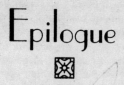

It was a warm April night. Our Alfa Romeo growled contentedly as Thomas and I drove up the San Diego Freeway from Newport Beach toward Los Angeles. My son, Perry, followed in his car.

"Thomas," I said nervously, "do you really think anybody will show up? Does anyone really care about Mamie Van Doren in 1984?"

"Hell yes, baby," he said. He checked the rearview mirror and changed lanes to get around a slower car. "I think you're going to be very surprised about the turnout tonight." He reached over and patted my knee. "Don't be so nervous, okay?"

I smiled and nodded at him. Thomas and I had come a very long way since the day we met in St. Petersburg to do *Will Success Spoil Rock Hunter?* We'd had to endure the disapproval of both our sets of parents for a time. And we had certainly had our personal ups and downs over the years since we'd first met. But time had given proof to the relationship. We felt like we had weathered the worst of the storm and were cruising now in safe if occasionally squally waters.

My nervousness tonight was because of a celebration arranged by Alan Eichler, my new public relations man. Alan had said to me some months before, "Mamie, why don't you get back in the business? You've been away from it too long."

"That's why," I answered. "I've been away from it too long. Nobody really remembers me."

"What?" Alan asked incredulously. "There's a whole new cult out there, Mamie. They're crazy about the 50's and 60's, they're trying to dress like everyone did back then, and they're watching your movies and *loving* them."

"You're kidding."

"I'm not. And they want to see more of you."

Alan is a very intense man when he gets going on something. And now he was in really high gear.

"Mamie, I want to arrange a tribute to you. We'll schedule it for the Nuart Theater on Santa Monica Boulevard, show three of your movies and invite Al Zugsmith and Aubrey Schenk, and Howard Koch to say a few words—"

"A few words over the body?"

"Cut it out, Mamie. I don't think you're ready to go to pasture yet. The press will have a field day. All the networks will be there, *Entertainment Tonight*, all the newspapers will want an interview."

"Alan, Alan," I said, "take it easy."

"Take it easy? You give me the word, Mamie. I can't do it unless you say yes. And when you say yes, be prepared to get back into it again, okay?"

So I said yes.

And here I was riding up to L.A. in a new dress. Scared silly. Wondering if anyone would actually come out to see three movies about wild teenagers made almost thirty years ago.

How the hell did I get into this? I asked myself. I began to think back through my life.

Life looks like a series of doors behind which loom alternate futures. I imagined what would've happened if the Universal talent scout on his way to the Bliss-Hayden Theater to see unknown Joan Olander in *Come Back Little Sheba* had had a flat tire and missed the performance.

Or if Gloria Grahame was suddenly taken sick and unable to play Ado Annie in *Oklahoma!*, and Richard Rodgers and Oscar Hammerstein were able to cast their first choice for the role: Mamie Van Doren.

Or if my phone was out of order the night Walter Winchell called to introduce Bo Belinsky.

Or if suddenly I had found the courage and strength to accept the offered role in *Will Success Spoil Rock Hunter?*

Of course, if I'd done *Rock Hunter* on Broadway, the chances are I'd never have been playing it in St. Petersburg, Florida, in time to meet Thomas.

I could have gone on and on with the what if's. But I'm afraid if I had done anything differently along the way, I would have missed Thomas and Perry and so much more. That's the way the cogs mesh in the universe. The fact is we get our futures the old-fashioned way—we earn them.

As we approached the Santa Monica freeway exit, my palms started to sweat.

Whatever comes of this, I told myself, good or bad, I will be satisfied with it. I will remember what dear, looney, smack-freaked-out Brother Dave Gardner used to say in his night club act when I would see him playing Gus Steven's Supper Club in Biloxi: "Happiness, dear hearts, ain't gettin' what you want. It's wantin' what you get." If nobody shows up at the Nuart, I'll accept it.

Thomas reined in the Alfa in front of the theater underneath a God-awfully big marquee that said: TRIBUTE TO MAMIE VAN DOREN. Thomas held the car door open for me, and I heard someone say: "There's Mamie!"

It was frightening for a moment to see the crowd of reporters and autograph hunters running toward me. They clambered for photos and microphone space, and the questions flew fast and furious. In the background, I could see Alan grinning from ear to ear.

When I finally got disengaged from the press, Alan took my hand.

"Did anyone show up?" I asked.

He laughed giddily. "Yeah, you might say that. The house is packed."

After two of the three movies were shown, Aubrey Schenk, Al Zugsmith, and Howard Koch said more nice things than anyone has a right to have said about them.

And finally it was time for me to speak. I whispered to Thomas that I didn't know what to say.

"I'm not worried," he told me. "You have that magic touch of always saying the right thing."

I dimly heard Howard Koch introduce me, and the applause thundered off the walls of the theater. I walked down the aisle with a bright spotlight in my eyes. As I stood in front of the cheering audience, there were tears on my cheeks.

"Thank you," I said. "I couldn't be any happier if I was getting an Oscar."

Filmography

1949–50	*Jet Pilot.* (Released 1957.) Director, Josef Von Sternberg (RKO). John Wayne, Janet Leigh, Jay C. Flippen
1951	*Two Tickets to Broadway.* Director, James V. Kern (RKO). Tony Martin, Janet Leigh, Gloria De Haven, Eddie Bracken
1951	*Variety Footlights* (RKO). Jack Paar
1951	*His Kind of Woman.* Director, John Farrow (RKO). Robert Mitchum, Jane Russell, Vincent Price, Tim Holt
1953	*Forbidden.* Director, Rudolph Maté (Universal International). Tony Curtis, Joanne Dru, Lyle Bettger
1953	*The All American.* Director, Jesse Hibbs (Universal International). Tony Curtis, Lori Nelson, Richard Long, Stuart Whitman
1953	*Hawaiian Nights* (Universal International). Pinky Lee

1954   *Yankee Pasha*. Director, Joseph Pevney (Universal International). Jeff Chandler, Rhonda Fleming, Bart Roberts (Rex Reason)

1954   *Francis Joins the WACs*. Director, Arthur Lubin (Universal International). Donald O'Connor, Julie Adams, Chill Wills, ZaSu Pitts, Lynn Bari

1955   *Ain't Misbehavin'*. Director, Edward Buzzell (Universal International). Rory Calhoun, Piper Laurie, Jack Carson, Reginald Gardiner

1955   *The Second Greatest Sex*. Director, George Marshall (Universal International). Jeanne Crain, George Nader, Bert Lahr, Kitty Kallen, Keith Andes

1955   *Running Wild*. Director, Abner Biberman (Universal International). William Campbell, Keenan Wynn, Walter Coy

1956   *Star in the Dust*. Director, Charles Haas (Universal International). John Agar, Richard Boone, Leif Erickson, Coleen Gray, James Gleason

1957   *The Girl in Black Stockings*. Director, Howard W. Koch (United Artists). Lex Barker, Anne Bancroft, Ron Randell, Marie Windsor

1957   *Untamed Youth*. Director, Howard W. Koch (Warner Brothers). Lori Nelson, John Russell, Lurene Tuttle

1958   *Teacher's Pet*. Director, George Seaton (Paramount). Clark Gable, Doris Day, Gig Young, Nick Adams

1958   *Born Reckless*. Director, Howard W. Koch (Warner Brothers). Jeff Richards, Arthur Hunnicutt, Carol Ohmart, Tom Duggan

1958   *The Beautiful Legs of Sabrina*. (Made in Rome at Cinecittà Studios.) Antonio Cifariello

1959   *High School Confidential!* Director, Jack Arnold (MGM). Russ Tamblyn, Jan Sterling

1959   *Guns, Girls, and Gangsters.* Director, Edward L. Cahn (United Artists). Gerald Mohr, Lee Van Cleef, Grant Richards

1959   *The Beat Generation.* Director, Charles Haas (Cinema Associates Inc.). Released as *This Regal Age.* Steve Cochran, Ray Danton, Fay Spain, Maggie Hayes, Louis Armstrong, Ray Anthony, Jackie Coogan

1959   *The Big Operator.* Director, Charles Haas (MGM). Mickey Rooney, Steve Cochran, Mel Torme, Ray Danton, Jim Backus, Ray Anthony, Jackie Coogan

1959   *Girls Town.* Director, Charles Haas (MGM). Retitled *The Innocent and the Damned.* Mel Torme, Gigi Perreau, Paul Anka, Jim Mitchum

1959   *Vice Raid.* Director, Edward L. Cahn (United Artists). Richard Coogan, Brad Dexter, Barry Atwater

1960   *Sex Kittens Go to College.* Director, Albert Zugsmith (Allied Artists). Tuesday Weld, Mijanou Bardot, Mickey Shaughnessy, Louis Nye, Pamela Mason

1960   *The Private Lives of Adam and Eve.* Directors, Albert Zugsmith, Mickey Rooney (Universal International). Martin Milner, Mickey Rooney, Fay Spain, Tuesday Weld, Paul Anka, Mel Torme

1960   *College Confidential.* Director, Albert Zugsmith (Universal International). Steve Allen, Jayne Meadows, Walter Winchell

1961   *The Blonde From Buenos Aires* (Argentinian Films). Jean-Pierre Aumont

1963   *Three Nuts in Search of a Bolt* (Adrian Weiss Productions). Tommy Noonan, Ziva Rodann, Paul Gilbert, John Cronin

1964   *The Wild, Wild West.* (German production.) Freddy Quinn, Rik Sattaglia

1964   *The Candidate* (Cosmat Production). Ted Knight, June Wilkenson

1966   *The Navy Versus the Night Monsters.* Director, Michael Hoey. Anthony Eisley, Pamela Mason, Bill Gray, Bobby Van

1966   *The Las Vegas Hillbillys.* Director, Arthur C. Pierce. Jayne Mansfield, Ferlin Husky

1966   *Voyage to the Planet of Prehistoric Women.* Director, Derek Thomas (Peter Bogdanovich). Mary Marr, Paige Lee, Aldo Roman, Margo Hartman

1971   *The Arizona Kid.* Producer, Cirio Santiago. Gordon Mitchell, Bernard Bonning

1985   *Free Ride.* Director, Tom Trbovich (Galaxy International Pictures). Gary Herschberger, Warren Berlinger, Dawn Schneider, Peter Deluise, Frank Campbell, Brian MacGregor